Mastering Academic Writing

Boba Samuels & Jordana Garbati

Sara Miller McCune founded SAGE Publishing in 1965 to support the dissemination of usable knowledge and educate a global community. SAGE publishes more than 1000 journals and over 800 new books each year, spanning a wide range of subject areas. Our growing selection of library products includes archives, data, case studies and video. SAGE remains majority owned by our founder and after her lifetime will become owned by a charitable trust that secures the company's continued independence.

Los Angeles | London | New Delhi | Singapore | Washington DC | Melbourne

→ SAGE Study Skills

Mastering Academic Writing

Boba Samuels & Jordana Garbati

SAGE

Los Angeles | London | New Delhi
Singapore | Washington DC | Melbourne

Los Angeles | London | New Delhi
Singapore | Washington DC | Melbourne

SAGE Publications Ltd
1 Oliver's Yard
55 City Road
London EC1Y 1SP

SAGE Publications Inc.
2455 Teller Road
Thousand Oaks, California 91320

SAGE Publications India Pvt Ltd
B 1/I 1 Mohan Cooperative Industrial Area
Mathura Road
New Delhi 110 044

SAGE Publications Asia-Pacific Pte Ltd
3 Church Street
#10-04 Samsung Hub
Singapore 049483

First published 2019

Editor: Jai Seaman
Editorial assistant: Charlotte Bush
Production editor: Katherine Haw
Copyeditor: Jane Fricker
Proofreader: Rebecca Storr
Indexer: Caroline Eley
Marketing manager: Catherine Slinn
Cover design: Sheila Tong
Typeset by: C&M Digitals (P) Ltd, Chennai, India

Library of Congress Control Number: 2018942957

British Library Cataloguing in Publication data

A catalogue record for this book is available from the British Library

ISBN 978-1-4462-9966-1
ISBN 978-1-4462-9967-8 (pbk)

Contents

About the Authors

Dr Boba Samuels holds a PhD in Education. She has taught writing at Western University, the University of Waterloo, Wilfrid Laurier University and the University of Toronto. Her research interests include writing pedagogy, disciplinary writing, rhetorical genre studies and writing centre administration. She lives and works in Toronto, Ontario, Canada.

Dr Jordana Garbati holds a PhD in Education and an MBA. She has over 10 years' experience teaching writing to undergraduate and graduate students at Canadian universities. Her areas of interest include business writing and communication, blog writing, and French and English as additional languages. She lives and works in Waterloo, Ontario, Canada.

Acknowledgements

Like other academic writing, a book is not simply a product of its author(s), but of a community of contributors both formal and informal. A lot of people helped us write this book. We would like to thank, first, Emmy Misser, the former manager of Wilfrid Laurier University's Writing Centre. Emmy was the original co-creator of this book before retirement lured her away and she passed the reins to Jordana. Emmy's love of language and passion for teaching excellence inspired the best in us, and she has been our mentor, colleague, friend and advisor. Much of our approach to writing instruction is owed to her guidance and example.

Second, we would like to thank our families and friends, who are too numerous to name. You know who you are. We couldn't have written this book, or much else, without your support.

Third, we'd like to thank the students we have worked with over the years and in particular those students and writing centre tutors who shared their work with us and allowed us to include it in this book. Your generosity and optimism never fail to amaze us. Thanks to Sarah Best, Brittany Bilsborough, Corinne Brassem, Amit Desai, Ali Greey, Monika Konopka, Kelly McDonald, Alexis Motuz, Carrie Palmer, Laura Reitzel and Matthew Shakleford-Lye.

Thank you to the wonderful folks at SAGE, who were endlessly patient and advised us along the way.

Finally, this book is dedicated to new generations of students who will embrace academic writing, perhaps tentatively at first, but then with increasing confidence. In our families, the newest generation – Duke, Reef, Holt, Giselle, Desmond, Eleanor, Quinn and Cole – is who we picture when we envision future students who will need our guidance. We're here for you.

Photo credits

Justin Dulewicz: antoniodiaz/Shutterstock.com
Eva Hibbard: iStock.com/NicolasMcComber
Devon Stratford: Monkey Business Images/Shutterstock.com
Belissima Wong: arek_malang/Shutterstock.com

Introduction

If you picked up this book, it's likely because you're curious about writing academically, advancing your writing skills, and learning about practical strategies to help you achieve your writing goals. Across the academic world, programmes and requirements vary, particularly in the terminology used to describe writing tasks. You may be writing an upper-year undergraduate paper, starting a Master's degree, or in the process of writing about your thesis data. This book is intended to help you with these tasks – and much more!

Academic writing is daunting for many people. It's not something that comes naturally. It takes practice, feedback and observation to master academic writing. If you're feeling like you're the only one who is struggling or who has questions about how to start writing or how to organize your writing, you're not alone. We've been there. Multiple times. Truthfully, writing this book was a daunting task for us! But by learning from the research and taking our own advice, we've accomplished our writing goals. The book you have in your hands right now is the result of many hours of thinking, reading, discussing and writing. And these things didn't happen in clearly defined stages. Academic writing is messy. It's complex. But once you move through the rough patches of the writing process, you'll achieve clarity, and you'll produce a piece of writing that you can be proud of.

We've approached this book from the perspective of the university writing centre. Writing centres are common in many areas of the world and increasingly being established in other areas; a variety of models exist. An academic writing centre occupies a privileged space where students come in confidence to get feedback on their writing before it is handed in for grading. Students come from every discipline and from every level of academic study. As writing centre professionals, we have worked with these students over many years, offering constructive feedback in a way that both honours their attempts and helps them move towards the rigorous standards and conventions demanded in academia. This perspective has allowed us to create a fictional cast of student characters for this book. Through them, we want to share with you what we have learned over many years of research and teaching.

Cast of Characters

The characters in this book were created to help you connect with the material in this book. They are fictional, but their problems are not. You will likely relate to more than one character and find commonality in terms of their writing successes or struggles. Our cast is as follows:

- Bellissima Wong: upper-year student in Sociology,

- Devon Stratford: upper-year student in Economics,

- Justin Dulewicz: first-year graduate student in a Master's of Anthropology programme, and

- Eva Hibbert: first-year graduate student in a Master's of Psychology programme.

Each of these four characters is inspired by the people we have met and have worked with in our time as writing centre professionals. The problems they face are real. The dialogues we have created in each chapter are based on real conversations we have had during tutoring sessions in our own university writing centres.

You will notice that our cast is diverse; the students whom you will meet in this book are pursuing different levels of study in a range of disciplines in the Social Sciences. In this book, we have included examples from different fields of study and authentic student texts so you can learn from real examples of the most common genres required in post-secondary education. The assignments we focus on may have different names in your discipline or programme, but it's likely you will face similar demands. Because our examples are real students' texts, you may notice in them errors (in grammar, in content, in style, etc.). Despite these errors, you can learn much from the examples, and we think it is important to present these texts uncorrected, as the students wrote them.

A Note about Language

The examples in this book are from the Anglophone world. They are based on our experiences as educators and researchers, and, like you, we read articles and books written by people from around the world (and sometimes in different languages, too). There are definitely differences in academic writing based on cultural context, but there are similarities, too. We want you to know that the instruction we offer in this book is likely to help you learn how to write academically in English or in other languages. Let's say you're writing a literature review in Portuguese – we think this book can help you! Once you have a good understanding of structure, genre, tone and voice, for example, in your first language, you more likely will be able to transfer this information to another language. Try it! And let us know how things work out.

Benefits to Students and Professors

For students and professors, this book will:

- clarify the rhetorical and genre demands of typical academic text types assigned to undergraduate and graduate students,
- provide models of effective academic behaviour in response to the challenges in writing each text type,
- provide writing instruction and support across multiple levels of university writing and encourage use of the book to support programme progress,
- provide dynamic writing instruction through the narratives of the characters' learning processes,
- use before and after samples of model texts to demonstrate the effects of revision and the aspects of writing that are addressed in each chapter,
- raise awareness of how people perceive and react to writing instruction and assignment expectations, and
- provide academic references in writing research to show evidence and support for the instruction.

Structure of Each Chapter

Each chapter is organized as follows:

1. An Introductory Story: In this section, you will be introduced to the character and his/her current struggle with writing.
2. At the Writing Centre: In this section, you will follow the character as he/she visits a writing tutor to learn about writing.
3. What You Need to Know: In this section, you will read about writing research and pedagogy and learn effective writing strategies through the analysis of authentic student texts.
4. Reader's Practice: In this section, you will have the opportunity to apply what you have learned in the chapter to practice examples, the character's writing, and to your own writing. Feel free to skip exercises for skills you feel confident about, though we recommend you do as many as possible. They are short and allow you to incrementally practise important elements necessary for your writing development.

5. Revision of Character's Writing: In this section, you will see how the chapter's character has revised his/her writing according to the instruction provided in section 3.
6. Summary of Key Points: In this section, you will find a summary of topics you should have learned in the chapter.

In the appendices, you'll find several full papers submitted by real students for use in this book. We have annotated them based on the writing instruction in the relevant chapter(s).

There is blank space at the end of each chapter. Use this page to take notes, doodle, write questions, draw diagrams, etc. We encourage you to engage with the book and write directly in it!

1

Developing an Argument

In this chapter, you will meet Bellissima Wong, an upper-year undergraduate Sociology student who finds it challenging to develop an argument in her writing. She has just received bad news on a draft she had handed in and realizes that she needs help. Along with Bellissima, you will learn:

- how to move from being a novice writer to an experienced writer,
- two models for argumentation: Toulmin and Rogerian, and
- the language of argumentation.

1. Intro Story: Bellissima Wong

Bellissima Wong closed her eyes tightly and sighed. A big sigh. When she opened them, the paper on the desk in front of her still looked the same, still had question marks in the margins, still had a request to 'please come see me' written at the end. She'd already made an appointment to see her professor tomorrow afternoon at 2 pm. She rubbed her eyes, dropped her cell phone on the dorm bed and wondered what her mother would have said if she'd told her the truth about how the academic year had started. But luckily her mother was far away in China, and Bellissima didn't have to face her disappointment yet. She'd told her mother that she was now very fluent in English after being immersed in university life for the past two years. Not quite a lie. She was much more fluent. But people spoke so fast. And reading still took so long. And writing ... sigh.

She looked again at the Sociology paper (see Student Text 1a) that had been returned to her in class two days ago. Two comments struck her: 'excellent description'. Thank goodness. If it weren't for that piece of good news, she surely would have cried. The next comment wasn't as good. 'No argument here. Don't recount. What's your point?' She had looked up *recount* in her translation dictionary: to tell the story or details of something. She knew that not writing an argument was a problem, but she wasn't quite sure about this *recount*. Wasn't she supposed to include details? The details had been hard to comprehend, too. There were articles about an incident from the past about cartoons, and religion, and Denmark. It was all quite foreign to her. She sighed again and hoped her prof was as nice in person as she seemed in class.

Student Text 1a

Essay on Danish Cartoons

Peter Goodspeed's article was called "Clash of civilization's orchestrated: Global protests were anything but spontaneous". The article said cartoons were seen in the newspaper Jyllands-Posten in September 2005 (A16). The newspaper's editor said cartoons were used in response to Danish illustrators fear of the Muslim community. Danish illustrators refused to work on children's picture book about Islam (ibid). Originally, twelve drawings were published. The Danish Muslim community protested but the Danish government ignored them. The Danish Muslim community used the original three cartoons plus three more cartoons to the Middle East. They wanted to create support for their protest (ibid). The community were angry because Prophet was not portrayed correctly. They were also angry because some Muslims did not approve of the depiction of Mohammed in any way. This was religious taboo. Furthermore, this resulted in a Muslim condemnation of Denmark. And also economic sanctions were against Denmark from Muslim countries. Moreover, public protests and attacks on Western embassies occurred (ibid). The Western media responded to the outrage by publishing the cartoons again. It also criticized a perceived Muslim hatred for free speech (ibid). Arab leaders said West attempted to "weaken and subjugate the Muslim world" by using cartoons. The Western leaders wanted to resolve the issue and called the implications indicative of a "clash of civilizations" (ibid).

2. At the Writing Centre

It was 9 am and Bellissima was sitting in the university writing centre, explaining to the student tutor that her professor had suggested she come for help before their meeting in the afternoon. The tutor, Eleanor, nodded her head.

Eleanor:	So your prof says you need to write an argument for this assignment, but you haven't done that. You're concerned that if you take out the details, the prof won't see all the research you've done on this topic, and won't see you really know what the topic is about. Is that right?
Bellissima:	Yes, I want to show that I know this was an important event, very controversial. But I don't understand why she doesn't want details about it. Don't I need evidence?
Eleanor:	Yes, of course. You do need evidence in academic writing. But that is only one characteristic of academic writing. You also often need an argument. In this assignment, in particular, we know that your professor asked you to write an argument about the Danish cartoon incident. So, can you tell me about what happened back in 2005?
Bellissima:	Yes. In 2005 a newspaper in Denmark published cartoons of the prophet Mohammed and many people were angry. Because of religion.
Eleanor:	I see. Do you think they were right to be angry?
Bellissima:	Hmm … maybe.
Eleanor:	Do you think the publishers knew the cartoons would make some people angry?
Bellissima:	Oh, yes.
Eleanor:	So, cartoons about religion were published even though it was known that some people would be upset. That's really interesting. Can you explain why you think this happened?
Bellissima:	Is that what my professor wants? She wants me to say *why* I think this happened?
Eleanor:	I think so, yes. She doesn't want you to simply tell her what happened. She wants you to explain why this was an important event. She wants you to examine what happened, come to some conclusion about it, and argue for your position on this event.
Bellissima:	I see. Not just tell what happened.

3. What You Need to Know

Have you received comments on your assignments as Bellissima described in her tutoring session? Has your professor ever given you a lower mark than you expected? Did this happen when you thought you had included good, detailed information in your report or essay?

For students who have moved successfully from their first years at university to more senior levels, the expectations for reading and writing can increase rather dramatically. Professors expect that the basics of how to form a compelling argument, how to identify key points, and how to marshal and present evidence are being polished rather than simply learned. They expect that longer and denser readings are analysed and responded to rather than merely comprehended. Professors and Teaching Assistants (TAs) often turn their attention to critiquing students' grasp of content and concepts, and expect to see more sophisticated and nuanced understandings – understandings that are clearly based in the discipline – than those of novice students. Many students however, have limited experience writing arguments. In other words, their content knowledge may exceed their knowledge of argumentation.

Novice–expert differences are, in fact, a good place to begin our exploration of the expectations for senior undergraduate writing. At senior levels, students will soon be expected to graduate and move into the workplace or continue to graduate studies. Yet Bellissima's paper demonstrates some of the characteristics of novice writing that her professor clearly expects she has moved beyond. For example, some students rely on what can be called 'the hamburger method' or '5-paragraph essay' for writing essays: an introduction (the top bun, 1 paragraph), a body section (the meat, 3 paragraphs), and a conclusion (the bottom bun, 1 paragraph). While simple to remember, this structure is insufficient for advanced academic writing.

In our analysis of Bellissima's sample text below (see Student Text 1b), you'll notice that she is taking a novice approach to argumentation. She uses background information as an introduction, provides no context, neglects to summarize key points of the reading, recounts multiple facts and details of the event, omits analysis, and fails to introduce a main focal point (thesis).

Other genres such as research reports that use an IMRD structure (Introduction-Methods-Results-Discussion; see Chapter 7 for additional information about IMRD) do expect background information in the introduction. We, however, are focusing here on argumentation.

Student Text 1b

Essay on Danish Cartoons

Peter Goodspeed's article was called "Clash of civilization's orchestrated: Global protests were anything but spontaneous".	Introduction
The article said cartoons were seen in the newspaper Jyllands-Posten in September 2005 (A16). The newspaper's editor said cartoons were used in response to Danish illustrators fear of the Muslim community. Danish illustrators refused to work on children's picture book about Islam (ibid). Originally, twelve drawings were published. The Danish Muslim community protested but the Danish government ignored them. The Danish Muslim community used the original three cartoons plus three more cartoons to the Middle East. They wanted to create support for their protest (ibid). The community were angry because Prophet was not portrayed correctly.	Recount of events

They were also angry because some Muslims did not approve of the depiction of Mohammed in any way. This was religious taboo. Furthermore, this resulted in a Muslim condemnation of Denmark. And also economic sanctions were against Denmark from Muslim countries. Moreover, public protests and attacks on Western embassies occurred (ibid). The Western media responded to the outrage by publishing the cartoons again. It also criticized a perceived Muslim hatred for free speech (ibid). Arab leaders said West attempted to "weaken and subjugate the Muslim world" by using cartoons. The Western leaders wanted to resolve the issue and called the implications indicative of a "clash of civilizations" (ibid).

Where is the thesis? What will be the main point of the argument?

Some distinctions between inexperienced and experienced writers are compared in Table 1.1.

Table 1.1   Distinctions between novice and expert writers

Novice/Expert distinctions	
Inexperienced writer	**Experienced writer**
Presents research as information	Presents research as support for an argument
Assumes the reader will see that the argument is obvious from the research presented	Makes the argument explicit by tying the research directly to reasons that form an argument
Summarizes the research	Shapes the research as an argument
Sees the research in isolation	Establishes the argument in the context of other arguments on the topic
Writes to pass the course	Writes as a member of the discipline to contribute to the discussion on a topic
Believes that writing one draft with some editing is good enough	Knows that writing requires several drafts, revision and careful editing
Writes for a general reader	Writes for a reader in the discipline

Source: Misser, n.d., adapted from Sommers & Saltz, 2004.

Expert students understand that the papers they write vary depending upon audience, context, and a number of other factors. Novice students, however, tend to see writing as *one thing*, a thing that shows what they know about a topic. In other words, writing demonstrates their content knowledge. But at advanced levels, academic peers *expect* that the writer knows her content and are looking for something more. That something is the writer's argument. That is what Bellissima's professor was looking for: not simply her awareness of an incident, but her understanding of the significance of the incident. She was looking for Bellissima to tell her *why* she thought the incident was important.

John Bean, a writing scholar, identifies a number of strategies that novice writers commonly use when they write academic papers and discusses why these strategies are ineffective (Bean, 2011). Check to see if you still use either of the two strategies below.

1. 'And then' writing

Students often display their knowledge using a sequential or chronological format. Bean calls this 'and then' writing because these texts are characterized by a series of events recounted in some order, often chronological and linked with 'and then'. Read the following text: 'Terrorism became an issue in 1999 when ____ happened. This led to ____, and then problems with ____. Then ____ developed ...' As this example demonstrates, such a text reads like a list of incidents strung together by 'and then ...' with no indication of any analysis, evaluation, or critique of the components listed. This is referred to as *a recount*: a description or listing of details about an event; for example, how you spent your day or the events that led up to the First World War. Recounts are useful when you want to clarify which set of details you are including in your discussion, but they do not substitute for explanation, critique, or argument. Writing only a recount suggests you know about the set of details on a topic that you've introduced; by extension, however, because you necessarily exclude other details (inadvertently or intentionally), the reader may infer that you don't know or perhaps are uninterested in the excluded details. This possible inference may explain why so many novice writers worry about 'what' to include in their writing: they are afraid of leaving out some important detail, which would indicate they lack knowledge. As a result, they focus on identifying as many details as possible but neglect to consider that this is not really what they have been asked to do at all.

2. The encyclopaedic approach

In this strategy, students provide extensive information about their chosen topic in a way that tries to be all-encompassing (thus avoiding the dreaded fear of omitting details). Rather than being comprehensive, however, this approach usually leaves a reader feeling overwhelmed and confused, and unsure of the writer's focus. For instance, when a student writes about what social media are, how they developed, who were the major people and companies involved, how they work, what are their uses, what problems they solve, AND what problems they create – well, a reader can be forgiven for wondering what the point of this text really is.

In contrast to novice students who use the two strategies above, expert students identify a clear focus for their writing. They understand that knowledge about most topics is vast and impossible to convey in its entirety; the expectation, therefore, is not that their writing includes all the details about an event or presents all the information about something, but that they specify *which details* are relevant to their focus. In other words, students must assess or evaluate their topic using some framework or criteria and let the reader know what they have concluded. This framework needs to be emphasized over details. Instead of 'Cars were created in the early 1900s, then popularized through the 1950s, and then abandoned in the 21st century', the goal is something more like, 'The history of cars can be traced from their creation in early 1900 to their growing popularity in the 1950s to their abandonment in the early 21st century as their environmental impact became recognized.' Notice in this example that we move from an 'and then' statement (details about cars in general) to one that provides a focus ('the history of cars') and a conclusion based on some type of analysis ('their environmental impact'). It is easy to see how this second statement could lead to an argument about the dangerous history of automobiles or the negative effects of automobiles on the natural environment. It is not so easy to see what the first statement would lead to – an explanation of why cars changed? A description of societal changes? An argument for the car as metaphor for civilization?

If 'and then' and 'encyclopaedic' approaches are ineffective, what should students do instead to rely less on recount and more on presenting an argument? Let's listen in again on Bellissima and Eleanor.

Bellissima: So I should tell what is the problem?

Eleanor: Yes, the problem–solution model is one conventional form in academic writing. You introduce a problem and then suggest what you think is a reasonable solution. What do you think is the problem in your Danish cartoons incident?

Bellissima: Hmm … well, it is about Muslims being angry that their prophet was shown in a cartoon.

Eleanor: So, the problem is that Muslims don't think a cartoon about the Prophet is funny?

Bellissima: Umm … not really. The problem is not about cartoons not being funny. Muslims, they were offended. This kind of humour is not done about their religion. Then the people in Denmark were upset because they believe they have freedom to say what they like, even about religion. They make fun of their own religions, and it is not a problem.

Eleanor: So it sounds as if the problem is cultural perhaps? Conflicting views about freedom of speech – especially how free people are to make fun of others' religious beliefs. If this conflict is the problem, does this incident also show us how to solve the problem?

Bellissima: Yeah, it shows we must be more understanding. We must try to see how other people believe and not just think all people must believe the same thing. Both sides are right, I think. It's hard to explain.

Eleanor: Yes, it is hard. It is a complex problem with no simple solution. That complexity is what you are required to examine in this assignment. The prof wants to see if you understand this complex problem and what you think about it.

The problem–solution model proposed by Eleanor, the writing centre tutor, is taken from Booth, Colomb, and Williams (2008), researchers who identified the context–problem–solution model as one way to introduce academic papers. In this model, the writer begins by providing some background information to situate the problem, then clearly identifies the problem, and then proposes a possible solution. The rest of the paper expands upon each of these elements, adding evidence and analysis as it builds towards a conclusion in which the solution is confirmed as the best possible one. This model is especially effective when the topic is a complex one and the writer wants to identify or propose a potential resolution for a problem.

In Bellissima's assignment, we could identify the following elements:

- The problem: the conflict between freedom of speech and limiting free speech to maintain peace.
- The context: the specific situation in Denmark in which cartoons of the prophet Mohammed incited anger, violence and worldwide controversy.
- The solution: greater cultural understanding is needed on both sides to avoid or minimize such problems.

Now, Bellissima needs to show the development of this argument in her text.

Expert writers need to know how to write effective arguments. Some writers may think this means they need to state their personal opinions. This is NOT the case. Opinions are personal views and beliefs, and these are often not based on evidence and analysis. Sometimes we believe things based on emotion or on preconceived ideas. One of the most important values in academia is that of supporting your views with evidence. You must actively search out evidence that might corroborate or challenge your views. By bringing together all of these different facts and perspectives, we are able to think critically about our topic so that we don't simply re-state whatever it is we believe. As academics, we re-think our beliefs and keep only those beliefs that we can support rationally with evidence.

Forms of Argument

Arguments can take various forms. The most common forms of argument in academic settings are called the Toulmin argument and the Rogerian argument. Stephen Toulmin (1922–2009) was a philosopher who proposed that western legal traditions have established a particular form of argument as pre-eminent. This form has as its central components a claim supported by evidence. Successful arguments marshal enough evidence to support a claim and demonstrate that it is better than alternative claims.

Carl Rogers (1902–1987) was a psychologist whose humanistic approach to patient care formed the basis for a different type of argument. In Rogers' model, opposing views are addressed through the establishment of common ground. Successful arguments provide a compromise that satisfies both sides. As a writer, you get to choose which type of argument will be most effective for your purposes and audience. Your discipline may also influence the form of argument structure that is most appropriate.

Toulmin Argument: The Win

The goal of the Toulmin argument is to present the strongest possible case for your position – to show that it is the best solution for a problem or the most comprehensive understanding of an issue. In essence, you want to 'win' the argument by presenting a stronger case than your opponent. To do so, Toulmin identifies a number of necessary and optional features. These include claims (statements or assertions of 'fact'), evidence (findings/observations about phenomena), warrants (links between claims and evidence), counter-claims (statements that contradict or oppose the initial claim), and rebuttals (refutation of the counter-claim). See Table 1.2 for an example of a Toulmin argument.

Table 1.2 Toulmin argument example

Claim	Muslims' religious beliefs are incompatible with some western cultural values.
Evidence	Attempts to make fun of Muslims' religious beliefs through cartoons resulted in violence and conflict in Denmark in 2005.
Warrant (provides link between claim and evidence, shows why they are related)	Depictions of the prophet Mohammed are prohibited in Islam.
Counter-claim	In the western world, even though making fun of religious beliefs is permissible under freedom of speech, doing so is limited in practice. Limits on values, therefore, are allowed.
Rebuttal	Actions that are legally permissible imply and often include reasonable limits but nevertheless have very broad applicability.
Restatement of claim	Therefore, if making fun of religion is an accepted practice demonstrating freedom of speech in Denmark, then Muslim beliefs that their religion is exempt from such practices are incompatible with this western value.

You may disagree with this argument and want to take a different position. But do you see how including the features identified by Toulmin forces us to create a deeper, more complex argument? The features identify points that can be elaborated upon and described more fully. In this way, you share your knowledge more effectively than by simply telling everything you know about the topic. You may even find that once you've carefully thought through these points you've changed your mind! (And that is the beauty of systematic critical thinking – the possibility that a different or better idea exists for you to discover. Critical thinking requires you to consider multiple perspectives on a topic.)

Rogerian Argument: The Win–Win

In contrast to the Toulmin argument, Rogerian arguments do not have the goal of 'winning' an argument over an opponent. Instead, the goal is 'win–win', so that all participants' views are acknowledged, and a compromise is reached that is acceptable to all. This type of argument is most useful when an issue is extremely polarized and participants may lack the openness or goodwill to change their positions. It is also useful in situations where there is genuine principled opposition, but collaboration is nevertheless required. The necessary parts of a Rogerian argument are finding common ground, clarifying both/all sides of the issue, and identifying a compromise that is acceptable to all participants. See Table 1.3 for a Rogerian argument example.

See Bellissima's revision (Student Text 1c) as she works to improve her original draft by incorporating an argument. As we can see, she is applying some analysis and thinking more deeply about the topic, but more work needs to be done to delete extraneous information and focus.

Table 1.3   Rogerian argument example

Common ground	Religious beliefs are susceptible to misunderstanding and controversy between cultures and individuals.
Common ground	Actions that are legally permissible or culturally appropriate are not always/should not be allowed in all contexts and situations.
Side A	Depictions of the prophet Mohammed are prohibited in Islam. Those who depict the Prophet deliberately offend Muslims.
Side B	Making fun of religious beliefs is permissible under freedom of speech in the western world. People who are offended are against the western world.
Compromise	Cultural clashes between offended Muslims and the non-Muslim public could have been avoided had greater cultural sensitivity been shown by both sides.

Student Text 1c

When I read Godspeed's article, I noticed several value and history terms right away. They were quoted and used by the author a lot. The terms referred to many different meanings of the cartoons. However, if the same people created the cartoons, the illustrations had the same purpose. But why was there so much confusion over the drawings and the meanings?

Research question

The answer to this question is to use the key theory in the Cultural Studies framework, created by Stuart Hall and he was one of the "founding fathers" of the discipline. Stuart Hall developed encoding/decoding. This means that audiences are not passive receptors of messages that are created and transmitted through media. On the other hand, audiences interpret cultural texts differently based on their socioeconomic status, the frameworks of knowledge, and the other individuals or institutions. They are "encoded" with the meaning intended. Furthermore, the text's meaning are "decoded" by the audience of the text according to the differences in the text that were mentioned. Stuart Hall describes three ways individuals can interact with the ideas or the values that are in a text. Stuart Hall calls these ways dominant, negotiated, and oppositional readings (101–3). First, a dominant reading occurs when the audience member completely accepts the original meaning of the message that the creator meant (101). Second, a negotiated meaning is from the partial acceptance of dominant values in a general level, and at the same time they are rejected in the specific instance in question (102). Finally, an oppositional reading completely rejects the meaning in the text, while at the same time also understanding it (103).

Background information and theory

Therefore, by examining the impact of these cartoons through a Cultural Studies framework, the Muslim response can be seen as both a challenge to Western hegemony and an attempt to define a Muslim identity.

Tentative answer = preliminary thesis statement

Bellissima's text has improved, but it still has problems with grammatical issues (e.g., articles, subject–verb agreement), word choice (e.g., confusion vs controversy) and sentence structure. She will be seeing writing centre tutors so that she can systematically apply her knowledge of grammar to work she is actually doing. We will address issues concerning word choice and language in more detail in Chapter 5 (Make Your Mark).

The Language of Argument

When you begin to write an argument, it can be helpful to use your own, familiar language to get your ideas down on paper, like Bellissima did, above (see Student Text 1c). Afterwards, you will need to revise to give your paper a more formal academic tone. You need to move from an informal 'think aloud' tone to a formal and precise academic tone (see Chapter 5). To write strong arguments, your statements need to be declarative (i.e., they need to declare something). They also need to include hedges or qualifiers so they're more precise and readily supportable. Hedges and qualifiers indicate the limits for claims, inserting the openness and possibility of uncertainty that are characteristic of careful academic thinking. See Table 1.4 for a comparison of general and precise language in Bellissima's sentences.

We revisit hedges and qualifiers in Chapter 5.

Table 1.4   Comparison of general and precise sentences

	General	Precise
Declarative claim	When I read Godspeed's article, I noticed several value and history terms right away. They were quoted and used by the author a lot. The terms referred to many different meanings of the cartoons.	The different meanings assigned to cartoons are related to the values and history of different groups.
Hedging	A text's meaning is 'decoded' by all readers.	A text *may be* 'decoded' for different meanings by a variety of readers.
Qualifier	Meaning is contextual.	Because audiences interpret cultural texts differently based on their frameworks of knowledge, meaning is *always* contextual.
Intensifier	Meaning is controversial.	Meanings may be highly controversial.

4. Reader's Practice

To help you see how your discipline handles language, underline the words in one of your readings that limit claims. This will help you become familiar with the conventions for qualifiers and hedges in your discipline.

You've now had a chance to read some of Bellissima's paper and to learn about expectations for advanced academic writing. What do you think Bellissima should do to improve her argument?

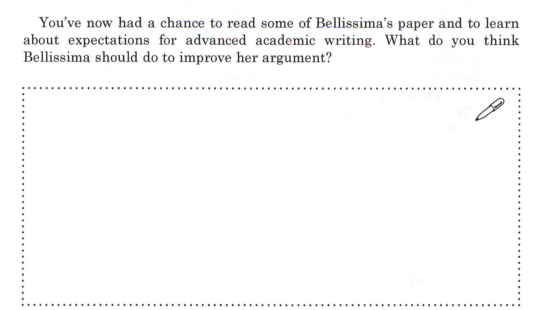

Read the paragraph below and identify Bellissima's main claim and the evidence supporting this claim.

Student Text 1d

One of the core issues at stake in this whole controversy is the nature of Muslim identity, and how both Muslims and those in Western societies view them. Cultural Studies looks at the creation of identity within groups and among groups as one of its central interests. As Hall explains, the media plays a central role in creating and sustaining identities through the transmission of values and ideologies associated with the group being defined in three ways (qtd in Seidman, 137) First the media presents a series of "cultural codes" that are based on hierarchal sets of binaries such as normal/strange, dominant/submissive, and strong/weak (ibid). Then the media places individuals within sociodemographic categories such as race, gender, or ethnicity, and applies the binary sets to these groups by ranking them; as a result of this categorization, individuals will read the meanings in texts differently depending on what group they have been placed in, as well as the meanings and values associated with that group (ibid). Hall also argues that our modern society is marked by this distinguishing of difference, and results in numerous intra-categorical conflicts and divisions that help form the identity of individuals belonging to that group (*Introduction*, 598). Bhabha also brings in an important idea that will be developed later, that the creation of identity in cultures is accomplished by repeating the same meanings over and over until they become natu-ralized; furthermore, these meanings must be directed at "the Other", a term which is recurrent in Cultural Studies (qtd in Davies, 103).

Did you find the following?

- Main Claim: media play a central role in creating and sustaining identities
  - Evidence 1: media construct identities in three ways: by creating a series of cultural codes; by placing individuals into categories; by ranking categories of individuals
  - Evidence 2: intra-category conflict (Hall)
  - Evidence 3: repetition of meaning so that it's naturalized and directed at 'the other' (Bhabha)

5. Revision of Bellissima's Writing

Now, read Bellissima's revised introduction. She thought it was a better version. What do you think?

Student Text 1e

Images of Identity: The Danish Muslim Cartoon Controversy in a Cultural Studies Framework

While they are often not considered to be a "serious" means of expressing personal or political viewpoints, **the power of cartoon images as a form of social commentary** should not be underestimated. A deceptively simple drawing can pass along an enormous range of ideas and values from the cartoonist to his or her intended audience, and in the right circumstances the impact of these meanings can be wide-ranging. Such is the case with the **recent events surrounding the publishing of a series of cartoons, first in Denmark and later across the Western world, depicting the Prophet Mohammed in an unflattering light.** According to the media, two opposing camps that are divided on the meaning of the caricatures have formed, with Muslims seeing the drawings as an attack on both their religion and their way of life, and Western countries viewing the Muslim response as an attack on free speech and democracy. **Sociological analysis of this incident and its fallout is best done through an interpretation of Cultural Studies theory,** because it is concerned with people's creation of identity and meaning as well as how audiences and cultural texts interact with one another. Application of this theory to the cartoon controversy will demonstrate how the creation of meaning from texts follows patterns laid out by such cultural theorists as Stuart Hall. **By examining the impact of these cartoons through a Cultural Studies framework, the Muslim response can be seen as both a challenge to Western hegemony and an attempt to develop and define a Muslim identity.**

The topic (political cartoons) is introduced and established in a specific context.

A problem (controversy over interpretation of cartoons) is identified and positions are explained.

The rationale for the analysis is stated.

Complex thesis statement presents a debatable view, substantive details, and a significant point.

If you would like to read Bellissima's complete paper with our detailed analysis, see Appendix A.

6. Summary of Key Points

In this chapter you learned:

- to assess your writing on the continuum of *inexperienced* ←→ *experienced* writers,
- about ineffective writing strategies ('and then' writing and 'encyclopaedic' writing),
- the difference between a recount and an argument and why arguments are preferred in academic contexts,
- about the context–problem–solution model of academic writing,
- two forms of argument: Toulmin and Rogerian, and
- about language to make your arguments more effective: hedges and qualifiers.

7. References

Bean, J. (2011). *Engaging ideas. The professor's guide to integrating writing, critical thinking, and active learning in the classroom* (2nd ed.). San Francisco, CA: Jossey-Bass.

Booth, W. C., Colomb, G. G., & Williams, J. M. (2008). *The craft of research* (3rd ed.). Chicago, IL: University of Chicago Press.

Misser, E. (n.d.). *Inexperienced vs. experienced writers*. Wilfrid Laurier University Writing Centre handout.

Sommers, N., & Saltz, L. (2004). The novice as expert: Writing the freshman year. *College Composition and Communication, 56*, 124–49.

8. Your Notes

2

Focusing a Research Topic

In this chapter, you will meet Devon Stratford, an undergraduate Economics student in his final year. He is completing a capstone[1] research project in his economic policies course. His professor gave him some instructions for this assignment, but they are vague, and he doesn't feel confident enough to email his professor with his questions. While he has freedom to choose his topic, he is interested in many areas of economics, so he is feeling overwhelmed by this freedom. Through Devon's experience, you will learn:

- about brainstorming your ideas (i.e., using mind maps and concept maps),
- how to narrow down a topic for investigation,
- how to use this topic to develop a research question, and
- about the functions and forms of thesis statements.

1. Intro Story: Devon Stratford

Devon shut the door to his room, muffling the sounds of his father and brother watching sports downstairs and his mother talking on the phone to relatives. He was feeling stressed. This capstone assignment for his policy course was not due until the end of term, but few check-in points with the professor were scheduled along the way. Worse still, he hadn't even chosen a topic. In his undergraduate economics courses, he had had little opportunity to practise writing, and he has avoided any writing-intensive courses that were offered as electives in his programme. He wonders now whether this might have been a mistake.

He looked at the calendar above his desk, marked to show mid-term exams looming in two weeks, and faced the fact that he had procrastinated long enough on this research project. He re-read his assignment instructions (see Box 2.1), then stared at the blank computer screen not knowing where to begin.

Box 2.1   Economics research paper – Assignment instructions

In this project, you will explore a research question and identify its relevance to policy. You should identify the economic theory that informs your research. In your analysis, you should decide if the current policies are appropriate and suggest alternative policies that could be better.

Before presenting your work, you should identify key pieces of literature that are related to your topic. Gather useful information from the library database sources, government documents, and other materials. Your review of the literature should be focused and clear.

Like most research, you are expected to have an empirical component. Your empirical evidence should include charts and graphs of basic data and some statistical analysis. Your empirical evidence should answer your research question. Based on your analysis, conclude your paper.

The next day, he walked into the writing centre to meet with Gigi, hoping this session would give him a starting point.

2. At the Writing Centre

Devon: So I have this major assignment to do in my economics course, and I'm feeling overwhelmed. I know a lot about economics, but this writing task is massive. There are so many things I could do, but I just don't know what my professor wants.

Gigi: Let's look at the assignment instructions. Hmm … I notice that you have a lot of flexibility with this assignment. This can definitely seem daunting. The possibilities are endless!

Devon: Exactly. It's huge!

Gigi: But this is also exciting. Now you have the chance to learn about any topic that interests you. You have very few restrictions here, so you can explore whatever you'd like.

Devon: I wish the professor had just told me what I should do. I could get straight to the research.

Gigi: Yeah. That might seem like an easier way to go. But you're in your last year, and professors expect that you can carry out an independent research project. Embrace

17

this freedom! Research what interests you even though you may be feeling overwhelmed.

Devon: Sure. Okay, yeah. So … where do I start? If I type 'economics' into the library search bar, I'll get way too many results.

Gigi: You're right! That topic is way too broad. Let's do some brainstorming. You need to ask yourself some questions. Make note of your answers. This can give you a good start.

1.   What are you interested in?
2.   What do you want to learn about?
3.   What have you learned about in the course?
4.   What texts have you been reading? What do you remember from these texts? What has stood out?
5.   Are you aware of a problem that needs solving?

Devon takes notes as Gigi asks these questions and gives him time to write. See Devon's brainstorm in Table 2.1.

Table 2.1   Devon's brainstorm

1. What am I interested in?	• foreign investment • housing markets • house prices • rising house prices • rising house prices in Australian cities such as Melbourne and Sydney • rising house prices in rural and urban areas overseas • pattern of house prices over time • equitable access to housing • foreign investment in housing
2. What do I want to learn about?	• I want to learn about the trends in housing prices in Australia and the impact this will have on people's ability to afford housing • impact of policies regarding foreign investment
3. What have I learned about in the course?	• house price trends • interest rate trends • mortgage rate trends • supply and demand of housing • urban vs rural
4. What texts have I been reading? What do I remember from these texts? What has stood out?	• statistical documentation from government websites • policies put in place to regulate foreign investment (e.g., Melbourne)
5. Am I aware of a problem that needs solving?	• impact of foreign investment on house prices • government policies regulating the housing market • choices available for domestic investors/homeowners if foreign investment increases housing prices

Gigi: So it looks like there are a lot of things that you know about economics. Is there anything here that really interests you?

Devon: Well, maybe house markets and government regulations. I don't know though.

Gigi: Okay. That's a good first step. Keep brainstorming. Let's try to narrow things down. What are your answers to the following questions?

1. What research have you done in this topic area?
2. Who are the scholars doing research in this topic area?
3. What conversations have you had with others about this topic? Are your opinions different? What have you learned?
4. What are your thoughts on the topic?
5. What are the possible lines of investigation?

See Table 2.2 for Devon's continued brainstorm.

Table 2.2 Devon's continued brainstorm

1. What research have I done in this topic area?	• government policy implementation documents • some historical trends • tax policies • house market trends in the past decade
2. Who are the authors that I have read who are doing research in this topic area?	•
3. What conversations have I had with others about this topic? Are our opinions different? What have I learned?	•
4. What are my thoughts on the topic?	• I think that the government policies that restrict foreign investment are a good thing. It will ensure that house prices stabilize for domestic investment. The people who need houses will be able to afford them.
5. What are the possible lines of investigation?	•

Gigi: You have a lot of ideas here. It seems that you are interested in the housing market specifically. You seem to be interested in both historical data and trends, as well as current issues regarding foreign investment and government policies. You could continue to answer the questions that I've posed and make more points when you look back over your course notes.

You now need to think of why you are interested in investigating these things and why others might be interested, too. In other words, what is the purpose of the research you want to do?

Here is a good template to help you identify and specify what you need to do. Can you complete the following fill-in-the-blank sentence?

> I am writing about _____
>
> because I want to find out what/why/how _____
>
> in order to help my reader understand _____.
> (Booth, Colomb, & Williams, 2008, p. 51).

Gigi left Devon with this task for five minutes. Student Text 2a shows how Devon completed this sentence template.

Student Text 2a

Devon's Sentence

I am writing about the current housing market in Australia
because I want to find out why/how foreign investment has forced the government to implement tax policies
in order to help my reader understand that tax policies regarding foreign investment can stabilize the domestic housing market and increase opportunities for domestic investment.

3. What You Need to Know

Can you relate to Devon's experiences and struggles? Have you tried to articulate a purpose for your work in a fill-in-the-blank statement such as the one above (Student Text 2a)? At first glance, this fill-in-the-blank statement may seem like a simple sentence to complete. But do not be fooled! It takes thinking and can be a challenge for many writers. You will need to think about a purpose for your research beyond your own interests. What do you want your reader to learn? What might you teach others as a result of your investigation?

As Devon's experience demonstrates, focusing a research topic can be an overwhelming task for both novice and expert writers. Brainstorming can be a helpful activity to get your ideas flowing and to think about the purposes of your research. It is good to begin by thinking about what you know, reflecting on what you have learned in an area, and identifying what interests you.

In addition to answering the initial questions to get some ideas flowing, you can create a mind map or a concept map to share your ideas.

Mind Maps

A mind map is a 'visual, non-linear representation of ideas and their relationships' (Biktimirov & Nilson, 2006). These maps show a network of related and connected ideas. Mind mapping encourages spontaneous thinking. It helps you to imagine and explore the associations between ideas (Davies, 2011). Mind maps can include text, images, diagrams, and different colours and line thicknesses to more clearly identify associations. Some people find the visual aspect of mind mapping particularly helpful.

The following are some suggestions you can use to create your map (adapted from Buzan & Buzan, 2000):

1. Place an image or topic in the centre.
2. Use images, symbols and codes.
3. Select keywords and make distinctions using a combination of upper or lower case letters.
4. Place each word/image alone and on its own line.
5. Connect the lines starting from the central image. The central lines are thicker, organic, and flowing. They become thinner as they radiate out from the centre.
6. Use colours (your own code).
7. Develop your own personal style.
8. Use emphasis and identify associations with colours and line thicknesses.
9. Keep the mind map clear by using radial hierarchy, numerical order, or outlines.

See Devon's mind map in Figure 2.1.

Concept Maps

A concept map is similar to a mind map, but it is more formal and structured, and it doesn't use as many images. The aim of a concept map is to document relationships between ideas and as such, it has 'a hierarchical "tree" structure with super-ordinate and subordinate parts (primary, secondary, and tertiary ideas)' (Davies, 2011, p. 282). Concept map elements include:

- a focus topic
- ideas and concepts related to the topic to be explored
- links using connective terms (verbs such as 'adjusts', 'determines', or prepositional phrases such as 'leads to', 'results from', etc.) to show relationships between concepts
- terminal concepts are the most narrowed concept applied to the topic
- examples may be added to terminal concepts (these are usually not bounded by a box or circle because they are not noted as concepts)

See Devon's concept map in Figure 2.2.

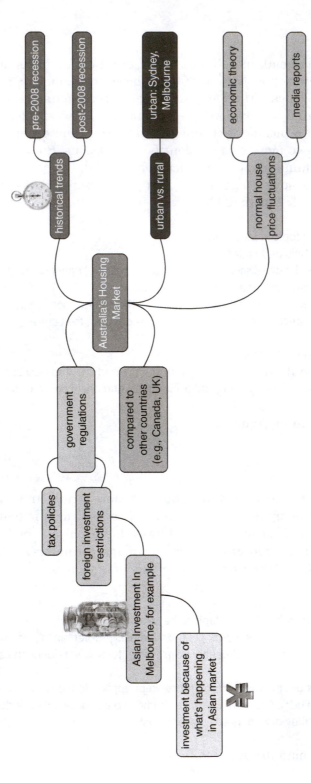

Figure 2.1 Devon's mind map

Note: Mind map created with www.mindmup.com/

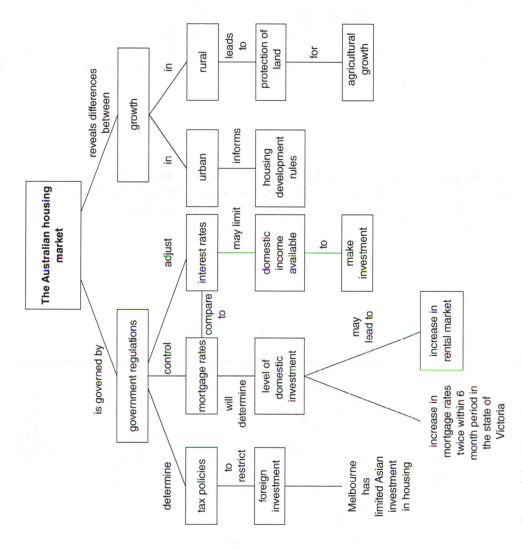

Figure 2.2 Devon's concept map

As a result of brainstorming (using a mind map or concept map), a topic worthy of investigation may emerge. A purpose for this investigation may become clear. You should give some thought to the broadness – or narrowness – of your topic.

Be careful here. A topic that is too broad will result in superficial research. But if you have decided on a very narrow topic, you may not find sufficient sources to develop your research paper. If you have a topic that is appropriately narrowed, then it will be easier for you to 'recognize gaps, inconsistencies, and puzzles' that you can turn into a research question (Booth et al., 2003, p. 44). In our experience, students often start with topics that are too broad.

Narrowing a Topic

You can think of the relationship between a topic, narrowed topic, research question and thesis statement like a bullseye (see Figure 2.3). In the centre of the bullseye is your thesis statement. We will explore thesis statements in the next section.

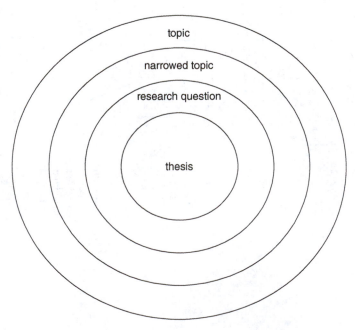

Figure 2.3   Narrowing the topic bullseye

On the outer edge of the bullseye, you will have your topic. It is still quite broad, and it will be difficult to get at your thesis statement if you stay out here. To move towards the centre, ask yourself the W questions: what, where, who, when.

Let us work through a simple example together (see Table 2.3).

Table 2.3   Narrowing a topic using W questions

Topic: Coffee shops

What	• What do customers do in coffee shops? • What are customers' motivations to work in coffee shops? • What are coffee shop owners' perceptions about making the coffee shop space into a work space?
Where	• Where are the coffee shops located that are most often used for work? • Where do customers position themselves in a coffee shop to set up their work stations? For what purposes? • Where does the coffee shop work culture exist? Does the coffee shop work culture exist everywhere in the world?
Who	• Who frequents coffee shops? • Who designs coffee shops so that they become enticing work environments?
When	• When do customers decide to use a coffee shop for more than just drinking a coffee? • When is the busiest time for coffee shops?

Look at all the possibilities for research! There are many options here, so you need to keep asking questions to identify topics that you can use to narrow your focus. For instance, instead of thinking about coffee shops all over the world, you could focus on coffee shops in one location (e.g., Australia). You also need to think about your discipline and your purpose for research. While the above questions may be valid questions for investigation, they may still be too broad or not relevant to your discipline. Develop some 'Why' questions to get at something really interesting – and more narrow.

If we continue to use coffee shops as the topic and we consider some of the W questions listed above, we can now brainstorm some 'Why' questions (see Table 2.4).

Table 2.4   Narrowing a topic using Why

Why	• Why has the Australian coffee shop developed into an enticing work environment for many customers? • Why do Australian students frequent coffee shops? • Why are students motivated to do their homework in coffee shops? • Why have coffee shops in Australia encouraged customers to work there?

A broad topic such as 'coffee shops' could be interpreted and investigated from so many angles. If you did a library search using the keywords 'coffee shop', you would have too many sources to sort through. A narrowed topic such as 'coffee shops as enticing work environments in Australia' is more manageable and would lead to more focused results in a library search.

From the narrowed topic, you can now formulate a research question. A good question enables analysis rather than a yes/no response. It therefore seeks to explain why or how something happens. A possible research question for this example is 'Why have coffee shops in Australia turned into places for customers to work?'

Your research question will guide your library search and be the guide for your complete investigation regardless if you are doing an analysis, a report, a reflection, or a full Master's thesis.

Thesis Statement

In the middle of the bullseye (see Figure 2.3), you will find your thesis statement. The thesis statement is the answer to your research question. At this point in your research process, your answer (thesis) is tentative. You may have a potential thesis statement at this point based on your prior knowledge, research, or conversations with others, but you will need to complete the research process before you confirm your thesis. We can call this draft thesis statement a 'working thesis'. See Table 2.5 for an example.

Table 2.5   Developing a working thesis statement example

Topic	Coffee shops
Research question	Why have coffee shops in Australia turned into places for customers to work?
Draft thesis	Australian students and people who work freelance positions or are self-employed conduct much of their business in local coffee shops because of the environment, the ambient noise and the community atmosphere.

We use this simple example to demonstrate the process of moving from a broad topic to a narrowed topic, to a research question, to a draft thesis. Can you follow the same process for your own work? Try it before moving on to the next section.

Function of a Thesis Statement

While you may think your thesis statement provides a solid answer to your research question, unless you do the research, you will not be able to justify your thesis statement. Let us now look to the function of a thesis statement, and strategies we can use to develop a strong one.

A thesis statement should be functional from both the writer's perspective and the reader's perspective. The thesis statement, however, serves different functions for each of these people. For the writer, the thesis statement encapsulates your conclusions, commits the paper to a specific focus, and helps you organize your text. For the reader, the thesis statement gives insight into the writer's conclusions, helps to anticipate the writer's argument, and, perhaps most importantly, provides a point of reference for the content of the entire text (Booth et al., 2003). Knowing about the function of a thesis statement can help you to construct a strong one.

So what are the characteristics of a strong thesis statement? In brief, the thesis statement is a short statement of the main point that will be discussed in the paper. It is usually one or two sentences long. The thesis statement is arguable, substantive and significant.

1. It presents an **arguable** premise. In other words, it presents something that could be debated.
2. It presents **substantive** content on a topic. It is not superficial, and it includes sufficient detail to be informative.
3. It indicates the **significance** of your topic. People are not left wondering 'so what?' after reading it.

Such a thesis statement is strong and provides a roadmap for the content of the report.

Review the thesis statements and their characteristics shown in Table 2.6.

In example 1 in Table 2.6, we see a thesis statement that can be argued – as in, someone could argue that coffee shops are *not* popular for people in the millennial generation. This statement, however, is not making a substantive or significant contribution to what we may already know about coffee shops. Coffee shops are popular for the millennial generation. Great. Why does anyone need to know this? Why does the reader need to care about this? What importance does it have on the reader's understanding of coffee shops or the millennial generation?

In example 2, we learn that 'People of the millennial generation are more productive when they work in coffee shops than when they work in cubicles.' While this may be an arguable and substantive claim, we are not certain of its significance. So this comparison exists. Great. Why should we care to learn more? Or to keep reading an essay about this topic? When we start to

27

Table 2.6   Thesis statements and their characteristics

Thesis statement examples	Characteristic checklist	
1. Coffee shops are popular for people in the millennial generation.	✓	arguable
	✗	substantive
	✗	significant
2. People of the millennial generation are more productive when they work in coffee shops than when they work in cubicles.	✓	arguable
	✓	substantive
	✗	significant
3. Although many workplaces expect employees to work in their offices, millennials prefer the atmosphere and informality of coffee shops to work creatively.	✓	arguable
	✓	substantive
	✓	significant
4. While coffee shops promote creativity and independence for millennials, employers may not value the work accomplished in such places in the same way they do in the traditional work environment.	✓	arguable
	✓	substantive
	✓	significant

ask these types of questions and realize the answers are unclear, we come to the conclusion that these potential thesis statements show simplicity rather than well-developed arguments.

Thesis statements are not all created equal. One way to ensure a complex and sophisticated thesis statement is to incorporate a paradox or conflict. To do so, you can use a subordinate phrase. Examples 3 and 4 in Table 2.6 above demonstrate a subordinate phrase at the beginning of the thesis statement (e.g., although … ; while …). The use of subordinate phrases introduces tension and draws in the reader. For example, instead of claiming that 'employers only value work conducted in the traditional work environment', we introduce contrast by showing how creativity and non-traditional work environments both create value. Such statements are more sophisticated and interesting than a simple declaration (e.g., example 1 in Table 2.6).

Depending on the purpose of your investigation and your research question, your thesis statement may take a different form. If your purpose is to analyse something, then you will need to break a whole into parts to see how the whole works. If you are comparing, you are assessing one thing against another. If you are doing an evaluation, you will need to make a judgement according to some norm. If you are creating an argument, you will need to be persuasive. If you are doing an interpretation, you will need to consider something in terms of a particular context. Finally, a reflection will require you to explore something in subjective detail. If the purpose of your research is unclear, you may end up with an inadequate thesis statement. Ensure, then, that your thesis statement reflects your goal.

You should recall that up to this point, we have talked about a working thesis statement or a draft working thesis statement. Why is this so?

Well, generating a thesis statement is a recursive process in that the thesis statement is very much connected to the evidence. The analysis of the evidence will direct and redirect your thesis statement development (Rosenwasser & Stephen, 2009). As a result of your library searches, your reading and your interaction with scholarly works, you will revise and reformulate your thesis. In fact, you may do this numerous times. Do not get so attached to your working thesis. If you are resistant to revision, then you may omit important findings in the research.

Recall this thesis statement:

> Australian students and people who work freelance positions or are self-employed conduct much of their business in local coffee shops because of the environment, the ambient noise and the community atmosphere.

Once you do some research, you may find that students do not, in fact, prefer to do their work in coffee shops, and freelance workers use coffee shops as spaces for client meetings. Your thesis statement would need to be revised so that it is accurate and reflects the content of your investigation.

4. Reader's Practice

Now that you've learned about narrowing a topic, try it out. Consider a current assignment, and use the following steps to identify a topic and narrow it appropriately.

Step 1: Brainstorm.

Answer the following questions to start generating some ideas about your research assignment:

1. What am I interested in?
2. What do I want to learn about?
3. What have I learned about in the course?
4. What texts have I been reading? What do I remember from these texts? What has stood out?
5. Am I aware of a problem that needs solving?
6. What research have I done in this topic area?
7. Who are the scholars doing research in this topic area?
8. What conversations have I had with others about this topic? Are our opinions different? What have I learned?

9. What are my thoughts on the topic?
10. What are the possible lines of investigation?

Step 2: Create a mind map or concept map to develop ideas and see connections between them.

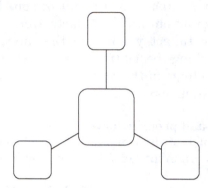

Figure 2.4   Blank mind map

Step 3: Complete the template below to identify your purpose.

I am writing about _____

because I want to find out what/why/how _____

in order to help my reader understand _____

(Booth et al., 2008, p. 51).

Step 4: Use the bullseye approach to narrow your focus.

Topic:

Who:

What:

Where:

When:

Narrowed topic:

Why:

Step 5: Formulate a tentative research question.

Step 6: Generate a working thesis.

5. Revision of Devon's Writing

Gigi: Welcome back, Devon. How has your brainstorming been going? Have you been able to narrow down your topic since we last spoke?

Devon: Yeah! Our session was really helpful. Thank you. I was feeling really overwhelmed when I walked in, but you broke things down for me and made the brainstorming process more manageable.

Gigi: Great. So where are you now in your writing?

Devon: As you may remember, I was working on a paper about the housing market in Australia. I just continued to think about what I know about economics, and I used my notes to do a library search. That helped me get an idea of what research already exists on the housing market. I printed off some articles that I thought could be helpful to me, too.

Gigi: Well done. Sounds good. Did you develop a research question?

Devon: Yeah. This is what I have now (see Student Text 2b).

Student Text 2b

Devon's Revised Text

Several urban areas in Australia have been experiencing increasing house prices for the last five years. In the major centres of Sydney and Melbourne, for example, average house prices have skyrocketed, leading to concerns about household debt. To calm the housing market down, Australia's government has proposed regulations about mortgage rates, mortgage insurance, and foreign investment. In this paper, I will analyze these regulations to determine their effectiveness in taming the market and their impact on the future of the housing market.

Gigi: Good work, Devon. It looks like you have really given this issue some thought, and you have a promising direction for your work. What are your next steps?

Devon: Well, I think I'll go to my prof. I feel like I really have something to talk about now! I want to make sure that she thinks my topic and research question are worthwhile. Then I might go back to the library to find some relevant sources. I know I have my working thesis, but I'm already getting a sense that I may have to change it.

Gigi: That's absolutely right. As you read more of the literature, you might learn that there are ideas that you had not previously considered. Keep going, Devon!

6. Summary of Key Points

In this chapter you learned:

- strategies and questions for brainstorming to generate ideas,
- suggestions for mind mapping and concept mapping to think about relations between ideas,
- the bullseye method for narrowing a topic and crafting a research question,
- how to identify the purpose of your research and construct a working thesis statement using a template (I am studying _____ , etc.), and
- how to increase the effectiveness and precision of your thesis statement.

7. References

Biktimirov, E. N., & Nilson, L. B. (2006). Show them the money: Using mind mapping in the introductory finance course. *Journal of Financial Education, 32,* 72–86.

Booth, W. C., Colomb, G. G., & Williams, J. M. (2003). *The craft of research* (2nd ed.). Chicago, IL: University of Chicago Press.

Booth, W. C., Colomb, G. G., & Williams, J. M. (2008). *The craft of research* (3rd ed.). Chicago, IL: University of Chicago Press.

Buzan, T., & Buzan, B. (2000). *The mind map book*. London, UK: BBC Books.

Davies, M. (2011). Concept mapping, mind mapping and argument mapping: What are the differences and do they matter? *Higher Education, 62*, 279–301.

Rosenwasser, D., & Stephen, J. (2009). *Writing analytically* (5th ed.). Boston, MA: Thomson.

Note

1. This may be called a culminating project or an undergraduate thesis depending on your location and discipline.

....

8. Your Notes

3

Entering the Academic Conversation

Integrity When Using Sources

In this chapter, you will meet Justin Dulewicz, a first-year Master's student in Anthropology. He is struggling with the organization and interpretation of source material. Further, he wants to ensure integrity in his use of these sources. Although he wrote a lot in his undergrad programme, he is finding the transition to graduate school more challenging than he'd anticipated. Through Justin's text samples, you will learn:

- how to synthesize source material and make connections between pieces of information,
- how to identify the significance of your sources,
- how to cite and use sources with integrity,
- about a model structure for academic paragraphs, and
- about four citation styles (overview only) to use references appropriately and avoid plagiarism.

1. Intro Story: Justin Dulewicz

Justin is planning to do his Master's research on Aboriginal issues in Canada. Currently, however, he is struggling with writing a literature review on the topic of the missing and murdered Aboriginal women of Vancouver.[1] Sitting in his apartment, surrounded by books and pages of notes, he knows he has read a lot about the topic, but he is challenged by how to make connections between sources, draw conclusions, and solidify his position within the literature. He feels as if he is drowning in readings. And while he is confident about his writing in general, he is not sure he is making any new contribution in his paper. He recalls ruefully that last term, one prof told him his writing needs some refinement.

He thumbs over his cell phone and clicks on a bookmark for the online scheduling system of the campus writing centre. He makes an appointment.

2. At the Writing Centre

Harrison: Hi, Justin. Nice to see you at the Writing Centre. How's everything going?

Justin: Hi, Harrison. Things are good. I just finished designing a website for a friend. That was fun. But I feel a little guilty for doing it because I should have been working on an assignment I have for my anthropology seminar course.

Harrison: Yeah, I know how that goes! I procrastinated so much when I was in dissertation-writing mode. I made appointments with the study skills teams to get advice on project and time management. Is that what brings you here today? Managing your proposal? Creating a timeline?

Justin: Ha! No, I'll be back next month for that. Today, I'm hoping you can help me with a lit review.

Harrison: Sure. What are you writing about? What are your concerns?

Justin: Well, I'm writing about the missing and murdered Aboriginal women of Vancouver.

Harrison: That's a big story. Do you have a research question?

Justin: Yeah, I think I do. I want to know about the reaction to this tragedy, in particular from local Aboriginal groups, women's groups, and the community. I'm interested in what effects these responses are having on developing solutions to prevent it happening again.

Harrison: Hm ... okay.

Justin handed Harrison a few pages of double-spaced text. Harrison scanned the first page and looked up at Justin.

Harrison: What have you read in the literature? Were you able to identify any themes in the readings about the issue?

Justin: Well, I think so. I mean, I'm trying. I think what I need to talk about is law enforcement – how police initially responded to the missing calls, how they were perceived by the local groups. It plays a big role in this issue. Also the media – what they reported, and violence, of course. And colonialization. I don't know. Maybe that's a start?

Harrison: Yeah, if these are themes that keep coming up in the literature you're reading, then these seem like a good place to start.

Justin: Okay. The problem is, I've read a lot about the topic. And I think what I've written isn't bad, but I feel like I'm not providing any answers. Then, a couple of profs have told me I need to do more interpreting of other people's work. I think I'm pretty good at reading and analysing and paraphrasing information. I feel like they're talking about something else though.

Harrison: Well, yeah, reading and comprehending are definitely part of interpreting. And you definitely will need to summarize all this information you're reading. But readers want to know what you have to say, too. Where do you fit in? What critique do you have of what you've read?

Justin: Well, I don't think I know enough to actually criticize what others have written about. I've only just begun my Master's. I can't really take on these experts.

Harrison: You may think you can't, but you can!

Justin: No, I can't!

Harrison: Of course you can! Don't think of critique as a negative – it doesn't mean to criticize or be negative. It means to respond thoughtfully. Think about academic writing as a type of conversation. Imagine you're having a conversation with a friend: you would listen to your friend, think about what she has said, and respond to what she said in a thoughtful way, as her friend. You might not agree with everything she said, but you might agree with some parts. In writing, you're sort of doing the same thing. You read, reflect on the ideas, and respond to the material – the literature – in an academic way. What I mean is – you respond in writing using the conventions of academic writing, just the same way you respond in conversation using the conventions of speech between friends.

Justin: Okay. That sort of makes sense, I suppose. Can you look at what I've written here? Have I done that? Used the right conventions? This part of my paper is focused on media. Like, how are Aboriginal issues portrayed in the media, and how does this portrayal impact public opinion. Have I responded thoughtfully?

Student Text 3a

Justin's Paper

Topic: Missing and murdered Aboriginal women of Vancouver

Research Questions:
1. How have local Aboriginal groups, women's groups, and community members responded to the tragedy?
2. What effects have these responses had on developing potential solutions?

Potential Themes:
1. Policing and law enforcement
2. Media: How are Aboriginal issues portrayed in the media, and how does this portrayal impact public opinion?
3. Violence
4. Social Movements
5. Colonialization

2. Theme – Media

Bourdieu analyzed the relationship between culture and media. He wrote a major text entitled *On Television* (1996) in which he addressed the concept of censorship in media, and how this can be used as a political and cultural tool (Bourdieu, 1996). Specifically, he discussed the concept of symbolic violence, which means the complicit relationship between media outlets and their viewers. Bourdieu (1996) argued that media, especially television, tends to focus on strong headlines and extraordinary news instead of providing the information that will help the general public and will support their democratic rights. Gauntlett, a media theorist, focuses on the relationship between media, gender, and identity. Gauntlett (2002) discussed how media portrayals shape ideas of masculinity and femininity, as well as appropriate gender roles. He compares how the expected gender roles were portrayed through media in the past, as well as how these portrayals change over time. Filion (1996) said that media shapes Canadian identity by its focus on both the maintenance of a national identity and on influencing Canadian market and cultural choices. Murphy (1998) examined the impact of true and false media representations on viewers and found that what viewers accept as true depends on viewer motivation as well as gender. Buddle (2004) examined the powwow and how this serves as a form of media that allows Aboriginals to participate in a cultural and political discussion. Buddle suggested that anthropologists are becoming increasingly interested in cultural forms such as the powwow as a way to analyze the relationship between cultural exchange, media, and cultural production. Harding (2006) looked at the history of Aboriginal news portrayal in Canada as well as how the dominant media discourse contributes to the maintenance of white power and perpetuation of stereotypes and social inequality between Aboriginals and non-Aboriginals.

Harrison: Wow, it looks like you've read a lot. You have referenced multiple sources here – Bourdieu, Gauntlett, Murphy, Harding. That's great. What do you think about what I've just read to you out loud?

Justin: Well, it's okay. I mean, there are references. I have proof, evidence that media affects relationships. That seems good. But it was kind of boring when you read it out loud. It was like a list of different points.

Harrison: Exactly. It was all evidence. No connections. No interpretation. Hearing it, we don't understand the connections *between* each piece of information. Why should the reader care about any of these studies or theories? You don't really tell us, do you?

Justin: Yeah, yeah. You're right. Hang on. I need to take notes here.

Harrison: Sure. Go ahead. So, the reader wants to know what you think about all this. What's your position? What's your take on all of this literature? What's your contribution to the conversation? It will be more interesting for you as a writer, and it'll be much more interesting for the reader, too, if you add your contribution.

Justin: Okay. I guess I'm still trying to figure out what that contribution could be.

Harrison: Good! Let's talk about the theme of media a bit more. I'll ask you some questions about what you've read and the information you found. Go ahead and take notes while we brainstorm ideas about how things are connected. Hopefully, your position will become more clear as we go along!

Justin: Great. I'm ready!

3. What You Need to Know

Information Organization

As you learned in Chapter 2, before diving into the actual writing of a literature review, a lot of pre-work is necessary. Moving from a general topic to a specific research question (even if it is just a draft question) is necessary to provide you with direction and focus.

Here we see that Justin has articulated a clear research question, and he has obviously started doing research. He has read enough in the area to have been able to identify themes (e.g., media) which will help him to organize his ideas when he writes. Justin's text itself, however, is not as clear and comprehensive as it could be. As Harrison noticed, Justin has summarized information from his sources, but he has not effectively drawn connections or interpreted the findings of the research he presents.

This chapter looks at how you can present research and enter a conversation – in writing – with scholarly work. This is an important skill to develop in your writing because it demonstrates your ability to read, think about and reflect on what you have read. It also leads you to your conclusions. Rather than being a *passive* receiver of information, you are becoming an *active* contributor.

There are several expectations of scholarly work. Your research should:

- be original,
- reflect the current state of the field, and
- be properly cited and referenced according to the conventions of your discipline.

When you work on a research project, you'll compile and read many sources that are related in some way to your research question. You may have spoken with a librarian about developing your database search skills. You probably have also collected a variety of sources – books, peer-reviewed journal articles, news articles, Internet sources – to help you to understand the context, any debate and issues surrounding your research question. These sources help you gain insight on your narrowed topic, and help you answer your research question.

To enter the conversation of scholarly work, one thing you need to do early on is evaluate the quality of your sources. Who are the writers and what qualifies them to write on this topic? Examine the purpose and contributions of each source. You may want to write an annotated bibliography to keep track of the information you have found (see Chapter 4 for an explanation of the annotated bibliography). Taking good notes (or writing a clear annotated bibliography) will help you to keep track of the conversation that is happening among scholars in your field. You can also keep track of your own thoughts and reactions to the information you are reading. For instance, writing in the margins of your articles can help you to critically engage with the text. This can help you remember later what points you found surprising or doubtful. Taking good notes is a skill worth developing because these notes will later help you to make sense of the information you have gathered, to categorize the information, and to start to draw some conclusions about what you have read. Through reading and re-reading your notes, you may also begin to see how a 'story' is developing about your research. You will revisit the 'story of research' in Chapter 6.

In the meantime, use the checklist below (Box 3.1) to guide your source evaluation.

Box 3.1   Checklist: Evaluation source material

When you read an article, think about the answers to the following questions:

- Who wrote this text? What do I know about this author? Do other scholars cite this author?
- Is the author qualified to write about this topic? How do I know?
- What type of article is this (e.g., review, empirical)?
- What is the purpose of the article?
- What is the author's argument/claim/hypothesis?
- How does the author support the argument? What evidence does the author use to support the argument?
- What data did the author collect? What methods did the author use to collect these data?

(Continued)

(Continued)

- What do I think about this article? What do I find surprising?
- What connections can be drawn between this article and others that I have read?
- What's the relevance of this article to my work?
- How do I intend to use this article?

Answering these questions will help you choose the articles you want to focus on.

Once you have chosen your sources and read them, you need to translate the sources into content that your readers will understand. It is your role as a writer to organize this information in an accessible format. In traditional research papers at the graduate level, this information is succinctly presented in a literature review (see Chapter 4 for more information about writing a literature review).

Organizing your research findings by themes, and discussing the findings in relation to one another are strategies that writers use to enter the academic conversation. By drawing connections between sources and identifying common threads in the research, you are making a contribution to your field. The connections that you see, for instance, may not be the ones that your classmates see. The choices you make about what to write and how to write – with thoughtful reflection and justification – demonstrate to the reader your position in the conversation.

How do you identify themes and see relations between ideas? You can use a mind map or concept map (see Chapter 2) to brainstorm ideas about what you have read and to see what thoughts emerge when you allow yourself free rein to consider anything as possibly relevant. For a more organized process, you could use a research matrix (such as the one in Table 3.1) to identify key authors, findings and trends within the literature. You should include your own categories, too, so that your matrix reflects ideas relevant to your work. When you are working with many sources – and a lot of data – the research matrix is a helpful organizational tool. It can help you spot themes and trends. For example, if you notice that your matrix contains a large number of studies that use similar methods, you might ask yourself why. Are these methods ones that are always used to study this topic? Is it possible other methods might yield different perspectives on the issue? Is this a point which you might draw attention to or critique as a limitation of current research? Perhaps your matrix identifies predominantly positive findings about a particular intervention or programme. You can use this information to draw conclusions about the likely benefits of this intervention, citing these studies as evidence.

Use the checklist in Box 3.2 to prepare and organize your sources.

Table 3.1 Blank research matrix

Research matrix

Topic:

Research Question:

Author(s)	Date	Title of Publication	Research Question/ Purpose/Goal	Theoretical Framework	Methods	Key Findings	Recommendations	What I think about this source?	What are the connection(s) to other sources?

Box 3.2   Checklist: Your guide to preparing and organizing sources

- Compile and read a variety of relevant sources (e.g., peer-reviewed journal articles, books, book chapters, government documents, Internet sources)
- Consult with an academic librarian about effective search strategies to ensure you've captured everything
- Track and record keyword searches
- Evaluate the quality of your sources
- Examine the purpose and contributions of each source
- Take detailed notes (i.e., about the source material, about your thoughts and reactions)
- Prepare an annotated bibliography
- Complete a research matrix
- Identify themes in your literature
- Draw connections between source materials

As you read through the research you have gathered, you should be able to find trends. For example, are there authors who are aligned in their views? What are the contrasting arguments that have been proposed? As noted in the checklist above, before you begin to write, it's wise that you identify themes in your research.

Paragraph Development

While the research matrix is a great tool to help you record your source information, identify the contributions of each source and see the connections among sources, it is only a planning document. Nobody sees this document except you and maybe your advisor. You now need to write about the literature in an organized fashion and comment on the source material. You need to *enter* the conversation rather than staying on the sidelines as an observer. You are probably asking, how do I enter that conversation? How do I do that in writing?

To effectively enter the scholarly conversation, you can use the structure of an academic paragraph as a framework. Effective paragraph development can greatly impact the quality and clarity of your writing. Many well-developed academic paragraphs follow a structure that looks like that shown in Table 3.2.

Table 3.2   Academic paragraph structure

Item	Function
Topic sentence	Identifies the writer's main point or subject
Elaboration	Defines, clarifies or makes the main point more specific (optional, but common)
Development	Gives support or evidence for the main point (e.g., data, facts, examples, illustrations, anecdotes, statistics, summaries of findings, paraphrases, quotations)
Interpretation	Shows the writer's interpretation of the evidence (facts don't speak for themselves)
Significance/Conclusion	States the writer's insight (what the evidence explains or its significance)
Transition	Carries the conclusion forward in the argument (optional)

Source: Adapted from Misser, n.d.

As you can see, this structure provides for the inclusion of both evidence from sources and interpretation from you.

How does this structure apply to an actual paragraph?

Read the following text that Justin wrote about sign languages for one of his anthropology courses.[2] Are you able to identify any of the paragraph elements noted above?

Student Text 3b

The first reason why sign languages should be considered real languages is because the brain patterns of sign language users resemble those of spoken language users. Neurobiological studies have shown that similar parts of the brain are active in both sign language and spoken language users while communicating. In one particular study, sign language users were presented with American Sign Language (ASL) ASL sentences and their brain activity was monitored with a Functional Magnetic Resonance Imaging (fMRI) machine. In the left hemisphere of their brains, the areas typically associated with language processing in spoken language users, such as the inferior frontal and the inferior parietal areas, were also active in sign language users (Newman et al., 2010, p. 674). This evidence is crucial because it shows that the human brain interprets sign language in a similar way as it interprets spoken language. Therefore, despite the fact that sign language users communicate with hand gestures, body gestures and facial expressions as opposed to sound, they have a language since their brains are working to process sensory inputs in the same way as are the brains of spoken language users.

Here is the same paragraph annotated according to the paragraph structure explained in Table 3.2.

Student Text 3b (annotated)

The first reason why sign languages should be considered real languages is because the brain patterns of sign language users resemble those of spoken language users.	Topic sentence
Neurobiological studies have shown that similar parts of the brain are active in both sign language and spoken language users while communicating.	Elaboration
In one particular study, sign language users were presented with American Sign Language (ASL) sentences and their brain activity was monitored with a Functional Magnetic Resonance Imaging (fMRI) machine.	Development
In the left hemisphere of their brains, the areas typically associated with language processing in spoken language users, such as the inferior frontal and the inferior parietal areas, were also active in sign language users (Newman et al., 2010, p. 674).	Development
This evidence is crucial because it shows that the human brain interprets sign language in a similar way as it interprets spoken language.	Interpretation
Therefore, despite the fact that sign language users communicate with hand gestures, body gestures and facial expressions as opposed to sound, they have a language since their brains are working to process sensory inputs in the same way as are the brains of spoken language users.	Significance

For the most part, Justin's text follows the paragraph structure we showed you, but you will notice that this particular paragraph does not have a clear transition statement at the end. As we said earlier, the paragraph structure we are presenting is common, but variation exists among paragraphs. In this case, Justin may include a transition phrase at the beginning of the next paragraph, or it may not be necessary at all. For instance, Justin may continue to write about the similarities of brain patterns between sign language users and spoken language users. The Significance sentence uses words (e.g., brain, process, inputs) that can be repeated in the first sentence of the next paragraph, serving as a transition. Alternatively, Justin may write about a second reason why sign languages should be considered real languages. Sometimes a transition sentence can be problematic and lead to the introduction of a new topic that is better left to the next paragraph. If in doubt, leave the transition out.

In reality, Justin's subsequent paragraph begins with: 'The second reason why sign languages should be considered real languages is because the learning process is similar to spoken languages. In fact, ...'

Using the academic paragraph structure as your guide, arrange the following sentences into a cohesive paragraph. Think about why you have chosen a particular order. Are you able to justify your decisions?

a. This is because no matter what type of language is being considered, an individual's ability to develop competency in a second language is affected by their first language.

b. A study of British Sign Language (BSL) acquisition in children is evidence to this fact.

c. An individual's native language impacts their ability to learn new ones in both sign and spoken languages.

d. This study compared a group of native signers (those who learned BSL as their first language) to a group of non-native signers (those who learned English as a first language and BSL as a second language).

e. Clearly, children who are properly exposed to sign language from birth will develop higher competency in it than those who learn it later on in life.

f. The researchers found that native signers were more accurate at picking out the non-grammatically correct sentences than were non-native signers (Cormier et al., 2012, p. 60).

g. The study compared these groups in terms of their ability to detect grammatically correct and incorrect BSL sentences (Cormier et al., 2012, p. 54).

h. The findings of this study are important when comparing the process of language learning in both spoken and sign languages.

Use this space to list the order you think these sentences should follow in a paragraph:

What helped you determine the order of the sentences? Were there keywords in each sentence that gave you a sense of how they should be arranged? Underline these keywords.

Now, check your version against the text's original form:

Student Text 3c

An individual's native language impacts their ability to learn new ones in both sign and spoken languages. A study of British Sign Language (BSL) acquisition in children is evidence to this fact. This study compared a group of native signers (those who learned BSL as their first language) to a group of non-native signers (those who learned English as a first language and BSL as a second language). The study compared these groups in terms of their ability to detect grammatically correct and incorrect BSL sentences (Cormier et al., 2012, p. 54). The researchers found that native signers were more accurate at picking out the non-grammatically correct sentences than were non-native signers (Cormier et al., 2012, p. 60). Clearly, children who are properly exposed to sign language from birth will develop higher competency in it than those who learn it later on in life. The findings of this study are important when comparing the process of language learning in both spoken and sign languages. This is because no matter what type of language is being considered, an individual's ability to develop competency in a second language is affected by their first language.

How did you do? Here is the annotated version of Student Text 3c.

Student Text 3c (annotated)

An individual's native language impacts their ability to learn new ones in both sign and spoken languages.	Topic sentence
A study of British Sign Language (BSL) acquisition in children is evidence to this fact.	Development
This study compared a group of native signers (those who learned BSL as their first language) to a group of non-native signers (those who learned English as a first language and BSL as a second language). The study compared these groups in terms of their ability to detect grammatically correct and incorrect BSL sentences (Cormier et al., 2012, p. 54). The researchers found that native signers were more accurate at picking out the non-grammatically correct sentences than were non-native signers (Cormier et al., 2012, p. 60).	Development
Clearly, children who are properly exposed to sign language from birth will develop higher competency in it than those who learn it later on in life.	Interpretation

| The findings of this study are important when comparing the process of language learning in both spoken and sign languages. | Significance |
| This is because no matter what type of language is being considered, an individual's ability to develop competency in a second language is affected by their first language. | Significance |

If you did not arrange the sentences in this order, you might be wondering why this order is the right one. Here are some strategies to use that can help:

1. Identify the subject in the sentence (i.e., Who is the sentence about?).
2. Identify keywords across sentences, especially if they are repeated; these words may be nouns or verbs.
3. Pay attention to *text cues* – words that indicate order, hierarchy, addition, or contrast (e.g., next, also, however).

Notice only sentences (b) and (c) have subjects that make sense at the beginning of a paragraph ('a study of British Sign Language (BSL) acquisition' and 'an individual's native language'). All the other sentences include pronouns ('this') or words that suggest a preceding idea, thus eliminating them as topic sentences. Maybe you're wondering why is (c) the topic sentence and not (b)? This is because there is a referent in (b) 'to this fact' suggesting that there is a prior fact which is being referred to. In addition, the subject 'an individual's native language' relates better to the remaining sentences than does 'a study of British Sign Language (BSL) acquisition', which is unconnected with some sentences such as (a).

Attending to the introduction and continuity of grammatical subjects can also build cohesion across a paragraph. At the beginning of the paragraph, we see the subject 'A study of British Sign Language (BSL) acquisition in children ...'. The subject uses a reference (this) at the start of the next section to refer back to this information that was presented in the first sentence. Gopen and Swan (1990) would label this as 'old information' – as in information that the reader already knows or is familiar with. Once the reader has been presented with familiar information, new information can be presented (e.g., this study compared ...). This new information is often presented starting with a verb (or predicate).

Not all paragraphs conform neatly to the academic paragraph structure model, remember, nor should they. Some paragraphs have specific purposes that don't require evidence, e.g., a description of a study's procedures. It is also less useful as a structure for an introductory paragraph or a conclusion. Nevertheless, this model is useful when you want to introduce and develop a point using evidence.

Another perspective on academic paragraphs in Humanities writing that is similar to this model is one proposed by Eric Hayot (2014) called the uneven-U (see Figure 3.1). In this model, the development of an idea within a paragraph is represented by a U-shaped line graph which shows movement closer or further from actual evidence – or the x-axis 'ground' (p. 62). The early sentences in a paragraph start high on the y-axis, identifying the subject to be considered and situating readers, preparing them for the evidence that will be presented (the lowest part of the U-shape). Then this evidence is interpreted (moving up the y-axis again) and considered in expanding contextualities, i.e., not just how the evidence relates to the paragraph's subject, but wider, to the subject of the paper, and then to the wider topic. In this way, the paragraph U-shape ends 'higher' conceptually than it began, giving the paper's argument a forward momentum. Feel free to use this model if it seems more clear to you.

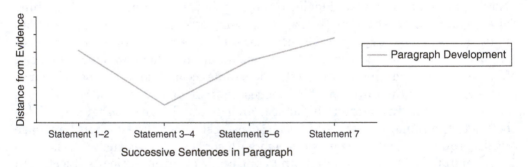

Figure 3.1   Paragraph development

Adapted from Hayot, 2014, p. 62

In addition to being a useful guide when writing a paragraph, knowing the typical structure of a paragraph can help when you read academic texts. For instance, the paragraph structure we've introduced suggests that a writer's evidence and source material will be located in the middle of a paragraph, so if you are trying to find out why the author is making a particular claim, you might scan the middle of several paragraphs to identify his/her evidence and sources. On the other hand, if you are wanting to summarize the key points of a text, you might take note of the topics identified in the first and second sentences of each paragraph. These are likely to reflect the writer's main points.

Efficient and effective reading is a skill that needs attention to build. Since the amount of reading (and re-reading!) you need to do as a graduate student is great, spending time practising effective reading strategies is time well invested.

Finally, paragraph structure can help you maintain focus and clear development in your paper. Get in the habit of reading over your paragraphs periodically as you draft your work or revise. When you read the first sentence or two of a paragraph and identify the subject you are discussing, you should see that the rest of your paragraph is about this subject. If you near the end of the paragraph and realize that you are now discussing a different topic, even if it is related (as it's likely to be), you need to stop and carefully consider whether you should cut and move this new idea to another paragraph. This type of 'topic drift' is particularly common in long paragraphs, near the end of paragraphs, and in transition sentences. If a sentence feels as though it's not quite about the topic you started out with, it probably isn't. Put it in another paragraph.

Citation Practices in Academia

As you've likely noticed in the examples presented thus far, when the author (Justin) references the work of other scholars, he follows the conventions of an academic citation style called APA. (APA stands for the American Psychological Association.) APA is only one of the many citation styles used in academic writing. As a novice scholar, it's your responsibility to learn about the styles used in your field (e.g., APA, MLA/Modern Language Association, Harvard, Chicago, Vancouver) and to use them accurately when you write. As an upper-year student or graduate student, you are expected to already have a basic understanding of in-text citations and reference lists. Whenever you're referencing work, research and ideas that are not your own, you have to acknowledge the original source in a way that is acceptable to your particular discipline.

Of course, citing sources is complex for a multitude of reasons, and many factors influence the decision to cite or not, including cultural factors, understandings of what is 'common knowledge' in the field, and difficulty in identifying source originators (Bloch, 2012). For example, in language studies, the concept that language consists of both spoken elements as well as gesture, intonation, etc. is common knowledge and would not need to be cited. However, these same points in education or in psychology would probably need to be cited. In addition, in an era when information is readily available on the Internet, but is often unattributed to a clear source, it can be difficult to know whom to cite and when. It is important, therefore, to take your cue from your disciplinary community. Pay close attention to how the researchers and scholars you are reading are citing their sources. Note what

Table 3.3 Comparison of citation styles: In-text citations and references list

Item	APA[a]	Harvard[b]	MLA[c]	Chicago[d]
In-text citation, one author	(Buddle, 2004)	(Bundle 2004)	(Buddle 2004)	[1] footnotes are used
In-text citation, two authors	(Nanda & Gregg, 2009)	(Nanda & Gregg 2009)	(Nanda and Gregg 2009)	[1] footnotes are used
Reference list, one author, journal article	Ryan, L. (2006). Rethinking social movement theories in the twenty-first century. *Sociology*, 40(1), 169–176.	Ryan, L 2006, 'Rethinking social movement theories in the twenty-first century', *Sociology*, vol. 40, no. 1, pp. 169–176.	Ryan, Louise. "Rethinking Social Movement Theories in the Twenty-first Century." *Sociology*, vol. 40 no. 1, Feb. 2006, pp.169–176.	Ryan, Louise. "Rethinking Social Movement Theories in the Twenty-first Century." *Sociology* 40, no. 1 (2006): 169–176.
Reference list, two authors, journal article	Weldon, S., & Gilchrist, E. (2012). Implicit theories in intimate partner violence offenders. *Journal of Family Violence*, 27(8), 761–772.	Weldon, S & Gilchrist, E 2012, 'Implicit theories in intimate partner violence offenders', *Journal of Family Violence*, vol. 27, no. 8, pp. 761–772.	Weldon, Sarah and Elizabeth Gilchrist. "Implicit Theories in Intimate Partner Violence Offenders." *Journal of Family Violence* vol. 27, no. 8, Nov. 2012 pp.761–772.	Weldon, Sarah, and Elizabeth Gilchrist. "Implicit theories in intimate partner violence offenders." *Journal of Family Violence* 27, no. 8 (2012): 761–772.
Reference list, one author, book	Heberle, R. (1951). *Social movements: An introduction to political sociology* (vol. 3). New York, NY: Appleton-Century-Crofts.	Heberle, R 1951, *Social movements: an introduction to political sociology*, vol. 3, Appleton-Century-Crofts, New York.	Heberle, Rudolf. *Social Movements: An Introduction to Political Sociology*, Vol 2. Appleton-Century-Crofts, 1951	Heberle, Rudolf. *Social Movements: An Introduction to Political Sociology* (vol. 3). New York: Appleton-Century-Crofts, 1951.

Item	APA[a]	Harvard[b]	MLA[c]	Chicago[d]
Reference list, two authors, book	Chomsky, N., & Herman, E. S. (1973). *Counter revolutionary violence: Bloodbaths in fact and propaganda*. Andover, MA: Warner Modular.	Chomsky, N & Herman, E 1973, *Counter revolutionary violence: bloodbaths in fact and propaganda*, Warner Modular, Andover.	Chomsky, Noam and Edward S. Herman *Counter Revolutionary Violence: Bloodbaths in Fact and Propaganda.* Warner Modular Publications, 1973.	Chomsky, Noam, and Edward S. Herman. *Counter Revolutionary Violence: Bloodbaths in Fact and Propaganda.* Andover: Warner Modular Publications, 1973.
Reference list, one author (organization), online source	Office of National Statistics. (2018). *Earnings and working hours.* Retrieved from https://www.ons.gov.uk/employmentand labourmarket/peopleinwork/earningsandworkinghours	Office of National Statistics 2018, *Earnings and working hours*, Viewed 14 June 2016, https://www.ons.gov.uk/employmentandlabourmarket/peopleinwork/earningsandworkinghours	*Office of National Statistics.* Earnings and Working Hours, 2018, https://www.ons.gov.uk/employmentand labourmarket/peopleinwork/earningsandworkinghours. Accessed 30 Mar. 2018.	"Earnings and Working Hours, 2018." Office for National Statistics, Accessed March 30, 2018. https://www.ons.gov.uk/employmentandlabourmarket/peopleinwork/earningsandworkinghours

Notes

[a] *Publication manual of the American Psychological Association* (6th ed.). (2010). Washington, DC: American Psychological Association.
[b] Monash University. (2012). *Harvard referencing guide.* Retrieved from http://guides.lib.monash.edu/ld.php?content_id=8481587
Snooks & Co. (2002). *Style manual for authors, editors and printers* (6th ed.). Milton, Queensland, Australia: John Wiley.
[c] *MLA handbook* (8th ed.). (2016). New York, NY: The Modern Language Association of America.
[d] *Chicago manual of style* (17th ed.). (2017). Chicago, IL: University of Chicago Press.

they cite and how they do it; for instance, whether they use integrated or non-integrated citations (see Chapter 5). Notice the words and phrases scholars use and how strong (or weak) their language is. What does this tell you about their perception of the source material?

Once again, we come back to the importance of reading. Although this is a book about writing, it should be clear to you now that you cannot become a strong academic writer unless you make effective, frequent and deliberate reading a regular part of your student life. Read not just for content, but to learn conventions and structures you need to use in your own writing.

Table 3.3 shows some of the differences between the APA, Harvard, MLA and Chicago reference styles (note that some publications and organizations may choose to use a modified version of a style). These guides are updated every few years. If you're looking for more information about these or other styles, consult the current style guides themselves.

4. Reader's Practice

Using the academic paragraph structure (see Table 3.2) as your guide, annotate Justin's paragraph (Student Text 3d).

Student Text 3d

The second reason why sign languages should be considered real languages is because the learning process is similar to spoken languages. In fact, it has been shown that children can even learn to sign faster than they can learn to speak. Deaf infants may begin to sign as early as 8 months old, while hearing infants usually begin saying their first words at around 12 months old (Anderson & Reilly, 2002, p. 99). Interestingly, hearing infants can also be taught to sign, and do so before they are able to speak. Their knowledge of sign language has even been shown to assist them with verbal language acquisition later on (Goodwyn et al., 2000, p. 98). This is evidence that sign languages are real languages because all children, both deaf and hearing, can acquire them quickly as long as there is proper exposure. In other words, communication via signing, and not by speaking, appears to be the more instinctive form of human communication. In the case of hearing children, it is only after they are sufficiently exposed to spoken languages that these languages replace their sign language use.

Compare your annotation to the one in Appendix B.

Now think about how best to organize your literature thematically, draw connections between sources, and identify your position based on what you've read. Work through the following exercises to get a better understanding of *what* you want to write and *how* you want to write.

Research Matrix

Topic:

Research Question:

Author(s)	Date	Title of publication	Research question/ Purpose/Goal	Theoretical framework	Methods	Key findings	Recommendations	What I think about this source?	What are the connection(s) to other sources?

a.   Complete a research matrix. Adjust the headings so that they are most suited to your work.

b.   Read your first article. Extract data pertinent to each category on your personalized matrix. For example, if your study has a theoretical framework that uses some form of critical theory, identify 'critical theory' under 'theoretical framework'. Try to be concise, but include enough details, so you can readily compare across studies.

List the themes that have emerged from your analysis:

1.   _____

2.   _____

3.   _____

4.   _____

5. Revision of Justin's Writing

Harrison: Hey, Justin. Welcome back. How has your writing been coming along?

Justin: Our last session was really helpful. Thanks! I thought I was a good reader and had analysed my articles, but I realized that this wasn't coming through in my writing. Our discussion last week about paragraph structure and interpretation helped me to analyse my own writing for several of the papers that I have been working on. I noticed that I summarized a lot, but didn't interpret much. So, I've revised the draft of my paper on missing and murdered Aboriginal women. Have a look.

Student Text 3e

Justin's Revised Text

Media and Missing and Murdered Aboriginal Women of Vancouver

Bourdieu, a prominent sociologist and social critic, analyzed the relationship between culture and media. He had a particular interest in television and journalism, and wrote a major text entitled *On Television* (1996). In *On Television*, Bourdieu addresses the concept of censorship in media, and how this can be used as a political and cultural tool (Bourdieu 1996). Specifically, he discusses the concept of symbolic violence. By this, he is referring to the complicit relationship between media outlets and their viewers. Media, especially television, tends to focus on strong headlines and extraordinary news instead of providing the information that will help the general public and will support their democratic rights (Bourdieu, 1996). In this sense, Bourdieu acknowledges how what is shown in the media is purposeful as is designed to influence the public in a particular way.

Another major theorist on media is David Gauntlett. Gauntlett focuses on the relationship between media, gender, and identity. In his major work, he discusses how media portrayals shape ideas of masculinity and femininity, as well as appropriate gender roles (Gauntlett, 2002). He also compares how the expected gender roles were portrayed through media in the past, as well as how these portrayals change over time. His work is key to this project because it not only addresses the ways in which media influences society, but also incorporates gender identity, which can be connected to the theme of violence against women. According to one source, media shapes Canadian identity by its focus on both the maintenance of a national identity and on influencing Canadian market and cultural choices (Filion, 1996). This means that media in Canada works to establish what constitutes our culture as well as what is apart from it, which has implications on who we view as Canadian and who we do not.

Since media is so intimately connected to identity, it follows that media also plays a role in the development and maintenance of stereotypes. Media impacts how certain groups of people are judged, and it can become hard for viewers to distinguish between real and fictional media portrayals. One study examined the impact of true and false media representations on viewers and found that what viewers accept as true depends on viewer motivation as well as gender (Murphy 1998). Female viewers tended to reject false stereotypes more frequently than men, but there was still acceptance by many women (Murphy, 1998). Identity and stereotyping are important parts of this research project as I want to determine how the media defines Aboriginals as well as how Aboriginals view themselves in relation to the rest of Canada.

A few authors have discussed the relationship between Aboriginal Canadians and the media. One author examines the powwow and how this serves as a form of media that allows Aboriginals to participate in a cultural and political discussion (Buddle, 2004). Buddle also addresses how anthropologists are becoming increasingly interested in cultural forms such as the powwow as a way to analyze the relationship between cultural exchange, media, and cultural production. Another study looked at the history of Aboriginal news portrayal in Canada as well as how the dominant media discourse contributes to the maintenance of white power and perpetuation of stereotypes and social inequality between Aboriginals and non-Aboriginals (Harding 2006). Aboriginal stereotypes are often negative and tend to assimilate various Aboriginal groups into one homogenous identity (Harding, 2007). Various stereotypes are involved in this portrayal, including that all Aboriginals are victims and that they are dependent on others to lead them and care for them (Harding, 2007). Perpetuation and acceptance of stereotypes results in misinformation, and promotes the idea that mainstream Canadian culture is very different from Aboriginal culture.

See annotated version of Justin's text in Appendix B.

Harrison: Looks like you've spent quite some time revising your work. I can see that you've moved beyond stringing together summaries. You've drawn some connections between different authors.

Justin: Yeah. I realized that I was not examining and developing the ideas presented in the articles. My first draft just looked like a list of information. After revising, I can now see that each paragraph has a clear focus. Writing topic sentences helped me organize the structure of my whole text, actually.

Harrison: Yes. I can see that.

Justin: I also tried to make more connections between sources in the development sections of the paragraphs. And I've tried to 'enter the conversation' with my interpretations – learning about THAT was so helpful! Now I know where to put what I think! But I'm still working on it.

Harrison: Great! Keep going! As you continue drafting and responding to your research question, you'll find you're better able to hold and maintain a position in each paragraph and throughout your whole text. And as you gain expertise in the discipline, your voice will become even stronger and more effective. Excellent work, Justin!

6. Summary of Key Points

In this chapter you learned:

- how to use a research matrix to organize and assess your sources,
- about the need to identify key themes or points across your sources,
- how to write about your evidence using a model for academic paragraph structure, and
- where and how to integrate YOUR interpretations and critiques of the evidence into your paragraph.

7. References

Bloch, J. (2012). *Plagiarism, intellectual property and the teaching of L2 writing.* Series: New perspectives on language and education. Bristol, UK: Multilingual Matters.

Chicago manual of style (17th ed.). (2017). Chicago, IL: University of Chicago Press.

Gopen, G. D., & Swan, J. A. (1990). *The science of scientific writing.* Retrieved from https://cseweb.ucsd.edu/~swanson/papers/science-of-writing.pdf

Hayot, E. (2014). *The elements of academic style: Writing for the humanities.* New York, NY: Columbia University Press.

Misser, E. (n.d.). *Paragraph structure: A writing centre resource.* Wilfrid Laurier University Writing Centre handout.

MLA handbook (8th ed.). (2016). New York, NY: The Modern Language Association of America.

Monash University. (2012). *Harvard referencing guide.* Retrieved from http://guides. lib.monash.edu/ld.php?content_id=8481587

Publication manual of the American Psychological Association (6th ed.). (2010). Washington, DC: American Psychological Association.

Snooks & Co. (2002). *Style manual for authors, editors and printers* (6th ed.). Milton, Queensland, Australia: John Wiley.

Notes

1. In Canada, discussions related to Aboriginal/Indigenous concerns are prominent. An ongoing controversy concerns the disappearance and murder of Aboriginal women across the country. To learn more, see information at the National Inquiry into Missing and Murdered Indigenous Women and Girls (www.mmiwg-ffada.ca/).
2. Note that this student text has failed to provide adequately in-text citations. For example, Justin's second sentence about neurobiological studies needs a citation. See Chapter 4 about writing with integrity.

....

8. Your Notes

4

Writing a Literature Review

In Chapter 3, you met Justin, who is a Master's Anthropology student. We learned with him how to use a research matrix to organize our sources and how to cite properly. In this chapter, we'll follow along as Justin synthesizes these sources into a literature review for his Master's thesis: a process which is integral to advanced scholarship and research. You'll learn about:

- pre-writing tasks, including analysing sources, writing annotated bibliographies and identifying themes,
- writing tasks, including how not to present your sources, and
- effective language and text cues used in literature reviews.

1. Intro Story: Justin Dulewicz

Justin opened his notebook and began sketching an outline of points. In front of him was a set of papers taped together end to end. Columns filled with pencilled-in notes filled these pages. 'The first point will be about definitions', he said to himself, scanning the taped papers and writing numbers into his notebook where he had written, '#1: definition'. 'Then what?' he frowned. 'Identity? Authenticity?'

After a few minutes staring at the taped pages, he shrugged and wrote '#2: identity' followed a few lines below by '#3: authenticity'. He had no idea if this was right. Maybe there was a less random way of choosing the order? And did he need to include all these sources? He'd never felt anxious about writing a lit review before, but he now found himself questioning what he really knew about lit reviews. 'Maybe it's different at the grad level?' he thought. He picked up his cell phone and scrolled to find what he wanted: the campus writing centre. He needed another appointment.

2. At the Writing Centre

Yisu: Hi, Justin, I'm Yisu. How are you doing?

Justin: Great, I'm starting to work on my thesis proposal. But I need help writing a lit review.

Yisu: Oh, yeah. Lit reviews are usually a stumbling block. They're definitely not easy to write.

Justin: Well, that makes me feel better! I don't know why it feels so much harder than using sources in my undergrad essays.

Yisu: It is different. For one thing, you are generally using lots more sources at the grad level.

Justin: Yeah, I've found about 50 articles that are relevant.

Yisu: Excellent! Have you read any of them?

Justin: I've read some, but not all. I kept collecting them, but I haven't had time to read them thoroughly.

Yisu: You should try to read things as you go, even briefly, to see what types of research exist, and to make sure you're staying on the right track. The next thing you need to do is figure out whether that is sufficient. Are you pretty confident that you found everything on your topic? You don't want to write a lit review for a project like a thesis when you're unsure if you are missing some significant area of research on your topic.

Justin: Here's the list I printed out. I went to the librarian, and she sat down with me and showed me how to expand my search using keywords and how to use the anthro databases. I saved tons of time by meeting with her 'cause I was just all over the place with my search. I'm satisfied that I've got what I need for the review now.

Yisu: Great! And I see that you've created a table summarizing all these sources.

Justin: Yeah. I came here last month and Harrison taught me how to make a research matrix. That's been really helpful. But I'm not sure what to do now. I thought I knew how to choose themes to talk about, but I feel like I'm randomly choosing to put a bunch of points in order, imposing some sort of structure, but maybe that's not the right order? You know?

Yisu: Hmm, that is a problem. Let's take a look at what you've got here.

3. What You Need to Know

Literature reviews are often given as academic assignments in advanced level courses and graduate studies. They also create the foundation for virtually all research studies, so researchers must, at some point, learn how to write an effective review.

Before starting, consider what **type of review** you need to write. Possibilities include:

- a systematic review: this focuses on a well-defined question and aims to answer this question from a narrow range of studies you have analysed (Arksey & O'Malley, 2005)
- a scoping review: this focuses on broader concepts and less specific research questions (Arksey & O'Malley, 2005)

You may be asked to write a different type of review particular to your discipline or field. While each of these may have a different focus, the general requirement is the same: a lit review needs to synthesize and evaluate the relevant academic research on a chosen topic.

There are a large number of tasks that comprise the writing of a lit review. We'll begin with those we can call *pre-writing* tasks, then look at *writing* tasks.

Pre-Writing Tasks

As the name suggests, pre-writing tasks are the things you need to do before you actually write a draft of your review. The pre-writing tasks that are helpful for writing literature reviews are as follows:

- search for relevant literature
- keep track of source material
- read sources carefully
- assess the quality of your sources using strategic processes
- analyse your sources by constructing a research matrix and/or question tree
- write an annotated bibliography of select sources
- identify themes and create a story

We will look at each of these items in the pages that follow.

Search for Relevant Literature

As Yisu suggested to Justin, the first place to start is with a **search for relevant literature**. Although you may be familiar with database searching already, we highly recommend making an appointment with an academic librarian at your university to ask for help in conducting a search, especially for a major project such as a thesis. Working with a librarian can ensure that you are using the most current and efficient methods in your search process. As we all know, technology and information availability change constantly these days, so reach out to the experts in this area: university librarians.

If you feel shy or nervous, get over it. Librarians are in the business of helping people find information.

Do not simply use Google Scholar or some other shortcut to identify research literature. I (Boba) once worked with a student in Pharmacy who confessed he'd identified the articles in his research paper's lit review using Google Scholar. He had, however, rather vaguely described in his paper a search strategy using recognized disciplinary databases. When I pointed out this was misrepresentation – a form of academic misconduct – he shrugged. The sources were the same, he said. When I suggested his choices may not reflect the full extent of research available, he disagreed. I then asked him to imagine having a brain tumour. Would he feel confident knowing that his neurosurgeon became informed about current developments in brain surgery by scanning articles in Google Scholar? He frowned. I asked him, would you feel confident, as a pharmacist, dispensing medication for a sick child based on what you read on Google Scholar? No, he admitted, but this isn't the same – this is just a course assignment. No, I told him. You are not *just* writing an assignment. You are learning and building the habits of professional practice. If you take shortcuts now, if you act unethically now, these will become habits you will likely continue later. And these habits may be not only worrisome, but also dangerous – to yourself or to others. So. Cultivate best practices. Even when you search for sources.

Keep Track of Source Material

We realize that keeping track of sources you want to read (or have read) can be overwhelming. Software exists to help researchers organize, sort and make notes about source material. Three software programs that we have used to manage our source material are Endnote, Mendeley and RefWorks. Doing some online research about these or other programs at the beginning of your research journey may save you time in the long run. Perhaps your university library has access to a particular program and offers workshops on using it. If you're working with many sources, it may be worth your time to talk to a librarian and attend an information session on source management software.

Read Sources Carefully

Once you have found relevant sources, you need to **read** them. You will now be faced with a common problem scholars complain about: finding enough time to read. As a student just becoming familiar with your field, you especially need to set aside significant amounts of time to read. In addition to time, however, effective reading strategies can help.

To read a large number of potential sources efficiently usually means you need to prioritize your reading. Start with an article's abstract and, if the abstract indicates the research may contribute something to your topic, put this article in the 'keep' pile. Abstracts that sound as though they are off-topic in some way or digress from your particular focus go into the 'exclude' pile. (These can either be physical stacks of paper or electronic files.) Keep track of the articles you discard – you may find you later want to reintroduce some of them, or you may need to explain why you are excluding particular works. Once you've identified the articles you will use, you MUST read them through. Not just the abstract. The whole article. Some students skim articles, cherry-picking useful bits and overlooking parts that seem less interesting or more difficult to comprehend. This is not a good habit to develop and, in fact, is contrary to the spirit of academic integrity. To respond to the community of scholars who are discussing your topic, you first must know what they are saying. That means you must read their work thoroughly. This doesn't have to be an entirely solitary endeavour. Meet classmates over coffee to discuss what you are reading. Meet your prof or advisor to discuss readings you find particularly challenging.

Assess Source Material

In addition to reading and thinking about your articles, you need to **assess the quality of your sources**. Although all academic articles in peer-reviewed journals undergo vetting by academic peers, it does not follow that all research is equally worthy. Some projects are beautifully designed, carefully conducted and elegantly written. Others have limitations or flaws that may or may not have been identified, methods that are sloppily carried out, and conclusions that aren't clearly supported. You need to know the strengths and limitations of your source articles so that you can use them appropriately. For instance, a study that is poorly analysed may still be useful as a contrast to one that is properly analysed and any difference in outcomes examined.

Some fields and disciplines such as Psychology and Health Sciences promote the use of **strategic processes** such as PICO to evaluate the quality of a research hypothesis or question. PICO stands for Participants, Intervention, Control and Outcome. These are four elements that should be identified and assessed when considering whether an experimental study is strong or weak. For instance, consider the following:

- Participants:
  o Who are the participants?
  o Are they an appropriate/relevant group to study?

- How were they recruited?
- Did the recruitment process minimize or introduce potential biases?

- Intervention and Control:
    - What are the intervention(s) and control(s) used in the study?
    - Is this intervention/control appropriate for the study in question?
    - Was the intervention/control operationalized properly?

- Outcome:
    - Were the reported results complete and accurate?
    - Were all relevant tests conducted and reported?
    - Are the results interpreted correctly and carefully?
    - Are overgeneralizations beyond the data avoided?
    - Are the author(s)' conclusions supported by the evidence?

To assess qualitative data, you can use resource guidelines for particular methodologies (e.g., ethnography), which provide a structure for assessing factors such as bias, authenticity and evidence of reflexivity. Triangulation is a common technique used to ensure the quality of qualitative studies. It requires researchers to use multiple sources of data to support and confirm their findings. Assessing your literature ensures not only that you understand more clearly what contribution a study makes, but also develops your ability to think critically and develop the attitudes and perspectives conducive to systematic research.

Remember that as you progress through your studies, you will continue to get more practice and to develop your assessment skills. Assessing the quality of a text is a skill best developed with guidance from experts in your discipline, and it will definitely take time to master.

Construct a Research Matrix

Constructing a research matrix is helpful when beginning the analysis of your literature (see Chapter 3). Such a matrix provides an overview of all your sources in an easy-to-scan table. We find it is easiest to do this in something like an Excel spreadsheet. Include in your matrix all relevant categories of information that you think might be helpful and group your studies according to these categories. Your research matrix should include headings and categories that you think are appropriate based on the studies you have found. By carefully examining your matrix, you can identify patterns or themes across your sources rather than thinking of them individually.

Write an Annotated Bibliography

While taking the extra step of writing an **annotated bibliography** may seem annoying and time-consuming, it can prove to be worthwhile when you are struggling to remember the reason you included a particular study in your 'keep' pile. This reason may turn out to be important and it might be easily lost. Students generally do not realize that one of the (few!) great advantages they hold over experienced scholars is the 'new' eyes they bring to a study. The freshness of perspective and curiosity that people unfamiliar with a topic bring to its study is one of the reasons professors find working with students so rewarding. With experience and repetition comes not only expertise, but also a tendency to see things in a particular way – the way we expect to see them based on our previous experience. Newcomers bring fresh vision and may see things experienced scholars overlook. An annotated bibliography is one way of recording what you think is important or interesting about a study when it is new to you.

To write an annotated bibliography, you usually write a brief summary of the research (e.g., what type of study it is, what it explores, its goals and its findings) and identify the reason you think it will be helpful in your project. For instance, you might say that one study provides an excellent description of a methodology that seems directly aligned with your topic. Another article may be useful because it provides a highly informative case study in a particular context.

An annotation consists of three parts: the citation in a recognized style format (e.g., APA, Harvard), a brief summary of the study, and a statement of the study's value to your work. Each annotation is relatively short; it is generally about a paragraph in length.

Identify Themes and Create a Story

Your final task as you prepare to write your lit review is to **identify themes** among all your sources. A lit review does NOT consist of a series of article summaries. Instead, it synthesizes the information provided in these studies to **create a story** about the research topic. The most compelling stories are those that involve controversy, missing pieces and searches for meaning. Identify the themes most prominently addressed across your sources by noting words and concepts that come up repeatedly. Do these themes interact in any ways? What story do you see your sources telling?

Review some common theme types in Table 4.1.

Table 4.1   Common theme types

Type of theme	Description across sources
Definitions	• Consistency and/or controversy regarding definitions of terms, especially of the main concept, but also of related concepts • How are your topic, concepts, or related terms defined across sources? Are contentions or distinctions identified or proposed?

Type of theme	Description across sources
Theoretical framework	• Use of an established or new theoretical (or methodological) framework for the study, its collection of data, or analysis and interpretation of data • What theory/theories have been applied to your topic?
Debate or dissension	• Disagreement between sources about some aspect of the topic, e.g., its applicability across specific contexts, the interpretation of some finding or data. Evidence for the existence of a debate or persistence of debate • What is debated about your topic?
Established knowledge	• Widely recognized facts or established views, seminal studies establishing foundations of the subject are summarized across sources • What is acknowledged as true about your topic?
Similar findings/ results	• The conclusions or findings of one study (effects, observations, etc.) are replicated or supported by conclusion/findings of other studies • Do a number of studies agree about some aspect of your topic?
Historical elements	• The impact of a historical event or perspective on your topic is described or implied across sources • How have different times influenced your topic?
Cultural elements	• The impact of particular cultural attitudes, differences among cultures, etc. are described • How do different groups view your topic?
Functions	• The purposes or functions of a thing or concept under study are addressed across sources • What are the different functions of this concept?
Representation/ semiotics	• The representations or meanings assigned to concepts are examined across sources • What is meaningful about concepts related to your topic?
Significant concern(s)	• Explication of some recognized problem or concern related to the topic • What have people identified as concerns about your topic?

Once you have found, assessed and organized your sources into themes (i.e., completed all of the pre-writing tasks), you are ready to begin writing.

Writing

Literature reviews are often written as a separate document or chapter (e.g., of a thesis or dissertation), so they require an introduction, main body, conclusion and reference list. Even when they are not meant to be stand-alone, a literature review will always resemble a story, with a beginning, middle and end. For example, your lit review may start by summarizing a prominent study that initiated new knowledge about a topic (beginning). You

65

might follow this by identifying a series of studies that replicated this prominent study and supported its findings (middle).You might provide brief details and explanations about these studies (middle). You might then draw attention to a group of scholars who refute the conclusions drawn from these studies and have proposed an alternative explanation (concern/problem). Finally, you suggest what information is needed to address this concern and propose your study to achieve this goal (end).

Strategies to Avoid

In Chapter 1, we identified two strategies that are mistakenly used instead of writing arguments: 'and then' writing and 'encyclopaedic' writing (Bean, 2011). See Chapter 1 for review because these two strategies are commonly misused in literature review writing as well. A third ineffective strategy is the 'data dump'. In this strategy, a writer presents large quantities of information but provides no indication for how this information is to be interpreted by the reader. It mistakes quantity of information for quality of synthesis of this information. Instead of dumping masses of facts and evidence on a reader, writers need to judiciously select data, synthesize them, and present this interpretation and conclusion to the reader in a lit review.

Text Cues

Having a mastery of language elements will help you to more easily present the themes, identify the research within that theme, and draw connections among your findings. For instance, text cues – signalling words – draw your reader's attention to how you have organized or structured the sources you've read. There are many types of text cues. Some suggest consensus, as demonstrated in the following sentence starters:

- Research indicates that …
- Several studies suggest …
- A number of studies examined …
- Many anthropologists agree that …

Transition words, on the other hand, draw attention to specific content (e.g., supporting, contradicting, extending, repeating):

- In addition, …
- Moreover, …
- However, …
- In contrast, …

Other text cues refer to your organization of information:

- First, ... Second, ... Finally, ...
- The most important reason is ...

Verb Tenses

Verb tenses in literature reviews are tricky, and a combination of past tense and present tense verbs is often seen.

1. Use past tense to describe the state of a study (i.e., that it happened, that it was carried out, that it was proposed, etc.) For instance, 'Smith and Jones (2015) **conducted** a study ...' or 'This project **examined** ...'. Use past tense to refer to actions carried out in such studies. For example, 'The researchers **interviewed** 10 patients.'
2. Use present tense when referring to the findings of a study that still hold, e.g., 'The factors leading to depression **are** ...' or 'According to Bernard (2015), relationships **follow** ...'.

Note the different tenses and uses in this correct sentence: 'The seminal study by Lee and Singh (2014) **showed** that policy interventions **affect** markets directly.'

See also Chapter 5 for more discussion of text cues, reporting verbs and other language elements.

4. Reader's Practice

Justin has started to identify themes from the reading he has done for his anthropology thesis about drug tourism and has compiled his thoughts in a personalized research matrix (see Chapter 3 for research matrix information). This matrix (see Table 4.2) of notes and ideas will help Justin to later organize his literature review. Like Justin, you will also be expected to organize and write about sources in a thematic way rather than about each source individually.

Use the matrix below as model for your own work. What themes have you identified? Recreate the matrix (and add appropriate headings when necessary) and start filling it in with the information you have read and analysed.

Theme	Reference	Summary	Notes

Table 4.2   Justin's research matrix

Theme	Reference	Summary	Notes
Definition: 'entheogens'	Blainey 2016 Cole-Turner 2014 Richards 2014	<ul><li>According to Blainey, 2016, 'entheogens' is a word derived from the Greek 'entheos'. It means 'the divine within' and these are used for spiritual purposes to connect the sacred through non-ordinary states of consciousness.</li><li>Cole-Turner (2014) as 'psychedelic drugs known to facilitate the occurrence of mystical states' (642).</li><li>They are recognized as the catalyst for powerful transcendent experiences (e.g., Richards 2014).</li></ul>	-important for setting parameters
Def'n: 'ayahuasca tourism' (also drug tourism)			
Def'n: 'shamanism'	Heinze 1991 Bowie 2000 Vitebsky 2000		
Historical views			
Negative effects	Dobkin de Rios & Rumrill 2008	<ul><li>These authors note that entheogens can negatively affect mental health if not taken in a proper context.</li><li>Since these new shamans are largely only out to make a profit, and often give westerners bad or even toxic drugs, many visitors have quite negative experiences, from panic attacks to heart arrhythmias and paranoia, to even death. The whole experience packaged and sold to naïve tourists is 'inauthentic, mimicking a watered-down shamanic religious tradition that has no history of proselytization' (77).</li></ul>	-compelling and rigorous study
Positive effects	W. Richards (2014) D. McKenna (2004) K.Tupper (2008) Strassman (2001)	<ul><li>Entheogens have the potential for mobilizing 'authentic' spiritual experiences.</li></ul>	

5. Revision of Justin's Writing

Yisu: Welcome back, Justin.

Justin: Hi, Yisu. Thanks for your help the other day. I realized that using a research matrix and identifying themes in the literature was really helpful. I had to adjust the matrix to fit my needs and interest, but it worked out well. I think.

Yisu: I'm glad to hear this, Justin. So you really did find the matrix useful?

Justin: Totally. At first, I felt like it might be a waste of time because I was stressed about getting pages written. But by doing the matrix first, I discovered how pieces of literature were connected.

Yisu: Yeah. Great. That's the point! It can be so overwhelming to read dozens of articles and then try to figure out how the info is connected.

Justin: Yup.

Yisu: So, what have you brought in today?

Justin: Well, I knew we wouldn't be able to go through my full document, so I just brought in my introduction. I thought you could get a sense of the themes that my lit review will explore.

Yisu: Great. Let's have a look.

Student Text 4

Justin's Introduction: Drug Tourism

Drug tourism, particularly *ayahuasca* tourism, is becoming increasingly popular in the Peruvian Amazon. Westerners come flocking in to the area, spending significant amounts of money on expensive *ayahuasca* resorts and 'authentic' curandero (native healer) experiences, hoping to find spiritual fulfillment and profound healing that they believe are inaccessible through ordinary western means. This research project focuses on the phenomenon of *ayahuasca* tourism through the lens of the popular *ayahuasca* resorts, particularly that of Blue Morpho Tours outside of Iquitos. The literature review that follows outlines the key framework for understanding entheogen tourism, and provides a multidimensional perspective for its interpretation. First, the review looks at entheogens themselves, defining the effects and uses of *ayahuasca* and its primary psychedelic component, DMT. Within this section, traditional shamanic uses of *ayahuasca* are considered, as well as the changing role of the Amazonian shaman and the rising popularity of new shamanic practices or "neo-shamanism" in both South America and the west. The second overarching area of study is that of tourism, specifically the category of "spiritual tourism" that *ayahuasca* tourism falls under. Though there are certainly many potential benefits to spiritual and indigenous tourism, this review also highlights the overly negative consequences of cultural appropriation and the

(Continued)

(Continued)

romanticization and objectification of the native "Other" that is involved. Finally, the topic of identity will be explored, specifically spiritual identity, and the ways in which *ayahuasca* tourism serves to reconstitute western spiritualties. This final section of the literature review looks at the ways in which the use of entheogens shape western spiritual encounters. However, though some previous research has been done on this topic, much work on the subject remains to be done. My own research intends to examine the ways in which westerners experience their own culturally-mediated hallucinogenic visions and spiritual formations, and how they "bridge the gap" between this and the indigenous context in which the drugs are administered.

See Appendix C for Justin's full literature review.

Yisu: Wow! You've really made some substantial progress since the last time we met. I'm impressed.

Justin: Okay. Great.

Yisu: Your introduction is fairly clear. You've started with some context. You've also introduced some key words like '*ayahuasca* tourism'. This info at the beginning definitely helps me – a reader who doesn't know about this topic – understand what's going on. Then, from what I've understood from your text, you have three main themes in your lit review:

- the effects of *ayahuasca*, including traditional shamanic uses of it and the roles – or changing roles actually – of Amazonian shaman, which could also be classified as 'neo-shamanism'
- a category of tourism called 'spiritual tourism' with an exploration of the positive and negative effects of it
- how *ayahuasca* tourism reconstitutes spiritual identity in the west and how the use of entheogens shapes western spiritual encounters

Have I got it right?

Justin: Yes. Great, Yisu! Thanks.

Yisu: Now that you have a clear organization to your lit review, you can of course continue with writing your paragraphs, but you should also continue to look at micro-level issues. I see you've used great organizational cues with words like 'first', and 'finally'. How are your transitions and text cues throughout the rest of your text?

Justin: Well, I can always improve the flow of this text with those types of words. I should help the reader along just a little bit more, I think.

Yisu: Yes. Sounds good. Keep at it. You can certainly work in the centre for a bit. Let me know if you need any help as you revise your work.

Justin: Thanks. I will.

6. Summary of Key Points

In this chapter you have learned:

- how to choose and organize sources for your literature review,
- how to write an annotated bibliography,
- how to use a research matrix to identify themes, and
- about text cues, transition words and verb tenses appropriate to literature reviews.

7. References

Arksey, H., & O'Malley, L. (2005). Scoping studies: Towards a methodological framework. *International Journal of Social Research Methodology: Theory & Practice, 8,* 19–32. Retrieved from http://eprints.whiterose.ac.uk/1618/1/Scopingstudies.pdf

Bean, J. (2011). *Engaging ideas: The professor's guide to integrating writing, critical thinking, and active learning in the classroom* (2nd ed.). San Francisco, CA: Jossey-Bass.

....

8. Your Notes

5

Using Voice to Make Your Mark

In this chapter, you will revisit Bellissima Wong, an international student from China who is studying sociology. You met her in Chapter 1 when she was working on developing a strong argument. Now, along with Bellissima, you'll learn how to make your own mark in your texts. That is, you'll learn how to better articulate your voice when working with source material. In so doing, you'll better connect with your reader and solidify your position in your writing. In this chapter you will learn about:

- metadiscourse, which are words in your text to guide your reader,
- integrating sources effectively and citation practices,
- formal and informal language impacting tone, and
- word choice.

1. Intro Story: Bellissima Wong

Bellissima sipped her coffee and only half listened to her friends crowded around the café table. It struck her that they each had such different voices, not only in their level of English proficiency, but also in the way they spoke – their confidence, their tone, what they were willing to say out loud. Recently, a TA had told her to better articulate her 'voice' in her writing, and she hadn't really understood what he meant. Now, listening to her friends, she wondered if there was a way to make voices sound different in writing too. She wanted her writing to sound more sophisticated and advanced. Several times, comments on her papers indicated a lack of 'flow', but she didn't quite know what this meant either. Certainly she hadn't been told how to fix 'flow'. In her upcoming session with the writing tutor, Bruno, she was determined to get to the bottom of the 'voice' and 'flow' problems.

2. At the Writing Centre

Bruno: Welcome back, Bellissima. It's nice to see you again. What would you like to work on today?

Bellissima: Hello, Bruno. I know my writing improved this term, especially with your help, but I still struggle with something called 'flow'. What does this mean? I think my papers are well-organized. I spend so many hours reading and thinking about my writing. It's not like English writers. Maybe I need to learn about flow.

Bruno: Oh, the 'flow' comment. Yeah, I've gotten that one before, too. Flow means how smoothly your paper is organized, how ideas flow – or connect – with one another, and even how your sentences are connected. Let's have a look at your text.

Bellissima: Okay. I brought in two body paragraphs in a paper I'm writing about a book.

Bruno: What is your whole paper about?

Bellissima: The assignment says to write about the ethnographic significance of a book called *The Gift of the Bride*.

Bruno: Okay, then. Let's have a look at the first body paragraph.

Student Text 5a

The novel addresses the issue of gender inequality. Substantial information is provided about patriarchal society of India and its affects on women. Julie is a professor of anthropology who teaches a class about culture and gender roles. She explains that in India, women are associated with the domestic sphere of reproduction and men are associated with public sphere of production and politics (Nanda and Gregg 2009:20). The domestic sphere is considered subordinate to the public. Women come to be considered subordinate to men and are given less power within the public sphere (Nanda and Gregg 2009:20). This domestic/public dichotomy limits women's work and social opportunities in India and in many other cultures.

Bruno: Okay. You may understand what your text is about, Bellissima, because you wrote it, and you read the book. A reader, though, may be confused because we can't follow your thought process. It might be too hard to see connections between ideas. It's also difficult to understand the context. For instance, you begin by referring to a novel, but you don't identify the novel or the author.

Bellissima:	Oh. I thought it was in the title, so I don't need to repeat.
Bruno:	No, putting information in the title is not the same as putting it into the body of your paper. It needs to be stated in the body.
Bellissima:	Okay. So what else do I do?
Bruno:	The good news is that there are many things you can do in your writing to improve flow and transitions. For example, you start your text sort of abruptly with 'The novel addresses the issue of …'. This suggests there is only one issue. Is this the only issue you're going to address in your paper, or just one of many?
Bellissima:	One of my many points.
Bruno:	Right. So if this is the first one, you can let your reader know this by writing something like, 'The first issue is …' or 'To begin …'. These words signal that more is to come later.
Bellissima:	Okay. That makes sense.
Bruno:	Another sentence is also unclear to me. You wrote: 'Julie is a professor of anthropology who teaches a class about culture and gender roles.' But who is Julie? You should introduce her to the reader.
Bellissima:	Julie is one of the main characters in the novel.
Bruno:	Great. You can insert this information quite easily by writing 'Julie, one of the main characters, …'.
Bellissima:	I see. I can understand how that would give the reader more information that I know about the book. Let me try to revise now to add information.
	Bellissima takes five minutes to revise her paragraph, then shows it to Bruno.
Bellissima:	Here's what I changed in the first paragraph (changes are bolded):

Student Text 5b

Bellissima's Revised Paragraph

To begin, the novel *The Gift of the Bride* addresses the issue of gender inequality. **Throughout the work,** substantial information is provided about the patriarchal society of India and its effects on women. **One of the main characters,** Julie, is a professor of anthropology who teaches a class about culture and gender roles. **In a lecture for her students,** she explains that in India, women are associated with the domestic sphere of reproduction and men are associated with the public sphere of production and politics (Nanda and Gregg 2009:20). **Since the domestic sphere is considered subordinate to the public,** women come to be considered subordinate to men and are given less power within the public sphere (Nanda and Gregg 2009:20). This domestic/public dichotomy limits women's work and social opportunities in India and in many other cultures, **especially in other patriarchal societies.**

Bruno: Great. Because you've added some more cues for the reader about context and connections, not only does the reader understand better what point you are developing, but also the text flows better. Let's look at one of your other body paragraphs.

Bellissima: How about this one on page 2? What do you think? Does this flow?

Student Text 5c

Gender inequalities develop in supposedly egalitarian societies as well, including North America. The association of women with reproduction is used as one of the main reasons for the exclusion of American women from military combat. The argument made by military officials is that women are not as useful as men in combat because they may become pregnant at any time, and become a burden to the rest of their team (Peach 2013:32). The biological capacity of women to become pregnant is being used to validate the complete exclusion of women from a particular job, which is a form of gender discrimination that limits their opportunities. The novel focuses on gender inequality within India. The ethnographic information presented in it is applicable to various societies.

Bruno: Well, since I haven't read the book, I don't really know how the ideas in the sentences connect to one another. For example, what's the connection between the first two sentences? The first sentence seems to be about gender inequalities while the second seems to be about reproduction and military careers.

Bellissima: Well, the first sentence – 'These types of gender inequalities develop in supposedly egalitarian societies as well, including North America.' – is the topic sentence. It is about gender inequality in 'egalitarian' societies. I've written the second sentence – 'The association of women with reproduction is used as one of the main reasons for the exclusion of American women from military combat.' – to show an example of this inequality.

Bruno: Great! If it's an example, tell the reader it is! You could insert the words, 'for example' in front of your second sentence. This will highlight to the reader and to you, too, what the purpose of that sentence is and its connection to the previous sentence. Do you see the difference?

Bellissima: Yes.

Bruno: Let's look at the final sentence in your paragraph. What is its purpose?

Bellissima: Well, I want to end the point. Draw a conclusion.

Bruno: Super. Tell the reader that's what you're doing. Maybe a word like 'thus' could help here.

Bellissima: Okay. I'll try to revise it. Give me a few minutes please. So, I need to give context for the reader and show connections between sentences, right? And tell the reader what I am doing.

Bruno: Yes. Give it a try.

After a few minutes, Bellissima shows Bruno her revised body paragraph.

Bellissima: Here it is: (changes are bolded) as was done in other sample texts.

Student Text 5d

Bellissima's Revised Paragraph

These types of gender inequalities develop in supposedly egalitarian societies as well, including North America. **For example,** the association of women with reproduction is used as one of the main reasons for the exclusion of American women from military combat. **In particular,** the argument made by military officials is that women are not as useful as men in combat because they may become pregnant at any time**, and thus** become a burden to the rest of their team (Peach 2013:32). The biological capacity of women to become pregnant is being used here to validate the complete exclusion of women from a particular job, which is a form of gender discrimination that limits their opportunities. **Thus, while the novel focuses on gender inequality within India,** the ethnographic information presented in it is applicable to various societies.

Bruno: Okay. This is also an improvement. Good work, Bellissima! Now I can see your voice as a writer come through. You – as the writer – are telling me – the reader – when you're giving an example, when you're summarizing, when you're pointing to specific pieces of evidence. This is important to keep the flow in your text and to help the reader follow along. Keep it up as you revise the other paragraphs in your paper.

3. What You Need to Know

In Chapter 3, you learned about how to enter the conversation in the texts you write. This goes beyond merely summarizing other scholars' work. The reader does not want to read a laundry list of source information. Instead, as you learned, it is your job as a writer to connect sources with one another, to make claims, and to interpret the sources you present. To do this, you will have to distinguish your position from that of the source author through the use of voice. In Chapter 4, you learned how text cues can help identify the way your sources are positioned and organized. In this chapter, we'll learn how voice identifies YOUR contribution to the topic.

While many may think that the author's voice comes through the text only by the use of 'I', in fact, this is not always the case. If there's a reflective element to your paper, then it would certainly make sense to use 'I'. More likely, though, the use of the first person pronoun (I) is not common in your discipline. In fact, you may not have seen it at all in the scholarly work you have read. Whether or not the first person pronoun is present in a text, all writing is voiced, even when disciplinary communication prioritizes objectivity.

At the beginning of this chapter, did you notice how Bellissima inserted her voice into her written examples? Did she use 'I'? No. But by using words such as 'to begin', Bellissima let the reader know about HER organization of her points. Later, when she wrote 'thus', Bellissima told the reader that she was about to draw a conclusion regarding the information she had just presented. These types of 'text cues' are signals to the reader about the structure the writer is imposing. Even though Bellissima didn't use 'I' within the paragraphs we showed you, she was certainly present in the text, guiding the reader. These words – and many other words and structures – improve the flow of the text, make it interesting to read, improve reader comprehension, and highlight the writer's voice. They also show that you understand how to use the 'voice of the academic'.

Metadiscourse

Writing is voiced mainly through the use of metadiscourse. Metadiscourse is the language you use in your writing to talk about your writing to your reader. It is writing about writing (Duke University, 2013); in other words, metadiscourse is used to 'talk' with your reader about the text. Metadiscourse happens at the sentence level. See the sample below.

Student Text 5e

This section of the paper will provide an overview of Esposito's work: *Immunitas: An Introduction*. I will provide a definition of community and immunity as it pertains to his paradigm. Using his arguments, I will demonstrate how the immunization of the individual, social and political body leads to the self-destruction of the very thing it is trying to protect.

In this sample text, the writer is telling the reader the organization of the text as well as her goals for the section. The writer refers directly to specific elements of the paper ('this section', 'an overview', 'a definition') that the reader will encounter. The writer also uses verbs to indicate what actions she will undertake in the text ('will provide', 'will demonstrate'). Finally, the writer indicates the subject doing the acting is both 'the paper' and 'I' ('the paper will provide', 'I will demonstrate'). To understand the impact of this metadiscourse, try this thought experiment: remove the metadiscursive language and evaluate the impact. For instance:

> An overview of Esposito's work, *Immunitas: An Introduction*, will be provided along with a definition of community and immunity as it pertains to his paradigm. His arguments demonstrate how the immunization of the individual, social, and political body leads to the self-destruction of the very thing it is trying to protect.

This revision is, of course, perfectly acceptable. In some disciplines it would be preferred to the original because it uses passive and third person constructions. The hard sciences (e.g., physics, chemistry) often prefer passive constructions. In this revision, note that the passive construction 'An overview … will be provided' is used. The revision is impersonal because it omits identifying who or what will be providing the overview. It also has less obvious 'flow' because it removes the personal actor 'I', leaving the reader to figure out how the ideas in the two sentences are connected to each other and presented in the text being read. This means it is more challenging and therefore might lead to misunderstandings. As well, the revision aims for an objective stance by using passive constructions rather than an obvious subject acting, but we are not fooled; we know the writer is lurking in the background, pulling the strings. This feels, arguably, vaguely manipulative. Is the writer trying to suggest greater credibility for her ideas by implying objectivity? Or is the writer trying to distance herself from these ideas? Who knows? Neglecting to mention the acting subject doesn't erase her.

Metadiscourse is useful not only because it guides the reader through your texts and aids in the communication between writer and reader, but also because it reduces a reader's cognitive load. Many academic texts introduce and engage with dense, complex information, and it can be hard to keep track of this information. By using metadiscourse, the writer helps the reader to understand the information presented with less cognitive effort by indicating how the information is organized and how it might be viewed. As mentioned above, metadiscourse can also help to ensure the reader understands the writer's goals, e.g., to introduce an example, to signal the conclusions the writer expects the reader to draw from the evidence. Finally, metadiscourse helps to build a relationship between the reader and the writer. In a verbal conversation, relationships are formed fairly directly between speakers. Speakers, for example, can repeat, restate and rephrase; listeners can interrupt, ask questions and argue. In writing, this form of dialogue does not exist. Metadiscourse, however, can facilitate communication and connections by reaching out from writer to reader, implicitly acknowledging that the writer recognizes the reader's needs (Swales & Feak, 2001).

Here are two more examples. Highlight the key words that you think show metadiscourse.

Practice Text 1

The purpose of this section is to sociologically analyze Esposito's concepts and arguments. I will relate the course theme of 'the body' to his concept of biopolitics in order to demonstrate how power and life interrelate. This in turn will demonstrate how the body has become a subject of power in modern society. Esposito focuses heavily on immunized societies therefore I will attempt to demonstrate how immunization mechanisms are portrayed using the policies surrounding immigrants in the United States.

Practice Text 2

The following exploration of Rosenblatt's theory reveals how transactional reading can provide individuals with the skills and confidence necessary for them to make their own way in the world.

Compare what you've highlighted to the corresponding texts below:

Practice Text 1 – Metadiscourse Highlighted

The purpose of this section is to sociologically analyze Esposito's concepts and arguments.	Telling the reader what the section is about
I will relate the course theme of 'the body' to his concept of biopolitics in order to demonstrate how power and life interrelate.	Showing a connection
This in turn will demonstrate how the body has become a subject of power in modern society. Esposito focuses heavily on immunized societies, **therefore I will attempt to demonstrate** how immunization mechanisms are portrayed using the policies surrounding immigrants in the United States.	Showing addition Showing conclusion

> **Practice Text 2 – Metadiscourse Highlighted**
>
> **The following exploration** of Rosenblatt's theory **reveals** how transactional reading can provide individuals with the skills and confidence necessary for them to make their own way in the world.
>
> Showing sequence and key point

Text cues and transitions maintain and direct the reader's attention (Gottschalk & Hjortshoj, 2004). We introduced these concepts in Chapter 4. Table 5.1 gives examples of uses of text cues (signals of voice) guiding the reader.

Table 5.1   Use of text cues

Purpose	Text cues
To indicate the writer's intention (e.g., to summarize, conclude, contrast)	To sum up Therefore However To review
To solicit the reader's response	Note that Consider now Recall that
To indicate the structure of the text	First ... second ... finally ... In what follows Three features of ...
To prepare the reader for what's to come[a]	In what follows This explanation will
To indicate logical conclusion	On one hand ... on the other hand ... As a result In the final analysis ...

[a] Hayot, 2014.

Integrating Sources

Text cues can be used to show your response to and framing of content. As we saw in Chapter 3, it is not enough to organize and summarize information, you should enter the conversation by introducing and responding to source material (Graff & Birkenstein, 2010). You might write:

- According to Smith (2015) ... . Smith's claim, however, omits ... .
- Smith (2015) insists that ... . Smith's data are confirmed by other researchers ... .
- On the one hand ... . On the other hand ... .

These examples indicate to your reader that you are directly engaging with other scholars' work.

Read the following paragraph and think about how the source material is identified and integrated into the text.

Student Text 5f

Institutional racism refers to the practices and processes of organizations which openly exclude minorities (Fleras, 2017). Structural barriers are recognized as obstacles for immigrants when searching for adequate employment. One of these barriers is the failure to recognize foreign credentials as equivalent to domestically obtained credentials (Frank, 2013). This discrimination is a result of preconceived opinions and stereotypes that have no valid reasoning behind them. Girard and Smith (2013) argue that it would take nearly ten years for immigrants to be considered skilled enough to work in a regulated occupation. Additionally, immigrants who received their education in Asia, Latin America, and the Caribbean are far less likely to be deemed skilled for certain occupations (Girard & Smith, 2013). Canadian immigrants are found to have three times the number of undergraduate degrees in comparison to Canadian born workers (Huffington Post, 2016). The current policies are devaluing the benefits that immigrants can bring to the Canadian workforce due to the restrictions and regulations. This systemic exclusion of immigrants from being employed in regulated occupations further demonstrates how Canada's multicultural model is false as it prevents institutional inclusiveness.

In this text, we see that the writer presented source material in her own words (paraphrased it), and cited the source material using in-text, parenthetical citations. In one instance, the writer began a sentence with the scholars' names (Girard and Smith). Finally, in the last two sentences, the writer offered her interpretation or position on the evidence. This variety in addressing evidence indicates a writer who has expertise in disciplinary expectations.

Integrating source material effectively is important to consider when you are entering the conversation. You can integrate sources by summarizing, paraphrasing, or using a direct quote. While most advanced level and graduate students have learned about these methods, you need to ensure that your execution now indicates awareness of your disciplinary conventions, not simply a good-enough attempt to record evidence. To refresh your memory and provide a more nuanced approach to integrating sources through summarizing, paraphrasing or quotations, consider the following:

- **Summary:** In a summary, you are using your own words to present material from a source in the most concise sentences possible. In a summary, you may present only an overview or main argument of a source. You may summarize a 10-page article in only three sentences. Or you may need a full paragraph. When details are irrelevant or the source does not warrant extensive discussion, write a summary (Booth, Colomb, & Williams, 2008).
- **Paraphrase:** Like a summary, when you paraphrase, you rephrase source material in your own words. You write about the source material in a clear and concise manner, and you include details from the original source. The purpose of paraphrase is not to introduce an idea in the shortest length possible, like summary. The length of the paraphrase may be even as long as the original source text because you provide details in your paraphrase, rather than an overview of the main point. The purpose of paraphrasing is to show your understanding of the source material and ability to communicate this understanding.
- **Direct quote:** A direct quote repeats the original author's exact words in your writing. A direct quote is identified with the use of quotation marks. Use a direct quote when 'the words themselves are evidence that backs up your reasons' or 'the words are strikingly original or express your key concepts so compellingly that the quotation can frame an extended discussion' (Booth et al., 2008, p. 189). Many disciplines – especially those outside of the humanities – frown on the use of quotations. In addition, overuse of quotations may suggest that you do not really understand the content and are unable to paraphrase it. So: be careful with quotations. They're trickier to master than it seems.

Disciplinary differences impact the use of quotations and summary because they reflect a discipline's epistemology. As a senior student, you need to understand how your discipline views the relation between knowledge and evidence, and you must learn the appropriate conventions that will mark your use of evidence as that of an 'insider' to the discipline.

Note that all three methods of integration require appropriate in-text citation identifying WHERE the source material is coming from. You must familiarize yourself with the reference style that is used in your discipline (APA, Harvard, MLA, Chicago, Vancouver, etc.). See the brief summary in Chapter 3. If you are a new graduate student, you will do yourself a huge favour if you purchase the style guide used in your discipline and use it consistently.

But back to the three methods for using source material. What is the effect of each of these methods? Which method do you use most often when you integrate sources? Why? Let's explore further.

A summary offers a panoramic perspective on a piece of text. We get an overview of the source material, but the specific details are omitted. A paraphrase offers a zoomed-in look at a source with some details included. A direct quote provides a close-up of a source, repeating a very small portion exactly. Table 5.2 might be a useful guide as you practise these three methods of source integration.

Table 5.2   Methods of source integration

Type of source integration	Purposes
Summary	• Rephrases source material in your own words • Presents an overview or main argument of a source • Is used when details are not important, or the source information does not require much attention or you have little space to elaborate • Presents a panoramic perspective
Paraphrase	• Rephrases source material in your own words • Includes key points from the source material clearly and concisely • Includes some details from the original source • Presents a zoomed-in view
Direct quote	• Repeats the original author's exact words • Includes quotation marks around the exact words • Is used when the original version is so compelling or elegant • Presents a close-up view

From Misser, n.d.

Remember that regardless of your integration method, it is your responsibility as a writer to *introduce* the source material and *respond* to it. Doing these two things will help your writing flow. See Chapter 3 about paragraph structure for strategies to respond effectively.

Read the following sentences and think about the differences in source use between them.

1. In India, women are associated with the domestic sphere of reproduction and men are associated with the public sphere of production and politics (Nanda and Gregg 2009:20)
2. Nanda and Gregg (2009) suggest that in India, women are associated with the domestic sphere of reproduction and men are associated with the public sphere of production and politics.
3. In 2009, Nanda and Gregg suggested that in India, women are associated with the domestic sphere of reproduction and men are associated with the public sphere of production and politics.

Why might a writer choose to introduce a source as in example 1? Or in example 2 or 3? What is emphasized differently in each of these sentences?

What you may have noticed is that the writer has placed emphasis on the material in three ways:

1. by focusing on the key idea (sentence 1)
2. by focusing on the researchers' findings (sentence 2)
3. by focusing on the time of the findings (sentence 3).

The way that you decide to introduce a source will also have an impact on the reader. Note that whether citation material (e.g., author's names and publication dates) is included within the text (integrated) or in a parenthetical citation after the sentence (non-integrated) makes a difference. In other words, citations in parentheses at the end of a sentence offer the most minimal acknowledgement to the authors – brackets, after all, are a method of including interjections and asides within a text. Moving the author or publication material to the sentence proper elevates its importance and draws attention to it. The question you need to ask yourself before you do this is whether this attention is warranted or helpful. Table 5.3 can help you identify and choose a method that meets your needs.

Table 5.3   Types of source integration and purposes

Type of integration	What do I want to emphasize?	Why would I use it?
1. Idea-focused integration	Idea	Information about the author is important, of course, but this information serves as reference material rather than part of the sentence that the reader is forced to read. Use parenthetical citation.
2. Researcher-focused integration	Research	Perhaps this author is a key scholar in your field. Perhaps you are following the author's research path. Regardless of your reason, by putting the author into the sentence, you are forcing your reader to read the author's name.
3. Time-focused integration	Time	In this time-focused integration, you may have noticed that the year is placed directly in the sentence rather than in the parenthetical citation. In this case, the chronology of the research may be important, so the writer has chosen to emphasize this by inserting the date into the sentence. The reader is forced to read the date and note it.

Reporting Verbs

When introducing source material, the writer should use an appropriate action verb. Notice in the sentence 'Nanda and Gregg (2009) suggest that in India ...', the author uses the verb 'suggest'. In the sentence 'Girard and Smith (2013) argue that ...', the author uses the verb 'argue'. 'Suggest' and 'argue' can be categorized as reporting verbs in that they report what a source has said. Do you see a difference between 'suggesting' and 'arguing'? What is the difference? Is it a difference in strength of claim or validity of claim? Reporting verbs vary in how objective/evaluative they are, in their positive/negative valence, and in their formality/informality (Swales & Feak, 2001). As an advanced writer, it is your responsibility to suggest to the reader how a claim could be interpreted. Other reporting verbs include: claim, propose, conclude, imply, describe, assert – get a writing handbook or begin to compile a list of the verbs commonly used in your field.

This section has walked you through strategies for source integration. It is important to remember that regardless of the type of integration, you must introduce and respond to source material as well as use an appropriate citation style to acknowledge the author.

Tone

We've spent the first part of this section looking at metadiscourse and integrating sources. The writer's voice becomes apparent through the choices she/he makes at the sentence level. Now, we'll be turning to the issue of tone and its role in voice. Why is tone important? Understanding and mastering tone will ensure your writing is formal for academic writing contexts. It is this formal tone that is the goal here because it is what is expected in many of the academic texts you'll write. This book, for instance, is written using an informal tone. We use contractions (e.g., 'don't', 'wouldn't') and address the reader directly (i.e., 'you'). In academic writing, this approach should be avoided.
Read the following sentence:

In contrast to Iser's phenomenological account, Rosenblatt's transactional theory focuses on the active role of each reader and, specifically, on what differences in image content might mean to and for individuals.

Unless you are familiar with the scholars Iser and Rosenblatt, this text might not mean much to you. Terms like 'phenomenological account', 'transactional theory' and 'image content' are academic, disciplinary jargon that the average reader may not be familiar with. Furthermore, this sentence uses an introductory phrase ('In contrast to Iser's phenomenological account') before the main part of the sentence; this structure adds complexity to the sentence. The sentence itself is long, composed of the introductory phrase, an interjection ('specifically') and a main clause. The combination of these elements creates a dense sentence with a formal tone, thus indicating a formal academic text.
Another way to represent the ideas in the sentence could be:

Rosenblatt focuses on the active reader and how differences in images are understood by individuals. This is called 'transactional theory'.

These are still formal sentences, but they do not use the level of jargon seen in the first version. This example is notably less dense in content. Does this sentence still seem academic to you?

Compare the two versions above to the one below:

Individuals don't understand images in the same way. A theorist named Rosenblatt teaches us about how readers are active when they read.

In this sentence, jargon has been removed as has the exact name of Rosenblatt's theory. In addition, a contraction – don't – has been used. This is an example of an informal text probably written for a novice audience.

In the three examples we've just looked at, you can see the variations in tone which progressively increase informality. Let's look a little more closely at how tone is used in a larger text.

Compare the following two sample introductions. Which one is formal? Why? Note the characteristics of each of these texts.

Example 1   **Characteristics**

The ethnographic novel *The Gift of a Bride* by Serena Nanda and Joan Gregg addresses many important themes about gender relations within the Indian diaspora. It is the story of an Indian bride named Anjeli who moves to New York City to live with her new husband Kumar after an arranged marriage. The novel revolves around Anjeli's experiences in her new home, with an emphasis on the abuse she is subjected to by her in-laws. The themes of the novel are intimately connected to kinship and gender not only within the Indian context, but also within the context of other cultural groups. In particular, the novel authentically addresses the issues of gender inequality, systemic violence against women, the experiences of immigrant men and women, and the critical role that anthropology plays in balancing cultural relativism with cultural defense.

Example 2   **Characteristics**

The novel, *The Gift of a Bride*, was written by Serena Nanda and Joan Gregg. This book is about gender relations in the Indian culture. Anjeli, an Indian bride, moves to New York City to live with her new husband Kumar after an arranged marriage. The story describes Anjeli's experience with her new home and the abuse she gets from her in-laws. Themes

---

86

> **Example 2** **Characteristics**
>
> of the novel include community and gender in the Indian context as well as other cultural groups. The novel really truly looks at unequal gender, violence against women, and the experiences of immigrant men and women. Also, it looks at the role that anthropology plays in balancing our understanding and defense of culture.

Example 1 is more formal. But why? What characteristics make it formal? Let's take a closer look (Table 5.4).

Table 5.4   Formal characteristics in example 1

Example 1	Characteristics
The **ethnographic** novel *The Gift of a Bride* by Serena Nanda and Joan Gregg addresses many important themes about gender relations within the Indian **diaspora**. It is the story of an Indian bride named Anjeli who moves to New York City to live with her new husband Kumar after an arranged marriage. The novel **revolves** around Anjeli's experiences in her new home, with an emphasis on the abuse she is subjected to by her in-laws. The themes of the novel are **intimately connected** to kinship and gender **not only** within the Indian context, **but also** within the context of other cultural groups. **In particular,** the novel **authentically addresses** the issues of gender inequality, systemic violence against women, the experiences of immigrant men and women, and the critical role that anthropology plays in balancing **cultural relativism with cultural defense**.	**ethnographic, diaspora** – the writer uses academic vocabulary/concepts from the discipline to show content knowledge **revolves** – this verb is specific and visual (compare to 'is') **intimately connected** – shows the writer's judgement **not only … but also** – correct use of grammar to indicate a complex structure **in particular** – text cue to focus topic **authentically addresses** – shows writer's judgement **cultural relativism, cultural defense** – academic vocabulary used in the discipline

Can you identify formal elements in the following text (labelled Example 3)? Underline words, phrases, or other elements that indicate a formal structure.

Example 3   **Characteristics**

The novel also addresses the importance of family honour in Indian society, which is a major factor in why women cannot escape domestic abuse. Indian women who decide to leave their husbands or who are sent away by them bring shame to their families (Nanda and Gregg 2009:34). This ideology of shame is also found in the Chilean **context**, where there is a lot of pressure placed on women to stay in abusive marriages (Parson 2001:264). Arguably, domestic abuse develops out of an ideological system of gender inequality where pressure is placed on wives to please their parents and their husbands no matter the situation. This pressure is not only found within the Indian context, but is a theme found in different cultures such as Chile, which broadens the implications of this theme in the novel.

Compare your analysis to that in Table 5.5.

Table 5.5   Formal elements in example 3

Example 3	Characteristics
The novel **also** addresses the importance of family honour in Indian society, which is a major **factor** in why women cannot escape domestic abuse. Indian women who decide to leave their husbands or who are sent away by them bring shame to their families (<u>Nanda and Gregg 2009:34</u>). This **ideology of shame** is also found in the Chilean context, where there is a lot of pressure placed on women to stay in abusive marriages (<u>Parson 2001:264</u>). Arguably, domestic abuse develops out of an **ideological system** of **gender inequality** where pressure is placed on wives to please their parents and their husbands no matter the situation. **Thus**, this pressure is not only found within the Indian context, but is a theme found in different cultures such as Chile, which broadens the implications of this theme in the novel.	• Academic vocabulary (factor, context) • Text cues are used to guide reader (e.g., also, thus) (bolded text) • In-text citations are used (in MLA format) (underlined text) • Disciplinary vocabulary is used (e.g., ideology of shame, ideological system, gender inequality) (in bold)

Word Choice

In this section, you'll learn about how you can convey your ideas precisely with the words you choose to use, and which types of words to avoid. In particular, we'll explore qualifiers and colloquialisms.

Qualifiers

Qualifiers – or hedges or intensifiers – are words or phrases that you add to another word to modify its meaning (e.g., 'likely' is a qualifier in the sentence 'People are **likely** to prefer tea on a cold afternoon'; 'really' is an intensifier in the sentence 'The student **really** dislikes multiple choice exams'; 'somewhat' is a qualifier in the sentence 'She only **somewhat** agrees with her colleague's argument'). Qualifiers give the reader clues about how confident you feel about the information you're presenting. These are important words in academic writing because they communicate to the reader whether you think your claims are certain or not (University of North Carolina, 2017). Over-use of qualifiers, however, can make you seem unsure of your facts and can also result in an informal text. Review the examples in Table 5.6.

Table 5.6   Using qualifiers

	Sentence	Degree of certainty of claim
1	The current policies **may** devalue the benefits that immigrants can bring to the workforce due to the restrictions and regulations.	• **may** indicates some uncertainty about this claim
	The current policies **devalue** the benefits that immigrants can bring to the workforce due to the restrictions and regulations.	• use of the verb (devalue) without a qualifier indicates a high level of certainty
2	Discriminatory practices **could be** analyzed using a sociological approach to prove that race and inequality are **likely** social constructions.	• **could be** and **likely** indicate uncertainty
	Discriminatory practices **need to be analyzed** using a sociological approach **to show** that race and inequality are social constructions.	• the lack of qualifiers indicates a definite assertion
3	Chinatown and Little Italy are **frequently** dynamic communities.	• **frequently** indicates that this is not always the case everywhere
	Chinatown and Little Italy **are** dynamic communities.	• the lack of qualifiers indicates that this is always the case everywhere OR in the particular case being examined

When making decisions about using qualifiers, you must distinguish between an absolute claim (i.e., something that is always true) and a particular claim (i.e., a claim with limited validity). Table 5.7 can assist you in choosing between absolute and qualified words.

Table 5.7 Word choice: Absolute and qualified[a]

Word Choice: Qualifiers

Absolute	Qualified
Will	May, might, could
Forms of 'be' (am, is, are, was, were)	May be, might have been, may have been
All	Many, most, some, numerous, countless, a majority
Every	Same as 'all' (above)
None/no	Few, not many, a small number, hardly any, a minority
Always	Often, frequently, commonly, for a long time, usually, sometimes, repeatedly
Never	Rarely, infrequently, sporadically, seldom
Certainly	Probably, possibly
Impossible	Unlikely, improbable, doubtful

[a] Table reproduced from University of North Carolina, 2017.

Most writing handbooks have lists of these words and their valence (making a word or claim stronger or weaker). An especially good resource is Graff and Birkenstein's (2014) *They Say/I Say* – see their appendices.

While qualifiers are useful in communicating your level of confidence in a claim to your reader, qualifiers can be overused. In addition, words such as 'a lot', 'very' and 'really' are informal qualifiers and out of place in academic texts. They do not add precision to your writing, and they can often be deleted altogether to make your writing concise. As a rule, avoid adverbs such as 'very' and 'really'. If you claim something is 'very important', how is a reader to determine how different this is from something that is merely 'important'? Or 'very, very important'? In academia, something is either important or it's not.

Table 5.8. shows how sentences can be made more concise by removing qualifiers.

Table 5.8 Making sentences concise

Original sentence	Remove qualifiers	Revised sentence
Social institutions are **really** expected to provide **a lot of** equal opportunities to each member of society.	really a lot of	Social institutions are expected to provide equal opportunities to each member of society.
Evidence suggests that the labour market is **very** damaged.	very	Evidence suggests that the labour market is damaged.
A lot of members must do more than just recognize that there are cultural differences.	a lot of	Members must do more than just recognize that there are cultural differences.

Colloquial Language

Colloquial language is informal or conversational language and includes slang. It includes errors in grammar that we overlook in speech but consider wrong in writing. This casual style of language is often acceptable for speech yet is avoided in academic writing. Using colloquial language (or colloquialisms) is unprofessional in writing and considered the mark of a novice. Review the following examples of colloquialisms and the suggested revisions (see Table 5.9).

Table 5.9   Using colloquial language

Colloquial language to avoid		
Term	**Example**	**Revision options**
Contraction	can't	cannot
	won't	will not
Cliché	only time will tell	become clear
	scared to death	frightened
	the writing on the wall	something that is already understood
Filler	basically	omit filler words
	even	
	just	
	well	
Split infinitive	She liked to often walk to work.	She often liked to walk to work.
End with a preposition (e.g., to, on, in)	He found a box to put the books in.	He found a box in which to put the books.
Slang (including text talk)	kids	children
	sorta	sort of
	I will see you @ the store.	I will see you at the store.
	The issue is btw the professor and his colleague.	The issue is between the professor and his colleague.
Conversational language (non-academic language)	look at	analyse
	the researchers said	the researchers concluded
Phrasal verb (verb + preposition or verb + adverb or verb + preposition + adverb)	works with	collaborates
	turn down	reject
	put up with	tolerate

There are many more examples of casual language that should be replaced with more formal academic language when you write. Pay close attention when you read to the vocabulary used in your disciplinary texts and try to add these words to your own writing when appropriate. As an advanced level student, you are expected to be learning and using the jargon of your academic discipline specifically, and formal academic vocabulary more generally.

Gendered Language

English is a language that relies on gendered pronouns. Currently, however, the use of these pronouns is controversial. In the past, the singular pronouns *he/him* were used to refer generically to all humans. This evolved to the use of *he/she* and *him/her*. We are currently in the process of accepting additional pronouns to refer more inclusively to gender, e.g., *their* as a singular, gender-neutral pronoun. While the use of such gender-neutral pronouns is acceptable and even expected in some disciplines, it remains grammatically unconventional and the subject of debate. To avoid controversy and minimize confusion, you can often use plural subjects and pronouns which are gender-neutral (e.g., *they/their*) instead of singular subjects and pronouns. For instance, instead of 'A student should present his/her concerns to the professor', try 'Students should present their concerns to the professor'. We recommend you become aware of the expectations in your discipline to guide your pronoun selection.

Wordiness

Precision in writing also requires you to pay attention to directness and wordiness. A number of strategies can help you to increase concision in your text. For instance, nominalization is the process of taking a verb and turning it into a noun (e.g., informs → information). Nominalizations convey a great deal of content in one word which is why they are appropriate to use to avoid wordiness. They are common in academic writing. But using nominalizations often means that you use fewer active verbs which can result in a less direct text.

Another strategy is to limit double verbs. For example, instead of 'try to study', you should simply write 'study'.

Expletives such as 'there are', 'it is', 'this is' are also wordy constructions. Delete these words and simply start with the subject. For example, instead of 'There are five studies that show ...', write 'Five studies show ...'.

Redundancy is a common error of wordiness. For example, 'In addition, he also claimed ...' uses three words ('in addition' and 'also') that mean the same thing. Only one is necessary.

Finally, sometimes we get into a bad habit of using a fluffy construction such as 'due to the fact that' or 'in order to'. These can be replaced by 'because' or 'to', respectively.

When we delete unnecessary words, we strengthen our writing by keeping the focus on the main ideas and actions. Remember that short, well-placed sentences clearly make your point, so key points should be strategically placed and short. Explications and descriptions can be made using longer and more complex sentences.

See Table 5.10 for more examples.

Table 5.10   Avoiding wordiness

Term	Original	Revision
Nominalization	The researchers experimented with multiple groups … People who are marginalized feel …	Experimentation with multiple groups … Marginalization makes people feel …
Double verb construction	This study helps explore factors … They are engaging in …	This study explores factors … They engage in …
Expletives	There are three factors to consider … It is clear that …	Three factors to consider are … Clearly, …
Redundancy	He is a man who … Past history shows …	He … History shows …
Fluffy construction	In order to test … She has the ability to …	To test … She can …

4. Reader's Practice

In the previous section, you learned about four aspects of making your mark (using your voice) in writing: metadiscourse, integrating sources, tone and word choice.

Read the following paragraph to raise your awareness of these four concepts. Circle metadiscursive words or phrases. Underline source integration and assess its effectiveness. Highlight words that indicate tone. Draw a box around questionable word choice. Revise the text to increase its level of formality.

Practice Text 3

The idea that people in romantic relationships basically have biased views of their part-ners is very present in common colloquialisms (e.g., 'love is blind,' 'seeing your partner through rose-coloured glasses') and definitely in the relationships literature. Operationally,

(Continued)

93

(Continued)

a person shows evidence of bias when they are asked to rate their relationship partner as systematically more positive or negative than what a certain reality benchmark would suggest (Gagné & Lydon, 2004). Most often, the direction of the bias people have about their relationships and relationship partners isn't very negative. For example, similar to how people typically underestimate their own faults and embellish their assets (Brown 1986), someone could tend to see more virtues in his/her partner than he/she perceives in the typical dating partner (Murray & Holmes, 1997), perceive his/her relationship more positively than outside observers (MacDonald & Ross, 1999), and see his/her relationship as being superior to other relationships (Van Lange & Rusbult, 1995).

Box 5.1 gives one suggested revision of the text. How similar is it to your revision?

Practice Text 3 – Revised

The idea that people in romantic relationships have biased views of their partners is present in common colloquialisms (e.g., 'love is blind,' 'seeing your partner through rose-coloured glasses') and the relationships literature. Operationally, a person displays bias when they rate their relationship partner as systematically more positive or negative than what a certain reality benchmark would suggest (Gagné & Lydon, 2004). Most often, the direction of the bias people have about their relationships and relationship partners is positive. For example, similar to how people typically underestimate their own faults and embellish their assets (Brown 1986), people tend to see more virtues in their partners than they perceive in the typical dating partner (Murray & Holmes, 1997), perceive their relationship more positively than outside observers (MacDonald & Ross, 1999), and see their relationship as being superior to other people's relationships (Van Lange & Rusbult, 1995).

5. Revision of Bellissima's Writing

Taking the advice of Bruno at the writing centre as well as her professors, Bellissima has made a conscious effort to make her mark in her writing. She has made notes about formal and informal language in English, metadiscourse, integrating sources, and using precise words to get her point across in a sophisticated style.

Bellissima is back at the writing centre to meet with Bruno to discuss her progress.

Bruno: Welcome back, Bellissima. What brings you in today?

Bellissima: I've been really trying hard on things like making my voice present in my writing and making sure that I'm sticking to formal language. Remember I was writing about gender inequality in a novel that I read? I want to show you two versions. I did a lot of revisions for the second draft.

Bruno: Great. Let's look at your texts.

Student Text 5g

First Draft

The systemic problem of domestic abuse and violence against women in Indian households, which develops because of gender inequality, is in the novel. Anjeli experiences so much verbal abuse by her mother-in-law. Her mother-in-law maybe would eventually arrange for Anjeli to be killed (Nanda and Gregg 2009:271–272). This isn't a true story. Abuse occurs in real-life society. Sometimes when the in-laws aren't so really satisfied with the dowry they've received from the wife's parents, they take their anger out on the wife (Nanda and Gregg 2009:32). Due to dowry demands and the economic strain it places on Indian families, female feticide is a common practice, with 36 million girls killed since the 1980s (Marceau 2007). Violence is a systemic issue in India, where murder is used to deal with economic and social issues created by gender inequality.

Student Text 5h

Revised Draft

Another important theme of the novel is the systemic problem of domestic abuse and violence against women in Indian households, which develops because of gender inequality. Anjeli is subjected to relentless verbal abuse by her mother-in-law, the woman who eventually arranges for Anjeli to be killed (Nanda and Gregg 2009:271–272). While this is a fictional example, these types of abuses and murders do occur in real-life Indian society. In cases where in-laws are not satisfied with the dowry they have received from the wife's parents, they may take their anger out on the wife (Nanda and Gregg 2009:32). Additionally, due to dowry demands and the economic strain it places on Indian families, female feticide has become a common practice, with 36 million girls killed since the 1980s (Marceau 2007). Violence has become a systemic issue in India, where murder is used to address economic and social issues created by gender inequality.

Bruno: It's good that you brought in two drafts. I can see the improvements. Could you underline what changes you've made in your revised draft?

Bellissima: Yes. I really feel my writing is stronger now. Thanks, Bruno!

Student Text 5h (annotated)

Revised Draft

Another important theme of the novel is the **systemic problem** of domestic abuse and violence against women in Indian households, which develops because of gender inequality. Anjeli is **subjected to relentless verbal abuse** by her mother-in-law, the woman who eventually arranges for Anjeli to be killed (Nanda and Gregg 2009:271–272). **While this is a fictional example,** these types of abuses and murders do occur in real-life Indian society. In cases where in-laws **are not** satisfied with the dowry they have received from the wife's parents, they **may** take their anger out on the wife (Nanda and Gregg 2009:32). **Additionally,** due to dowry demands and the economic strain it places on Indian families, female feticide has become a common practice, with 36 million girls killed since the 1980s (Marceau 2007). Violence has become a **systemic issue** in India, where murder is used **to address** economic and social issues created by gender inequality.	Transition (another …) Precise, engaging language (subjected to, relentless) Academic vocabulary (fictional) No contractions (are not) Qualifier (may) Text cue about structure (additionally) Academic vocabulary (systemic problem, systemic issue, to address)

6. Summary of Key Points

In this chapter you learned:

- how to identify and use metadiscourse to guide your reader,
- about three methods to integrate source material (summary, paraphrase, direct quotation) and their differences,
- how voice varies through the use of tone, and
- how to use qualifiers, hedges and intensifiers to increase precision in your writing.

7. References

Booth, W. C., Colomb, G. G., & Williams, J. M. (2008). *The craft of research* (3rd ed.). Chicago, IL: The University of Chicago Press.

Duke University. (2013). *Graduate school scientific writing resource: Metadiscourse.* Retrieved from https://cgi.duke.edu/web/sciwriting/index.php?action=meta_discourse

Gottschalk, K., & Hjortshoj, K. (2004). *The elements of teaching writing: A resource for instructors in all disciplines.* New York, NY: Bedford/St. Martins.

Graff, G., & Birkenstein, C. (2010). *They say/I say* (4th ed.). New York, NY: W. W. Norton.

Hayot, E. (2014). *The elements of academic style: Writing for the humanities.* New York, NY: Columbia University Press.

Misser, E. (n.d.). *Source integration strategies.* Wilfrid Laurier University Writing Centre handout.

Swales, J. M., & Feak, C. B. (Eds.). (2001). *Academic writing for graduate students. A course for nonnative speakers of English. Michigan series in English for Academic and Professional Purposes.* Ann Arbor: University of Michigan Press.

University of North Carolina. (2017). *Qualifiers.* Retrieved from https://writing-center.unc.edu/tips-and-tools/qualifiers/

8. Your Notes

6

Preparing a Scholarship Proposal

In this chapter, you will meet Eva Hibbert, a new Master's student in Psychology who is writing a research funding proposal. With Eva, you will explore this high-stakes writing genre that many graduate students face as complete novices: writing a scholarship application (alternatively called a grant application or research funding application). High stakes? Yes, you could receive substantial research funding if you are successful versus none if you are not. As well, the inclusion of a prestigious award on your CV can open doors for other research opportunities, including academic jobs. The strategies in this chapter can be applied to any type of highly persuasive texts such as proposals for business and non-governmental organizations. But you may be like us: we had zero experience writing such an application (heck, even reading such applications!) before we were told in the first month of our graduate programme that we needed to write one. Although this could be a stressful situation, there are ways to minimize the anxiety.

You will learn:

- the demands of high-stakes proposal writing,
- a model that can be used to guide proposal writing and other persuasive texts such as application letters, and
- rhetorical concepts to consider: ethos, logos, pathos.

1. Intro Story: Eva Hibbert

Midnight, and the bluish glow from the computer illuminated Eva's face as she peered at the screen, reading intently. 'Good', she thought to herself. 'This is good. I think Etienne will like it. Done.' She clicked to save the file again, just to be sure, then attached it to an email and hit 'send'. She turned off the computer. Etienne should be in his office by 8:30 am and reading her draft. She'd stop in at 9:00 am to see what he thought.

Etienne: A really good first effort, Eva! This project really should get funded, I think. I suggest you take it to the writing centre for help with revision before submitting the application.

Eva: Is there something wrong? Did I make a mistake?

Etienne: Grant and funding applications are special documents. It is important to learn how to present them most effectively, especially for first-year graduate students like you.

Eva: Oh. You mean I haven't written the proposal properly? Is my writing – bad?

Etienne: I didn't say that. I suggested it might be more effective. The writing centre can help.

And with that, Etienne turned around, and Eva realized she was being dismissed.

2. At the Writing Centre

Cory: So this is your first grant application? And your Master's supervisor suggested you come here for some help?

Eva: Yes. He said grant applications are special documents and the writing centre can show me how to make mine more effective.

Cory: He's absolutely right! I love it when faculty know about our work and refer students to us.

Eva: Here's my draft. I thought it was pretty good. I followed all the instructions and I've always been an excellent writer. I'm not sure what the problem is. He didn't say.

Cory: You're in luck! I actually really enjoy working with students on their grant applications. So, can you tell me what it is you want to do?

Eva: It's here, this part. This is my research project.

Cory: I see. But can you explain to me what you want to do? What's your project about?

Eva: Well, it builds on the work I did in my undergrad research project in psychology. I'm looking at the perceptions of change room spaces by the gay – LGBTI (lesbian, gay, bisexual, transgender, and intersex) – community.

Cory: Hmm. You mean inclusion of the LGBTI community in change rooms?

Eva: Yes. That's right. It's actually even more complicated than that.

3. What You Need to Know

Most graduate students begin their studies with enthusiasm for their particular field and an overwhelming interest in an issue or question related to that field. You may be one of those students who is eager to talk about your work to anyone who will ask. (If not, perhaps you should reconsider your field?) If you have a willing audience, take advantage of the situation and use it to practise talking about your research interest.

This 'talking' is important because it gives you practice in articulating ideas about your work and gives you a chance to hear someone's response to those words and ideas. Whether we communicate orally, in writing, through technology, or any other way, communicating is always based on shared attention to an idea or thought – a writer and a reader, a speaker and a listener, responding to each other. Successful communication provides benefits to both parties.

When students write papers about topics that interest them, however, they often forget about this requirement to engage with a reader. They sometimes act as if everyone is as excited about their topic as they are. They can become overly focused on the topic itself, and write at length about new findings in the field, questions and controversies taken up by current or former scholars, background information, methods and historical contexts, and do it all using jargon that may or may not be comprehensible to the audience. While this enthusiasm in oral communication is endearing in the view of some people and annoying to others, it is not an effective approach to engaging people when writing.

Engaging the audience holds particular importance when you write documents that must convince that audience to materially support you and your work. Research grants and research scholarship proposals are such documents: you need to convince an audience to give you money to carry out a particular research activity. You need to convince them that YOU are worthy to receive their confidence (and money) and that your project is one that deserves funding.

This is significantly different from a perspective that sees grant writing as a primarily transactional research activity, i.e., you show the need for a particular research project and, if this need is confirmed, the project is funded. This perspective is a rational, objective perspective. It also completely overlooks the emotional and interpersonal aspects of research. It is helpful to remember that asking people to support your work is as much about human engagement as it is about research activity. Learning how to write effective grant proposals, then, requires attention not only to research content, but to the rhetorical situation inherent in asking for funding.

So, what do you think might be important to tell an audience if you are asking them for money to support you? Imagine you have $100,000 in your bank account. Identify which of the following items would convince YOU to give that money to someone for their research:

a. Credentials of the researcher
b. Your own interest in the project
c. World-wide impact of the project
d. Ability to complete the project quickly
e. Trendiness of the topic
f. How expensive the project will be
g. The extent of others' work on the same/similar projects
h. The enthusiasm of the researcher
i. Whether the project is on the 'cutting edge' of knowledge
j. Whether the researcher is an expert in the topic
k. Whether the researcher has experience doing similar projects
l. Whether the project will lead to further research or provide conclusion for a current concern

So, who are you going to give your money to? Someone who is bold, enthusiastic, but has little experience in a field? Someone doing a sexy, controversial project that will attract widespread attention because it addresses a current issue? Someone who is meticulously planning a small but long-term study in an area of particular interest to you? Or a new scholar in an established field who has identified a gap in existing knowledge that may have significant practical implications?

Perhaps you can see benefits to funding each of these researchers – which suggests that there is not one 'correct' way to have a successful funding proposal. Instead, it depends on a number of factors, such as the researcher's experience, prominence of the topic, extent of prior and current research on the topic, and impact of the project, among many others. Students who depend only upon an explication of content on their topic – like Eva – are likely to overlook these other factors. Simply put, content knowledge (expertise) is not enough.

*   So how do you include more than content in your scholarship proposal?
*   What, specifically, do you include?
*   What does it mean to address your credibility as a researcher?
*   How do you talk about your experience?
*   What does writing about the prominence of your topic actually look like?

To answer these questions, we can turn to the seminal work of linguist John Swales. Swales' research analysing successfully published research articles provides a model for the 'moves' that effectively introduce research ideas to a reader. He calls this the CARS model: Create A Research Space (Swales, 1990) (see Table 6.1).

Table 6.1   The CARS model

Move	How to do it
Establish a territory	• Make a centrality claim, • Make a topic generalization, and/or • Review the literature.
Establish a niche	Narrow your focus by • identifying a *gap*, • posing a *question*, • *extending* existing research, and/or • *contradicting* an existing position.
Occupy the niche	State how your proposed study can best *fill the niche by* • articulating your purpose(s) or goal(s), and/or • outlining your methodology, claims, hypothesis, and/or contributions to knowledge.

Adapted from Swales, 1990.

Let's see how the CARS model can be applied to scholarship proposal writing.

Establish a Territory

Make a Centrality Claim

Let's say your research is on how tax policy affects entrepreneurship. You could begin your grant application by saying, 'My proposed research project looks at how tax policy affects entrepreneurship.' Direct, yes. Engaging of the reader, not so much. This type of statement reflects a writer-centric view of research: telling what you, the *researcher*, are doing. But recall that you are trying to communicate with people who have $100,000 in their bank accounts and are trying to decide which project to fund. To really make an impact, you need to go beyond simply identifying your topic to actually convincing your reader that it is important and fascinating. In other words, you need to switch to a reader-centric view.

One way to address a reader's attention is to make a centrality claim, which means that you identify your topic as central to public interest or to current research interests. If, for instance, your government has recently proposed contentious tax policy changes, you could say:

'Recent proposals to make tax laws more equitable have generated widespread outcry from small business owners (Doe, 2017) and critique from accountants and the finance sector (Jones, 2017; Smith, 2017).'

If no such public interest is handily available and the interest is primarily that of other scholars, you could say:

> 'Many economists have debated the merits of using tax policy to encourage growth in entrepreneurship in Canada (Jones, 2017), the UK (Smith, 2017), and the US (Doe, 2017).'

These types of centrality claims are engaging because they draw the reader's attention to the fact that a lot of people think this is an important topic. Many other people besides you, one lonely researcher, are invested in examining it. This topic is getting public attention. Even, this topic is sexy!

But, you might be saying to yourself, my topic isn't getting any public attention. Nobody here is arguing publicly about tax policy. What can *I* do?

Make a Topic Generalization

If you can't make a claim that your proposed research topic is central in importance to the world, your country, or your field, you may be able to make claims about the current state of knowledge on your topic. In other words, you can make a topic generalization, such as:

> 'Tax laws in Germany have received scant attention from the public and, apart from periodic reviews by various government bodies, have been little changed in over 25 years. Until Smith and Jones' (2012) study of the impact of tax law on entrepreneurship, growth in small businesses was not connected to tax law. Their study, however, established that taxation policy can contribute to regional economic growth by encouraging entrepreneurship.'

In this example, the writer acknowledges that her topic is not 'sexy' in the eyes of the public or even many researchers because it is not generating a great deal of attention. Nevertheless, she presents the reader with a summary of what is known or accepted to be true about the topic. Adding references to existing source material supports your claims about that general understanding or consensus on your topic.

Key phrases when using topic generalizations may include:

- The effects of … are well established …
- XXX has been shown to influence …
- The relation between … and … is known to rely upon …

Review Items of Previous Research

A third step in establishing the territory of your work is reviewing previous research. This step is probably the most familiar one to students because it refers to the process of summarizing content knowledge. When you're reviewing items of previous research, you're pointing to key pieces of scholarly work that will – or have – informed your line of enquiry. You can take the opportunity to provide significant details about a particular study – or studies. You'll likely keep the name(s) of some scholars within your sentences rather than burying them in a parenthetical citation or footnote. For example:

- Smith's (2014) study of …
- Jones' (1990) theory of …

See Chapter 5 for information about integrated and non-integrated citations and when to use them.

But the CARS model does not suggest you use only one method to establish the territory. Often a combination of steps will most effectively give the reader context. For instance, you can combine a centrality claim with a review of previous research, reinforcing how much attention has been devoted to your topic.

Depending on the stage you're at in your research and the extent of publications on your topic, the 'establishing the territory' portion of your proposal may be relatively short and succinct. This is no reason to worry. There is no benefit in presenting a lengthy review of the literature at this point (nor is there space to do so) because, although your reader is interested in the context, what he or she really wants to know is, what is the problem?

Establish a Niche

Identify a Gap

There are four ways to establish a niche within the CARS model. It will be up to you – the writer – to determine which way is most relevant for your work. Identifying a gap may be the easiest strategy to use, so we'll start with that.

When you identify a gap, you clearly articulate that research on something is missing and therefore required. Your reading of the literature on your topic should alert you to where the gaps lie. If you have not been able to find an answer to the question that interests you, that is a gap. Be careful not to minimize or dismiss any research that you considered when you identified a potential gap because, frankly, you are far too junior to be making those types of judgements! In fact, as a researcher (whether you are a novice or established scholar) you are expected to demonstrate humility in the search for knowledge; one way of doing this is to acknowledge your predecessors' contributions, even as you point out that research on some aspect of the problem is still required. You can identify a gap in the area by using phrases such as:

- There is little research in the area of ...
- It has yet to be discovered ...
- The extent to which ... remains unclear.

The grammatical construction known as subordination can be particularly useful here. Subordination involves juxtaposing two ideas within a sentence, placing one in the background and one in the foreground through the use of specific words and punctuation. You could say, for instance:

'Although the processes involved in disseminating information through social media are widely known and used, little research has examined the impact these processes have on users' motivation to share confidential information.'

In this sentence, a common understanding about social media is presented as background information against which the interesting observation that we know little about one particular aspect (impact on 'x') is presented as a gap. Note the introductory clause beginning with the subordinating conjunction 'although' followed by a comma, and then the main point in a clear and direct clause. Together, they make a complex sentence which is interesting both in content and in structure.

Pose a Question

Another way to establish a niche within a broad territory is to pose a question that has yet to be answered within the literature.

For example, you might make a topic generalization and follow it by writing:

- How does ... influence ...?
- In what ways can ... determine ...?
- Which model best accounts for ...?

Clearly articulating a question worthy of investigation gives the reader the sense that there is research to be done. In addition, inserting a question into your text has an important rhetorical function. It directly addresses your reader and brings that reader in by inviting him/her to consider the question.

Extend Existing Research

Perhaps you think research is necessary to *extend* some really interesting work; that is, a model or theory needs to be explored in a new way. Perhaps a particular intervention has been tested with X group and Y group, but you wonder if it is effective with Z group? If extending a current line of research or a tradition will provide significant new information in your field, then you could use this strategy to establish your niche.

Sample phrases include:

- It is necessary to build on our understanding of …
- The model needs to be extended to determine …
- By expanding on the work of Smith and Jones, …

Contradict an Existing Position

Contradicting an existing position is perhaps the most dramatic of the steps in establishing a niche. This is a bold move. Here, you're essentially proposing a different direction than the scholars who have come before you. You are offering a counter-claim – an opposing viewpoint – to one that exists in your field of research.

For example, you might write the following:

- While Smith (2016) argues …, this reasoning is flawed because …
- Existing studies have failed to account for …
- These approaches are unreliable in that they …

As you might notice, the language of contradiction is strong – failed, flawed, unreliable – and if you opt to use this step, the reader will definitely expect you to support your position clearly and confidently. It is, however, an effective way of getting attention and showing confidence by stepping up to contribute your voice to the scholarly conversation (Li, 2008).

Using one or more of the 'establish a niche' steps will persuade the reader that research in your area is required. The reader will be convinced that there's a hole in our knowledge and that it needs to be filled.

You are now perfectly positioned to tell the reader how YOU are going to fill this hole with your research project. Now, it's your job to occupy the niche.

Occupy the Niche

You'll likely want to occupy the niche by announcing the goals of your work and providing details about your project. You may find this the easiest section of the proposal to write because it involves describing concrete actions, but you'll need to think carefully about what level of detail to include, your language (watch out for jargon!), and consistency between what you have already presented (in the territory and establish a niche section) and your own project.

Articulate your Purpose or Goal

In this step, you articulate the purpose(s) or goal(s) of your project. It is often best to be direct and explicit with this important move. Consider where you want to put this statement: at the beginning of a description of previous research or after? After a centrality claim? Before a description of your project's methods?

A clear statement might begin:

- The purpose of my research is to …
- My project will determine whether …
- The proposed study will identify …

Outline Your Methodology, Claims, Hypothesis, and/or Contributions to Knowledge

After stating the overarching purpose(s) or goal(s) of your work, you'll want to outline your methodology, claims, hypothesis, and/or contributions to knowledge. All researchers work within particular frameworks or perspectives recognized in their discipline. You need to align your work with one or more of these frameworks to show that you will be drawing from assumptions and understandings that are relevant and supported by others. You need to describe what you will actually do – your methods – and you need to do so at a level of detail that is appropriate to your level of study. For instance, if you are a student just entering a Master's programme, you will not be expected to have the level of detail and sophistication in your methods that a second-year doctoral student should have. But you may very well be expected to articulate a theoretical framework that will influence your data collection. In addition, just as you made your study's purpose clear in a direct sentence, you should make your research question or hypothesis equally clear. You might even consider putting this question in a separate paragraph with a subtitle so it can't be missed.

Summary of CARS

What the CARS model can do is provide you with strategies to demonstrate that you are learning to become part of an existing research and disciplinary community. This community has a history, and interests, and goals, and language that its members share and value. These values differ across disciplines, but there are also values that are recognized widely across all research fields. By demonstrating that you are trying to participate in the research community using its recognized behaviours, you indicate to the reader that you also share in the community's values and therefore ought to be recognized (with funding!).

Rhetorical Appeals: Ethos, Pathos, Logos

The CARS model you have just learned will help you present your research project in moves that rely on evidence and reason. This is referred to as *logos* – an appeal to logic, one of the three central concepts from classical rhetoric. The other two are *ethos* (appeals to credibility) and *pathos* (appeals to emotion).

Preparing your scholarship proposal requires you to draw on all three rhetorical appeals:

- *Ethos* refers broadly to an appeal to credibility. In the context of grant applications, it shows the reader that you have the expertise or experience needed to carry out your project. In other words, your proposal demonstrates that you are situated to successfully carry out and complete the research study you described. This might be through demonstrating a long-standing commitment to the work, particular skills development, or related work experience.
- *Pathos* refers to an appeal to emotion. In the context of grant applications, it demonstrates how your project connects you to the wider community through values, engagement and disciplinary or cultural norms. For instance, a long-standing interest in a field of study should be conveyed through a sense of engagement or passion about your topic which readers value. It has been found that reviewers evaluate a researcher's engagement with the topic when they are assessing projects (Lamont, 2009).
- *Logos* refers to logical, rational presentations of research and evidence. In the context of a grant application, this can be seen in a concise review of the literature, demonstrating a need for your study; relevant details explaining your own study; and an acknowledgement of the contributions your study will make to the field.

4. Reader's Practice

Consider your research project and fill in the tables below.
Which move will you use to establish territory in your application?

Move	Example for my study	Use?
Centrality claim		
Topic generalizations		
Review items of research		

Which move will you use to establish a niche in your application?

Move	Example for my study	Use?
Identify a gap		
Pose a question		
Extend existing research		
Contradict an existing position		

Which move will you use to occupy the niche in your application?

Move	Example for my study	Use?
Articulate purpose/goal		
Identify theoretical framework		
Identify methodology		
State claims/hypotheses		
Contribution to knowledge		

Turning to *ethos*, consider your credibility by checking the list below. Which items merit inclusion in your application? Check all that apply.

Ethos:

- ☐ completed previous research on related topic
- ☐ pilot study planned or completed
- ☐ received previous funding
- ☐ received scholarship/award/recognition
- ☐ published research
- ☐ have specific technical/lab/methodological skills (e.g., statistical software, data analysis, lab procedures, etc.):_____
- ☐ experience as a research assistant
- ☐ teaching experience
- ☐ work experience
- ☐ relevant courses taken:_____
- ☐ student of _____ (relevant faculty member)
- ☐ conference presentations, invitations, attendance
- ☐ other _____

Now consider how you will engage emotionally with your reader.
Pathos:

- ☐ show personal connection to project
- ☐ identify long-standing or historical connection to topic
- ☐ demonstrate significance of study to society
- ☐ use of vocabulary that suggests engagement, passion, and/or innovation
- ☐ show connection to disciplinary community
- ☐ demonstrated sense of 'story' in your application
- ☐ other _____

Take a look at the first paragraphs of Eva's scholarship proposal draft. Identify evidence of her use of rhetorical appeals (pathos, ethos, logos).

Student Text 6a

While serving on the Canadian women's boxing team, and as a three-time Canadian champion, I have visited change rooms around the world. As an androgynous female athlete, entering the women's change room can be an alienating experience. I am regularly met with nervous or hostile stares and often directed to the men's change room. In 2015, returning to Toronto between competitions, I observed a phenomenon that compelled me to return to University of Toronto to pursue a Master's degree.

   Entering the change room at the U of T's Athletic Center, I observed that the reactions I'd grown accustomed to were replaced with welcoming nods from other women in the change room. At this time, an installation for the Pan-Am Games, The Change Room Project (CRP) was on display (Fusco et al. 2015). Large posters with quotations from lesbian, gay, bi, transgender, intersex, and queer (LGBTIQ) participants were mounted in visible areas. These quotations gave change room users an opportunity to look inside the vulnerability that LGBTIQ often experience in this space. For example, "In the change room I dress as quick as possible. I'm afraid if I make eye contact, I'll get beat up (John, transgender athlete)." My Master's research pursues the hypothesis that the CRP offers a model which can alter perceptions of diverse bodies, previously rendered unintelligible in the change room (Sykes 2011).

Compare your analysis with our analysis below (**pathos**, *ethos*, logos).

Student Text 6a (annotated)

While serving on the Canadian women's boxing team, and as a three-time Canadian champion, I have visited change rooms around the world. **As an androgynous female** athlete, entering the women's change room can be an alienating experience. I am regularly met with nervous or hostile stares and often directed to the men's change room. In 2015, returning home between competitions, I observed a phenomenon that compelled me to return to university to pursue a Master's degree.

Entering the change room at the university's Athletic Centre, I observed that the reactions I'd grown accustomed to were replaced with welcoming nods from other women in the change room. At this time, an installation for the Pan-Am Games, The Change Room Project (CRP) was on display (Fusco et al. 2015). Large posters with quotations from lesbian, gay, bi, transgender, intersex, and queer (LGBTIQ) participants were mounted in visible areas. **These quotations gave change room users an opportunity to look inside the vulnerability that LGBTIQ often experience in this space. For example, "In the change room I dress as quick as possible. I'm afraid if I make eye contact, I'll get beat up (John, transgender athlete)."** My Master's research pursues the hypothesis that the CRP offers a model which can alter perceptions of diverse bodies, previously rendered unintelligible in the change room (Sykes 2011).

As you can see, sometimes your sentences overlap and serve more than one purpose, e.g., they demonstrate both ethos and pathos or logos and pathos. See Eva's final draft (annotated) in Appendix D.

5. Revision of Eva's Writing

Let's listen in on Cory and Eva to see how she has progressed in her writing.

Cory: Welcome back, Eva! How's the grant application?

Eva: I cannot believe how much better it is! I went home and re-wrote the whole introduction. I moved a lot of the information down so I could include the CARS moves that you taught me.

Cory: Good for you! So let's see what else we can improve.

Eva: What I'm really struggling with now is telling 'why is this relevant?' I want to bring in elements from CARS and the rhetorical appeals you taught me, but I'm a little stuck. Here are my initial notes.

Student Text 6b

Why is This Research Relevant?

Gender trouble in men's vs. women's rooms is becoming a growing issue (stat?) (source)

(Continued)

(Continued)

Provides a barrier to using athletic and recreational facilities and programs (source)

For trans and gender non-conforming [Define jargon] the change room is a space with high incidence of violence and harassment

While gender neutral bathrooms are being used as a solution, gender neutral solutions aren't likely to offer big solutions

Because infrastructure for men and women's rooms are already in place. Expensive and unlikely to be converted to gender neutral. (source)

Also, gender neutral raises safety issues and barriers for Canadians eg muslim women

Identify the niche: Unaddressed: what to do? Canada hasn't figured out a solution to this societal puzzle.

Fill the niche: My research question asks what is the most effective/economically feasible approach to improve perceptions of inclusion and safety of participants using men's and women's change rooms. I hypothesize that …

Cory: You have a good starting point here. What do you want to do with this information?

Eva: Well this explains why my study is so important.

Cory: So this should probably be included at the end of your application, right? After you describe your proposed study?

Eva: Yeah. Exactly. But it's also background information.

Cory: So you need to refine these notes to make clear, concise points, and end on one strong, memorable key note. Evaluators aren't machines – yet! They react to proposals that convey passion, engagement, interest and confidence. You can convey these by including something about yourself, if that is relevant and discipline appropriate, but they can also be conveyed through word choice. The language you use needs to convey your expertise, but also your respect for your readers by not talking above them. Avoid jargon that is unrecognizable to academic insiders, but use appropriate terms to indicate your knowledge of the field.

Eva: Use terminology, but not too much?

Cory: I know, it's tricky! You'd rather have a simple answer, no? What about other words? Verbs, for instance. You want verbs that are active and what I call 'visualizable' – you can picture what they look like. So say, 'I analysed' or 'I calculated' not 'I did' or 'Analysis showed'. And avoid using too many words. You want your writing to be direct and concise.[1]

Eva: Slow down, Cory. I can't believe I have so much revision to do … again! Let me take a few minutes now to draft a conclusion.

See Student text 6c

Student Text 6c

Significance: We, as scholars, are aware that LGBTIQ participants experience discomfort in change rooms, but do not yet understand how to diminish this discomfort. This case study will improve the literature by helping to characterize the nature of these challenges. The change room is a space where a lack of progress for LGBTIQ individuals is most evident, due to the vulnerability of nudity. My research presupposes that the CRP offers a model to mediate this space, and seeks to further examine the CRP's potential for making the change room a more inclusive space for all bodies, regardless of difference.

Cory: Let's have a look. I see that you've reiterated the gap in the literature when you wrote 'but do not yet understand'. You've also clearly articulated the niche you're occupying when you wrote 'This case study will improve the literature by …'. What you wrote here relates to an appeal to credibility as a researcher because you're aware of what the disciplinary community values, which demonstrates *ethos*.

Eva: Thanks, Cory. I think I get it now. I'll refine the rest of my proposal this week and come back with another draft next week.

(See Appendix D for Eva's draft and final annotated scholarship proposal.)

6. Summary of Key Points

In this chapter you learned:

- about the complexity of persuasive genres like research/grant proposals,
- the CARS model for introducing your research,
- considerations of rhetorical appeals (ethos, logos, pathos), and
- the importance of precise and formal word choice (see also Chapter 4).

7. References

Lamont, M. (2009). *How professors think: Inside the curious world of academic judgement*. Boston, MA: Harvard University Press.

Li, X. (2008). Learning to write a thesis with an argumentative edge. In C. Pearson Casanave & X. Li (Eds.), *Learning the literacy practices of graduate school: Insiders' reflections on academic enculturation* (pp. 46–57). Ann Arbor: University of Michigan Press.

Swales, J. (1990). *Genre analysis: English in academic and research settings*. Cambridge, UK: Cambridge University Press.

Note

1. Thanks to Y-Dang Troeng for setting out the elements of this grant writing approach in her Laurier Writing Centre workshops (Wilfrid Laurier University Writing Centre, Waterloo, CA).

....

8. Your Notes

7

Writing about Data

In this chapter, you will revisit Eva Hibbert, whom we first met in Chapter 6 when she was writing a research grant application at the start of her Master's programme. It is now several months later and Eva is working on a research project with a colleague. She has collected a great deal of data and is struggling with their presentation, reporting and interpretation. In most studies, data are examined in the results or findings sections of the research report. This section is usually preceded by an introduction and methodology and followed by a discussion. This structure is the standard IMRD structure – Introduction-Methods-Results-Discussion – which is common in the social and hard sciences. This structure, of course, is often adapted for the purposes of specific disciplines, fields, or research projects. Examine a number of published studies in your discipline to see how this structure is used or revised to suit specific requirements. One notable area of difference is in how data are presented.

In this chapter, you will learn:

- the difference between reporting and interpreting data,
- considerations for presenting data in different formats (e.g., graph, table, figure),
- differences when reporting qualitative vs quantitative data, and
- the language of data reporting.

1. Intro Story: Eva Hibbert

Eva looked at the three piles of paper stacked in front of her on the desk. Many papers showed tables of numbers with highlighted sections and scribbled notes in the margins. Other papers had bulleted lists of points. Behind her, on the computer screen, a document page was open and half-filled with text under the heading 'Findings'. Eva scowled. 'Why did I think collecting so much data was a smart thing?'

Tonya: Hey Eva! ça va?
Eva looked up at her office mate and grimaced.

Tonya: That bad, eh? I told you you collected too much data. You should have done one simple study for that project, not two little ones. But did you listen to me? Mais, non!

Eva: Okay, okay. You win. But don't pretend you're not having problems writing about all those interviews you conducted.

Tonya: Yeah, you've got me there! I know there are points I really want to make, but it's hard to know where to even start sometimes.
A long pause.

Eva: Maybe it's time I went back to the writing centre.
Tonya grinned. 'Me too!'

2. At the Writing Centre

Jean-Paul: Congratulations on completing the data analysis for this project, Eva!

Eva: Thanks, but now I've got all these results and data and I don't know how to start explaining it all. I mean, I've got a bunch of tables. But my writing just seems to repeat everything that's in the tables. I know that's not right, but I don't know what I should do instead.

Jean-Paul: It is difficult to talk about data. On the one hand, you want to explain to your reader everything you see in these data. On the other hand, you must not repeat what the table presents.

Eva: Exactly! How do I know what to say and what NOT to say?

Jean-Paul: Why don't we start with an example? Imagine you have a chart of data about this writing centre. You have data about the size of this space. Yes, it is small, right? You have data about the large number of books and handouts that we have available – very helpful, no? You have data about the location – in the basement, at the far end of the building. Sad, but what can we do? You have data about the lack of windows, the number of tables and chairs, the colourful posters on the walls. So what do these data tell you?

Eva: Well, that the writing centre is a small, but cheerful and busy space.

Jean-Paul: Ah! Yes, I can see this. Do you know what these data tell ME? They say that the writing centre is small and poorly located, far from other academic units, in a badly-ventilated basement that is difficult for students to find.

Eva: Hmmm. Okay. Same data, different story. So you're saying I should not repeat the data, but tell the story?

Jean-Paul: Brilliant! Yes, tell readers the story you want them to see. Or they might create their own story, which may be quite different.

3. What You Need to Know

We have all heard the adage, 'Numbers don't speak for themselves.' This is especially relevant for researchers who are presenting data – be they numerical or not – in their written reports. While presenting data is integral to research and especially to thesis and dissertation writing, students can often be so preoccupied with collecting, recording, analysing and summarizing these data, that they overlook the importance of explaining to a reader what story the data are telling. It may seem perfectly evident, but it probably isn't. You are now an expert on your data, after all. Along with your supervisor, you have probably considered every possible interpretation of the data. But your reader has not. Your data may, in fact, make no sense to your reader. It is up to you to explain what the data are showing and tell the reader how this relates to the research question you set out to explore. Do the data provide the expected answer? Or is it unexpected? Is it a weak answer or strong?

One way of concisely and directly telling this story is to reiterate the research question and provide the answer according to what the data indicate. This question/answer structure may look something like:

> 'This study sought to explore the factors involved in successful drug treatment programmes. Analysis of the five longest-running treatment programmes in the country demonstrates that a combination of internal and external factors leads to success. Table 1 presents these internal factors, and Table 2 presents the external factors. As can be seen, internal factors relate to … .'

In this example, the first sentence reiterates the research question, while the second sentence provides the answer to this question. The third sentence tells or **signals** to the reader where/how the data supporting this answer are presented, and subsequent sentences summarize these data concisely.

Why is this a useful structure? Because you have probably identified your study's goals or hypothesis much earlier in your report, probably at the end of your literature review section. You need to remind your reader what exactly you are looking for in your data. Then you need to tell what you found and guide the reader through a presentation of the relevant data. See Table 7.1 for a question/answer structure example.

Table 7.1   Question/answer structure example 1

Research question/goal:	What factors are necessary for successful drug treatment programmes?
Answer/story:	A combination of internal and external factors are necessary for success.

(Continued)

Table 7.1 (Continued)

Signalling towards data:	Table 1 and Table 2 present these factors; see Table 1 ...
Summarizing of data:	Internal factors relate to a, b, c ...; external factors relate to x, y and z.

Many studies include a variety of data collected through different methods. Ensure you systematically present summaries of all the data, organizing their presentation to logically follow the questions driving your research.

Presenting Data Concisely

Options for data presentation outside of standard prose include tables, graphs, or figures. Such visual representations are highly effective, especially when you have a lot of data you need the reader to see. Make sure, however, that you use a form that is most effective for telling your data story. Tables, for example, are most useful when you have a number of variables that are related to a point/s of interest; for example, company revenues (point of interest) could be shown in a table that shows different revenue streams by month (variables), along with subtotals and totals. In such a table, the months of the year could be listed horizontally across 12 columns, while the rows could be labelled with the different revenue streams. This quickly allows a reader to see how revenues in any particular stream change over the year by reading left to right.

Graphs are used when you want to visually present the relation between two (or more) variables; for instance, as the number of practice events increases (plotted along the x-axis), expertise in a sport increases (plotted on the y-axis). Multiple lines can trace different relations demonstrated by the data collected.

Finally, figures are particularly helpful to visualize proportions, for instance, the relative numbers of in-person, online, or hybrid courses available at a college. Pie charts, for example, are helpful here.

With the advent of sophisticated computer programs, a huge variety of data presentations is at your fingertips. Flow charts, Venn diagrams, and any number of visual strategies are available. One particularly interesting consideration is infographics, which are meant to represent data in an easily interpreted pictorial form, e.g., 'wordles' of common terms related to a topic. A wordle is a computer-generated word cloud that displys the frequency relationship in a set of words. In these popular depictions, the frequency of terms is related to the reader by their relative size in comparison to other terms and their proximity suggests how close is the association between those terms.

Many students need to create a poster or other visual representation of their research at some point in their academic careers. Also, if you are presenting at a conference or teaching a lesson, you will likely be creating a PowerPoint presentation or some other visual prompt. If these tasks are expectations in your field or programme, we strongly suggest you invest time in learning about effective use of visuals. There are many good resources that can guide you in creating visual data representations. One such resource that we have used is a book called *Presentation Zen* by Garr Reynolds (2011). You might also want to view TED talks online for inspiration about how to effectively incorporate compelling visuals into your presentation.

Appendices are often used to present extensive datasets. For instance, many graphs, charts and figures are placed in appendices. See a style guide for guidance about placement, titles and other necessary details. By using appendices, you increase readability and avoid getting readers bogged down in too much data. In addition, another benefit of providing access to your data is that readers can make their own judgements about your interpretations and your study's validity.

Presenting Qualitative Data

If you are analysing qualitative data, you often present your data and its interpretation together rather than separating the data into a table or figure and your interpretation in prose. This methodology means your signalling towards and summarizing of data will be different, relying primarily on prose; for instance:

> 'A prominent reason students avoid fully online courses is that they are socially isolating. According to Mary, a first-year Arts student, "doing a course by yourself in your dorm room feels lonely. It's not like going to class in a room where you see people." Similarly, Jason, a second-year history major, noted, "online discussions often feel like you are just posting your ideas into a void. You don't always get a response from anyone." On the other hand, some students identified …'

In this example, the first sentence references the research question (why do fewer students take online courses?) and provides an answer. The following two sentences signal to and present data (quotations from students). The third sentence introduces a second possible, contrasting, answer (presumably followed by presentation of data) (see Table 7.2).

This example shows how you can refer to the data you have collected and integrate a 'story' about these data into your report by summarizing and interpreting them. The 'story' in the example above begins with a goal to understand reasons behind student choices about courses, then develops by introducing an answer. Data are presented to support this answer. But wait – a contrasting answer is suggested, with data introduced to support it.

Table 7.2   Question/answer structure example 2

Research question/goal:	Why is enrolment in online courses lower than in-person courses?
Answer:	Online courses are socially isolating.
Signalling towards data:	(text cues that refer to direct quotations taken from the data collected) According to …, participant X said, etc.
Data summaries:	Representative direct quotations taken from data collected.

A resolution is reached. It may not be as exciting as a spy caper, but it definitely has its own narrative arc!

In Chapter 3, we discussed effective paragraph structure and the importance not only of presenting data, but interpreting these data in subsequent sentences within a paragraph. The ideas presented here, as you can see, overlap with this structure, reinforcing the roles of evidence (data) and interpretation.

In qualitative research, it may be more difficult to see the separation of Results (or, more correctly, Findings) from Interpretation/Discussion because of the reliance on prose and themes rather than numbers or statistics for reporting. In addition, methodological requirements for qualitative research blur the line between data and analysis, including beliefs that findings must emerge from the data, and that 'objective' data outside of interpretation do not exist. But the same principles specifying particular rhetorical action in each section nevertheless apply. In the Findings section, the data are presented and interpreted; in the Discussion, the interpretations are applied to the research question and generalized out to reach a conclusion. Using our earlier qualitative example, the Findings section of a paper on online course preferences might state, 'A prominent reason students avoid fully online courses is that they are socially isolating. According to Mary, a first-year Arts student, "doing a course by yourself …"' (interpretation followed by data evidence). In the Discussion section of this same paper, you might write, 'This study identified three themes under which students' reluctance to enrol in online courses could be categorized: the isolation of online courses, their pedagogical weakness, and lack of applicability to credentials. The first of these themes was most prominent, especially among entering students …'

If you are doing a qualitative study, begin now to pay attention to the ways that researchers in your field present their data and report on them in various sections of their published articles. There is tremendous variation between and within disciplines, so you may need to become familiar with a number of approaches to find one that best suits your project and data.

Presenting Quantitative Data

In a traditional thesis or report, when writing a Results or Findings section, students are often cautioned to present only what is observed or analysed and to leave interpretation to the Discussion section. It is worth noting, however, that despite this expectation, published research articles regularly include elements of 'interpretation' in their Results (Swales & Feak, 2001). Nevertheless, in research that is primarily quantitative, this separation of reporting and interpreting data is fairly easy to carry out, once you get the hang of it. For instance, in the example study exploring factors that are related to successful drug treatment programmes, the Results section could begin by presenting summaries of the raw survey data, and these summaries would then be used to identify factors of relevance. These factors might be grouped into tables of internal and/or external factors (or some other categories). The sentence used to introduce this tabular data presentation would note the relations between and among these data, for instance:

> 'In addition to six internal factors, survey responses indicated four external factors contributed to the success of these drug treatment programmes. See Table 2.'

A more detailed exploration and explanation of the relations among these factors, however, and how they answer the research question should be left to the Discussion section. Often this section begins with a recap or reminder of the goal of the study, as mentioned earlier. For example, the Discussion section of this drug treatment paper might begin, 'This study sought to explore successful drug treatment programmes and hypothesized that internal factors were primarily responsible for their efficacy. Our findings, however, indicate that a combination of both internal and external factors are integral to success …'.

It can be challenging to become proficient in distinguishing between the ways to talk about data in the Results/Findings section of your paper and in your Discussion. Again, we advise you carefully read exemplary studies in your field and pay close attention to how the researchers talk about their data. Make note of phrases or language you find compelling or commonly used and mimic these in your own writing.

The Language of Data Presentation

Presenting data requires precision. The terminology and jargon associated with presenting different types of data are highly restricted and often discipline-specific or methodology-specific. For example, the word 'significant' has a prominent statistical meaning and is highly associated with inferential statistical testing. It would be wrong to use this word in a quantitative study when you are not referring to its statistical meaning. You could not, for instance, say 'The most significant factor associated with drug treatment programme success is ...' *unless* your study used statistical testing to compare all the factors identified. If you want to indicate simply what is the most prominent or common factor (rather than a statistically significant factor), you might say, 'The most prominent factor associated with ...'. While a novice may not notice the difference in terminology, experienced researchers certainly will and will look favourably on your precision.

Other common problems when discussing data include ensuring clarity around causation. Again, if you are in a field that regularly conducts experiments designed to test hypotheses, you will be familiar with the need to be precise about causation. 'Avoidance of online courses was caused by three factors' is a strong and simple claim. It suggests a direct link between an outcome (avoidance of online courses) and a specific number of variables. 'Avoidance of online courses is related to three factors' is a less strong claim, suggesting not causation, but a more complex, perhaps indirect relationship tentatively involving more than the three factors identified.

It's commonly recognized that many people confuse causation and correlation. While this problem is generally addressed by appropriate framing of the research question and data collection, you need to make sure you don't make confusing claims when you interpret data. Ensure that you are clear about these differences and how they are discussed in your discipline.

On a related note, many students are reluctant to use 'because' in their writing when it is perfectly obvious they mean causation. For instance, 'Participants were asked to respond to the survey online as it was more convenient.' In this sentence, it is clear online responses were requested BECAUSE it was more convenient, i.e., convenience prompted the decision to request online responses. So the sentence should read, 'Participants were asked to respond to the survey online because it was more convenient.' We suspect many students avoid using 'because' because they have been traumatized by rules about not starting a sentence with because. They have perhaps overgeneralized this rule to avoid using because anywhere. But it's not necessary. Use because. Even at the beginning of a sentence (provided it introduces a subordinate clause that you follow with a main clause!).

Another area that causes problems is the use of verb tenses when reporting study results. You may recall from Chapter 4 our discussion of verb tenses used when referring to past events or those with ongoing implications. When reporting on findings, it is common to use past tense (e.g., 'found', 'showed', 'participated'). This is because findings/results sections usually recount a narrative about events that happened in the past. In the discussion section, however, there is generally a combination of verb tenses: past tense is used to identity specific results or procedures done at some previous point, but present tense is used to indicate conclusions regarding the research question or hypothesis; e.g., 'Interviews *indicated* [past tense – recount] that students *prefer* [present tense – conclusion] on-campus classes to online courses.' The best advice we can give you for developing the language of data presentation is to carefully read and analyse texts in your field. Presentation of data is at the heart of what researchers do and each field has very definite views on what needs to be said and how. See Eva's sample text at the end of this chapter for an example of what is expected in social psychology.

4. Reader's Practice

Exercise

Analyse the data in Table 7.3 and write one sentence that is appropriate to present your finding for a Results section and one sentence for a Discussion. Remember that interpretation is limited in Results sections.

Table 7.3   Example data

Date	Temperature in degrees C
5 May	10
6 May	11
8 May	13
10 May	14
12 May	16

Results:_____

Discussion: _____

Compare your answers to ours below:

Results: As indicated in Table 7.3, the temperature rose steadily over one week from 10 to 16 degrees.

Discussion: In late spring, as expected, temperatures tend to rise steadily after reaching a weekly low.

5. Revision of Eva's Writing

Eva is back at the writing centre, showing Cory a draft of her Results section.

Cory: Wow, Eva, you have done a great job on this draft! At your last visit, we didn't talk about the overlaps between the Method section and the Results, but you got it perfectly.

Eva: I did what you suggested and analysed a number of really good articles in psychology to see how the researchers I admire write their reports. I noted they had a section in Method for 'Participants' that reported some data about who participated in the study, and then sections for describing the research procedure and the types of measures or tests that were used.

Cory: And did your analysis help you with the Results too?

Eva: Oh, yes! I wasn't sure about the wording for talking about main effects, but several of the studies I read included this, so I got a good sense of what I needed to say. And what do you think of the Discussion?

Cory: You have done a really good job reminding your reader about the study's goals, and then stating your conclusions and generalizing out about why this is an important finding.

Eva: Thanks, Cory! This was the hardest thing I've written yet. But now I feel pretty good about looking at my thesis data. I'll see you for help with that next year!

Student Text 7

Eva's Sample Text

Method

Participants
A total of 1537 (1094 females) participated in this study. The mean age for participants was 19.05 (SD = 2.55). Participants received course credit in exchange for their participation.

Procedure

All participants completed this study as part of a larger questionnaire administered to students at the beginning of the semester. Embedded in the large questionnaire were our measures of interest. Measures that were given in conjunction with our measures are not of interest in the current study and thus will not be discussed further.

Measures

Personal Legitimacy. To measure personal legitimacy of female appearance norms (i.e., the extent to which people think the appearance norms for females are legitimate), participants rated their agreement with the following item: I agree with the sociocultural norm for thinness and beauty for women and think it is legitimate. Ratings took place on a 7-point scale, ranging from 1 (strongly disagree) to 7 (strongly agree).

Social Legitimacy. To measure social legitimacy of female appearance norms (i.e., the extent to which people think that others believe the appearance norms for females are legitimate), participants rated their agreement with the following item: I think other people agree with the sociocultural norm for thinness and beauty for women and think it is legitimate. Ratings took place on a 7-point scale, ranging from 1 (strongly disagree) to 7 (strongly agree).

Results

A mixed-ANOVA was conducted with legitimacy (personal vs. social) as a within-subjects variable and gender (male vs. female) as a between-subjects variable. Results revealed a main effect of legitimacy, with participants rating the social legitimacy of female appearance norms ($M = 4.85$, $SD = 1.55$) higher than the personal legitimacy of female appearance norms ($M = 3.13$, $SD = 1.66$), $F(1, 1535) = 713.49$, $p < .001$. While only 22% of participants actually agreed with the appearance norms for females (calculated as the number of participants in the sample who indicated that they somewhat agreed, agreed, or strongly agreed with the norms), they believed that 65% of other people agreed with the appearance norms (calculated as the number of participants in the sample who somewhat agreed, agreed, or strongly agreed that others agreed with the appearance norms for females). That is, consistent with an idea of pluralistic ignorance, people perceived others to be much more accepting of appearance norms for females than they were themselves.

There was also a main effect of gender, with males ($M = 4.29$, $SD = 1.22$) having higher legitimacy ratings than females ($M = 3.86$, $SD = 1.22$), $F(1,1535) = 38.74$, $p < .001$. Overall, males were more likely to rate the personal and social legitimacy of appearance norms for women higher than females were.

Both of these main effects were qualified by a significant Legitimacy X Gender interaction, $F(1,1535) = 86.85$, $p < .001$ (see Figure 1). Although both genders displayed the typical pattern of pluralistic ignorance (rating social legitimacy higher than personal legitimacy), the difference between social and personal legitimacy was significantly greater in female participants (Mdiff = 2.016) than male participants (Mdiff = .97), $p < .001$. This indicates that female participants (versus male participants) perceived a larger discrepancy between their personal endorsement of appearance norms and what they perceived others' endorsement to be. More specifically, it seems that although both males and females had similar perceptions of how much their peers endorsed appearance norms (i.e., the social legitimacy of norms; $p = .29$), females personally endorsed appearance norms less than males ($p < .001$).

(Continued)

(Continued)

Discussion, Limitations, and Future Directions

The purpose behind this research was two-fold. Our first objective was to demonstrate that people display pluralistic ignorance when it comes to female appearance norms. This objective was met in Study 1. Consistent with the idea of pluralistic ignorance, participants thought that others endorse appearance norms for females more than they do themselves. That is, although people indicate that they do not personally endorse appearance norms for females, they believe that others do. This finding is consistent with previous research demonstrating that people often overestimate the extent to which others prefer a thin woman (Cohn et al., 1987; Jacoby & Cash, 1994; Rozin & Fallon, 1988).

Although consistent with previous literature, our results are distinct in a couple of ways. First, our study directly examined the disconnect between private judgements of legitimacy and beliefs about social legitimacy. Much of the previous work has asked people what they prefer in a female body type and what they think other people prefer. Researchers then use the discrepancy between these two preference ratings to make inferences about overestimation of a norm (e.g., female thinness). In contrast to this previous work, we directly asked participants about how legitimate they think the norms are and how legitimate they think that others perceive the norms to be. For our purposes, these types of questions allowed us to directly test the hypothesis that people overestimate the extent to which other people think the appearance norms for females are legitimate. Overestimating how legitimate others think appearance norms are is harmful to individuals because, despite the fact that they don't personally buy into these norms, believing that other people do buy into these norms leaves the person feeling judged and inadequate. If a person believes that the majority of other people think the norms presented in the media are legitimate, their own personal questioning of the norms will be silenced, leaving them to publicly endorse unhealthy attitudes, and behave in ways that are consistent with how they think other people believe they ought to behave.

The ubiquity of images that females are constantly bombarded with on a daily basis via the media is extremely dangerous for females' physical health, psychological well-being, and relationships. One method of potentially countering these negative effects is to dispel the erroneous belief that others think the norms portrayed by these images are legitimate and worth pursuing. The current research represents the beginning of an interesting investigation into this idea, with the ultimate goal of helping females feel more satisfied and comfortable with their appearances.

6. Summary of Key Points

In this chapter, you learned about:

- writing a 'story' when reporting data,
- the difference between reporting and interpreting data,
- concisely presenting data in different formats (e.g., graph, table, figure),
- conventions for presenting and discussing qualitative and quantitative data, and
- the importance of precision in language for reporting data.

7. References

Reynolds, G. (2011). *Presentation Zen: Simple ideas on presentation design and delivery* (2nd ed.). Thousand Oaks, CA: New Riders.

Swales, J. M., & Feak, C. B. (Eds.). (2001). *Academic writing for graduate students: A course for nonnative speakers of English. Michigan series in English for Academic and Professional Purposes*. Ann Arbor: University of Michigan Press.

8. Your Notes

8

Writing Collaboratively

In this chapter, you will revisit Devon. He's working on a group project for one of his courses, and this is the first group assignment he has had to work on in this course. He – and his group members – are learning not only about new content in the area of business (project management), but also about how to produce a written report that is cohesive and consistent in terms of the writing style, tone, language, etc. Through Devon's experiences, you'll learn how to approach collaborative writing and how to make your writing consistent across the group. In this chapter, you will learn about:

- the group writing process,
- providing and receiving feedback,
- common frustrations and pitfalls, and
- identifying individual strengths/weaknesses.

1. Intro Story: Devon Stratford

Devon and four other students sat around the table in a glass-walled student work room, each with their laptop open in front of them. They were working on their group project and feeling tired. Devon gets along well with his peers, but feedback from professors has always been the same – 'increase consistency in style', 'work more collaboratively', 'it sounds like four very different people wrote this paper', and 'keep style of writing consistent throughout the report'.

Devon's group has recognized the flaws in their previously submitted work, and have decided to learn more about how to write collaboratively to ensure their current report is consistent in its written style and presentation. Devon has volunteered to take his group's work to the writing centre for initial feedback and advice.

2. At the Writing Centre

Francesca: Hey Devon. Welcome back. How's it going?

Devon: Hi Francesca. I'm in trouble. I'm working with this group on an assignment, and our writing is all over the place. On other group assignments, profs always write things like 'inconsistent style' or 'this seems pieced together' or 'write more collaboratively'. It's annoying. I don't know what to do.

Francesca: Oh, right. Yes. Group writing can be rough, can't it? What's your usual strategy?

Devon: Well, we're all tight on time. So we usually just divide up the work, then copy and paste our individual work into a document, then submit it. One person usually edits the document before we submit. We contribute based on strengths. It's efficient.

Francesca: Yes, this may seem like an efficient way to get a group task done, but it really is just a start. When you write a document with others, you need to work more collaboratively. That means that you're doing more than just cutting and pasting individual work into a common document. You need to discuss, provide feedback to one another, decide on writing style and format, and then, yeah, revise throughout the process and proofread before you submit it to your prof.

Devon: Yeah, well, we're not really doing all that.

Francesca: Did you bring anything to show me today? What are you working on?

Devon: Yeah, here are a few pieces from me and the group. For this assignment, we had to plan a project for a community. Our group chose to create a plan for a community garden for a local non-profit organization that provides meals to families in need. We figured that if the organization had a community garden, it could then use the produce in its meals. This will save the organization money and ensure more healthy meal options, too. We're really excited about the possibilities.

Francesca: Cool. Sounds like a fun project.

Devon: Totally. It is fun. There are so many components to our project though, and we haven't started really putting anything together. We had to submit a project proposal a while ago. Our prof approved it. Then, based on that proposal, we started to expand the individual requirements of the project and assignment steps. Here's what we have so far. I brought five documents. Here's how we divided up the work.

First, here's our writing plan. We used headings from the course assignment.

Student Text 8a

Deliverables as per Outline

Written reports (one per group) (25 marks) (Aug 2)
Complete Baseline Project Plan consisting of:

1. Project Overview Presentation to Senior Management (or Investors if appropriate). This report can refer to the Microsoft Project file (or other software) when appropriate.
2. It must include all elements of a complete project plan

    a. Charter/Scope – Devon
    b. Work Breakdown Structure (WBS) – Lilly
    c. Network – Lilly
    d. Schedule – Lilly
    e. Budget – Lilly
    f. Resources – Barbara
    g. Risk Analysis – Chloe

3. Microsoft Project file or other suitable software output

    a. Two Status Reports – Concise, aimed at senior management to demonstrate project update:
    b. The planning process – 1 page max – a few bullet points is acceptable if they are clearly written – Devon
    c. Detailed updates (at one-third and two-thirds of the way through the project) addressing developments (once the plan is complete) – 1 page max, conciseness is valued – Andrew

Francesca: This is interesting. I see that you have noted the assignment goals and the various expected components for your report. And you've assigned people to each task, too.

Devon: Yeah. Some of these items were taken directly from the assignment instructions like in number 3a where it says 'concise, aimed at senior management to demonstrate project update'. We divided up the sections as you can see in number 2.

Francesca: I see that. It seems like a reasonable start to me. How did things progress from this outline?

Devon: Well even though we drafted this division of work and assigned tasks to different group members, we did need to talk about each of our components since there was overlap. A decision that was made for the Work Breakdown Structure (WBS), for example, impacted other components. We needed to talk about these things as a team before individuals could make progress on their assigned sections.

Francesca: I'm glad you realized this. It happens all the time when items are divided up too early in the research and writing process. Ok. What else did you bring in today?

Devon: The second document is Chloe's risk management plan.

Student Text 8b

Risk Management

Step 1: Risk Identification

A crucial step in risk management is determining a laundry list of all potential risks the project could face. This step of the management process is considered to be most important as the project is still in designing/planning stages and the costs associated with mitigating/avoiding/transferring the risks are the lowest. The following is a list of all foreseeable risks:

Risk Breakdown Structure		
Risk Category	**Risk #**	**Risk**
Technical	1	Quality of soil is found to be compromised, unable to produce high quality vegetables without land reclamation
	2	The plant varieties chosen did not do well in the area (becomes obvious before project is turned over to the organization)
	3	Unable to prevent critters (rabbits, mice, snails, etc.) from getting into the garden and eating plants
External	4	Unexpected frost after May 24 (Date of Planting)
	5	Inclement weather pushes back schedule as volunteers cannot work outside when raining
	6	Summer is unseasonably cold, and garden produces minimal yield. Making the overall project unsuccessful
	7	The organization unhappy with the yield/setup of garden
	8	Rototiller not available for days needed, holds up schedule
	9	Local community feels the garden is a "free-for-all." Helps themselves to vegetables as they wish
	10	Excessive flooding due to topography of where the garden plot is located
	11	Health and Food Safety regulations have not been considered when implementing a "farm to table" program for the organization's customers
	12	Not Enough/Too much Sun.
	13	Vandalism by vandalism hooligans
Organizational	14	The organization unable to secure the minimum funding required for garden project
	15	Local garden centres unable/unwilling to donate seeds and seedlings to project
	16	Project does not generate enough interest among the volunteers

(Continued)

131

(Continued)

Risk Breakdown Structure		
Risk Category	**Risk #**	**Risk**
	17	Volunteers are not physically fit enough to garden for extended periods of time
	18	Volunteers lack in gardening know-how.
	19	Volunteer gets hurt while gardening
	20	No leadership established among the volunteers. Keeping motivation up difficult to do
	21	Conflict among members of the volunteer community, makes scheduling volunteer hours more difficult
	22	Difficulty communicating what has been done (and what needs to be done) to volunteers from one day to the next
	23	Estimated plot size not large enough to make vegetable yield worthwhile
	24	Underestimated the increased cost in water and hydro bill

Step #2: Risk Assessment

Risk assessment is easily measured using a Risk Severity Measured. The graph below captures all identified risks based on the likelihood of occurring and the impact its occurrence would have on the garden project. For simplicity purposes, the matrix uses risk numbers from the Risk Breakdown Structure (RBS) above.

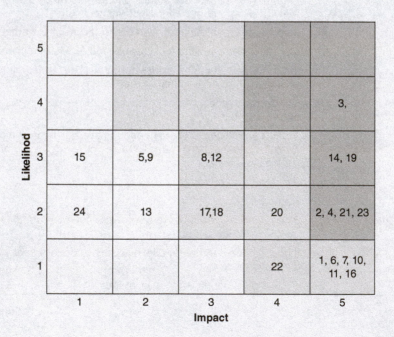

Step 3: Risk Response Development

It is obvious that there are many potential risks associated with the garden project, but many are low impact and unlikely to occur. For the purposes of a Risk Response Development, only those risks identified as "High Risk" (dark blue in colour) will be analyzed further in terms of appropriate response and contingency plan.

Risk Event #	Response	Contingency Plan	Trigger
2	Retain	Purchase additional plants of strains proven to do well	Plants die within first week of being in ground (before turnover to the organization)
3	Mitigate	Install a more efficient fence, capable of keeping rodents out	See bite marks on the plant leaves or vegetables
4	Retain	Replant as much as possible using money from Management Funds	Plants dead after overnight frost
14	Avoid	Have them pay upfront before work begins.	No Trigger
19	Transfer	Ensure the organization has the proper liability insurance to cover accidental harm to volunteers	Near-misses in the garden with volunteers
21	Mitigate	As part of volunteer orientation to garden, do team building exercises	Internal strife
23	Retain	Mark as a lesson learned for next season	Report from the organization indicates harvest not big enough to be worthwhile

Devon: The third document is Lilly's project priority plan.

Student Text 8c

PROJECT PRIORITY MATRIX

The priority matrix establishes priorities for the time, cost and scope, which all have an impact on the overall quality. Given that the project is under a strict deadline to ensure that planting takes place no earlier or later than May 24th, 2018, the only available option is to optimize time. Cost is constrained because the budget available to complete the

(Continued)

133

(Continued)

project is fixed based on the donation received by the non-profit organization. It is acceptable to not meet the original parameters for the performance criterion as 2018 is the first year that the organization will have a vegetable garden and as such, will be using the 2018 year as a test platform from which to learn for future years. The priority matrix has been established in cooperation with the non-profit organization's goals, and therefore it is not anticipated that there will be any significant management implications as a result.

	Time	Performance	Cost
Constrain			●
Enhance	●		
Accept		●	

Devon: The fourth document is my communication plan.

Student Text 8d

THE ORGANIZATION GARDEN PROJECT - COMMUNICATIONS MANAGEMENT PLAN

Author / Originator	Target Audience	Objectives	Communication Vehicles	Frequency	Setting
Project Manager	The Organization Leader	• Negotiate project scope, including deliverables, timeline, and budget	Face-to-face meeting	Once	The Organization Office

Author / Originator	Target Audience	Objectives	Communication Vehicles	Frequency	Setting
Project Manager	The Organization Leader	• Provide project status updates at one-third and two-thirds through the project timeline	Face-to-face meeting	Twice	The Organization Office
Project Manager	Suppliers	• Negotiate best pricing for supplies required. Do not go over the maximum estimate. Try to negotiate discount.	Face-to-face meeting	Once at the beginning of the project	Supplier's Location
Project Manager	Labour	• Ensure volunteers are aware of the project scope and deliverables. • Educate volunteers on the work breakdown structure (WBS).	Face-to-face meeting	Once before the project begins; once near the start of the project; ongoing communication with labour crew	The Organization Garden
Financial Lead	Project Manager	• Provide financial status update to project manager.	Email	Weekly	every Monday
Volunteer Coordinator	Project Manager	• Provide updates on volunteer training, progress, and	Email or Face-to-face meeting	Weekly	every Monday

(Continued)

(Continued)

Author / Originator	Target Audience	Objectives	Communication Vehicles	Frequency	Setting
		regarding preparation and planting of garden			
The Organization Leader	Community Members	• Connect with the The Organization community to share information about the preparing and planting of the garden. • Share news of project completion at the end of the project.	Email or news-letter	Once before the project begins and once at the end of the project	Via The Organization network

Devon: And, finally, the fifth document is Andrew's progress report draft.

Student Text 8e

Progress Since Last Report – **Need Devon's Part as a reference**

Problems and Issues Since Last Report

Actions and resolution of earlier problems – **Need Devon's part as a reference**
Since the last progress report, we have had a couple of new issues arising. Firstly, there have been some slight changes to the scopes regarding the quality of the fence and vegetables in the garden. Secondly, there have been some delays in the schedule due to bad weather and volunteers not showing up on time. Thirdly, our inventory of tools and seeds were stolen and damaged by critters, respectively. These new problems have caused us to modify the scope, budget, and schedule.

Current Status of Project

Costs Incurred and Reduced and Slight Changes to the Scope:

The cost of fence increased to **$303.85** because one of the volunteers, who is a contractor, recommended a couple of changes. Firstly, they recommended for us to use a gate instead of leaving an opening in the fence. Secondly, they recommended for us to use better quality posts as the ones we had were unlikely to go past two winters. The benefit of using stronger posts is it will prevent further costs in the future. For example, if in the future if the poor-quality posts were to fall it would take down other aspects of the fence as well, which would increase the cost to fix the fence. Installing good quality posts right now will ensure such damages and costs will not be incurred in the future. Lastly, the volunteer recommended we increase the perimeter of the fence to allow for some walking space. These changes in the quality of the fence did not increase the duration to build the fence as the process did not change significantly.

Another source of the incurred costs was some of the tools were stole and the seeds we had planted were eaten by critters. These issues were easily fixable as we simply had to repurchase the lost goods and replace them, which costed us **$213.89**. The costs of the tools and seeds were also not significant enough to cause any delays in the schedule. We also decided to place the tools in the built shed and lock the doors this time around to prevent further theft. The lock costed us **$20.00**.

The last cost incurred was a scope change regarding the plants we planted. The non-profit organization decided to change the plants they wanted planted so it cost us time and money to change these plants. It took us roughly **0.25 days** and costed us **$108.00** to replace these plants.

The above costs incurred were countered by some saved costs. Specifically, we received a donation of 50 tomato plants from local gardening centers, which allowed us to save the amount of money we spent on plants. The funds we saved were used to repurchase lost tools and seeds and the remainder were used for the costs incurred from the fence. In total, we saved **$437.50** due to these donations from the gardening center.

Scheduling Issues:

Some volunteers were not showing up on time due to their personal schedules so the amount of time they committed per day was decreased by roughly **1–2 hours**. This has been a cumulative trend and it is an understandable risk as these individuals are giving their free for these activities. The result of these attendances has led to us being **1 day behind overall**.

Another factor that has increased the duration of the project is bad weather. Rainy days meant the workers were unable to work outside on the activities. When we added the hours of rain we ended up finding ourselves with **2 waste days**.

The corrective measure we took for these delays was informing the non-profit organization about them. We wanted to communicate clearly the progress of the project and

(Continued)

(Continued)

wanted to avoid surprising the organization. These delaying factors were beyond our control and there was simply nothing we could do. Perhaps next time, we could have used volunteers and paid workers, which would have increased the chances of the workers showing up on time as some of would be paid for it.

Francesca: Right. Okay. It's good that each person in your group is contributing content, but, to me, everything seems disjointed. You'll need to not only make each part connect to one another and explain this connection to the reader, but you'll also need to write in a consistent format.

Devon: I know. But it's so hard. And it's too much work for just me to do all of that.

Francesca: Exactly. You're not expected to do everything, Devon! You need to do this *collaboratively*. So take what you learn here today with me back to your group. And next time, all of your group members should attend a Writing Centre session.

Devon: That's gonna be hard! But what do I do now? What do you mean about making things connect?

Francesca: Well, I mean, what is the connection between the risk identification and the priority plan? Can you explain this to me?

Devon: Sure. Well, the priority plan analysis is important because there could be so many individual tasks required in setting up a community garden, so we need to articulate the priorities clearly so that our team's project priorities align with the organization's goals. Not only that, but by first articulating the priority matrix, we'll better articulate the timeline and scope for the project.

Francesca: Okay. So that seems like, in terms of organization, the priority plan needs to come before the risk information. Could you tell me more about the risk document?

Devon: Yeah. So, with any project, there are things that you may not be able to control. In the risk identification and analysis document, our team has noted some risks. We tried to figure out ways to deal with these risks so that we can still execute our project plan according to our identified project scope and timeline.

Francesca: Yeah, this makes sense. Now, in terms of writing style, even if you look at just these two documents – the risk document and the project priority document – you should notice some differences. I mean, look at the organization of paragraphs or even the font. They're different! If you handed them in as they currently are, your prof would certainly be annoyed at the inconsistency. Imagine you were giving this report to a boss, he or she wouldn't be happy to see something that looks like puzzle pieces instead of a finished puzzle. You know what I mean?

Devon: Yeah. Totally. I get it. I mean, we should keep everything consistent – from the font to the paragraph indentation to the language we use. Even as I look at those two documents now, I can see that the risk document is basically just one long list, but the priority plan document has a paragraph of explanation. We need to write more paragraphs, I think.

Francesca: Let's look at the two other documents – the communication plan and the progress report. The communication plan is just a table without an explanation. How would the reader know how this is connected to everything else?

Devon: Yeah, well we should write a paragraph that explains its function and how it fits into our project plan.

Francesca: Good idea. Finally, look at the language used in the progress report. Do you notice anything?

Devon: Um. *Devon takes a few minutes to look over the documents.* Yeah, I notice that the group member that wrote the progress report uses 'we' everywhere in this document. The other team members didn't.

Francesca: Exactly. This is inconsistent. As you write the final report, you and your group members need to decide if you're going to write in the third person or use 'we'. Your professor – or other readers or your future bosses – will want this to be consistent. Your document will be easier to follow and much more professional.

Devon: Yeah. True.

Francesca: We're just about out of time now, Devon. What are you going to do after you leave here today?

Devon: Well, I'm going to report back to my group in terms of what I learned – like overall organization and language consistency. I'm also going to tell them about style – like paragraphs for every section and even things about font and paragraph indentation. We want our document to be professional, and all of these things will help!

Francesca: Great. And feel free to make another appointment with me, but bring your full group next time!

Devon: Sounds good. Thanks.

3. What You Need to Know

Collaborative writing can take many forms in the post-secondary environment. Some professors may assign a culminating project that is comprised of smaller components (Speck, 2002). Alternatively, professors may include collaborative writing tasks during class while other professors may require students to combine in-class and outside of class group work (Speck, 2002). In graduate school, writing collaboratively (in writing groups or circles, for example) can help people 'join the conversation in their scholarly disciplines' (Paré, 2014, p. 18). Studies have shown that complex collaborations exist in many fields and can result in the production of everything from corporate reports to institutional texts to peer-reviewed publications to novels (see Paré, 2014). Collaborative writing tasks promote cooperative learning and a student-centred teaching approach. As you may have noted with Devon's experience, he was working on a large, complex, collaborative writing task. These complex writing tasks are the main focus of this chapter, since you may experience such tasks during your undergraduate and graduate degrees as well as beyond school in various workplaces.

While some writers may think that writing in a group is an efficient and time-saving venture because of the division-of-labour approach that is often used, in fact, group writing is time-consuming and requires substantial effort and engagement from all writers. As Devon experienced, the divide-and-conquer approach can result in documents that are disjointed and inconsistent. While this approach results in individuals each creating content, this is not enough to produce a professional, well-written final document. Devon – and you, too – will not only need to consider how one component fits with another component but also how to write more collaboratively to ensure that organization, paragraph development, tone, voice (and other concepts that you have learned in this book!) are consistent.

The Group Writing Process

The group writing process is similar to the individual writing process in that it takes writers from the initial draft stages to revisions to proofreading the final document prior to submission. Individual components within the process, however, can differ between individual and group writing tasks. Consider the following steps as you prepare for a collaborative writing task:

1. **Identify the goal of the paper**: All group members must discuss the goal of the paper. Do you have a writing prompt?

2. **Start early**: Although this is a common piece of advice for writing, in group writing, this is especially important. Starting early will allow time to make revisions, to accommodate group members' schedules, to adjust research and writing approaches if necessary, etc. Expect your paper to go through multiple iterations to ensure a unified and consistent piece of writing.

3. **Brainstorm**: In Chapter 2, you learned about brainstorming ideas using mind and concept maps. The same strategy can apply to the group writing process, but here, all group members should contribute ideas. You and your peers should generate as many ideas as possible, and each idea should be equally valued at this point. No suggestions should be eliminated. If you do not already know your topic, you will likely settle on one during this brainstorming stage. Have you identified a problem that requires a solution?

4. **Outline**: Use an outline to structure the ideas from your brainstorming session. In other words, you should have a clear focus and points to be developed. The items you put in the outline should address the goals of your paper. This outline could serve as the framework for your paper. You can outline as a group to ensure that everyone is on the same page in terms of goals and outcomes. Have you developed a potential thesis statement from the research/knowledge you already have?

5. **Research**: You learned about gathering research in Chapter 2. In this step, it will likely benefit your group to divide the work. If you have completed the outline stage, then you will likely see natural points of division for the research step. Can you narrow your thesis statement at this point? Are you able to articulate the purpose for your paper?

6. **Discuss progress**: This a step that you do not generally have a chance to engage with during individual writing tasks unless you discuss your progress with a peer, a writing centre professional, a professor, or others. This is an essential part of the writing process for group writing. In this step, you should meet with your group to discuss your individual research findings. Think about the following questions:

   a. How will the individual research contribute to the goals of the assignment?
   b. How will the individual research be integrated? Organized into sections?
   c. Do any revisions need to be done to the outline?
   d. Does the overall structure of the paper need to be altered at this point to integrate the expected – or new – research findings?

   Remember that the writing process is 'recursive and sloppy, full of loops that can take the writer back to previous locations (the library, the thesis) …, including dead ends' (Speck, 2002, pp. 40–1). It's okay if you and your group members feel like things are not linear or completely clear at this point in your writing process.

7. **Write**: Write the essay/report/draft together. One way to do this is via an online/shared platform such as Google Docs or a shared file in Dropbox or Outlook. By using an online, shared platform, all members of the group can contribute to the document's various sections at any time while other members can view the changes as they're made.[1] Using a shared platform also assists during times when groups cannot meet to discuss progress in person. Since each member is responsible for the paper, not just their initial sections or research, a shared platform can provide the place for individuals to contribute to the overall document.

8. **Read**: Each member is responsible for the final product; as such, each member should read the entire draft throughout the writing process and especially towards the end of the process. Think about the following:

   a. Does the paper achieve the goals of the assignment?
   b. Are there sections that need more work (e.g., more research, reworking of ideas, elimination of unnecessary info)?
   c. Are there clear transitions between sections and ideas?
   d. Is the format and writing style consistent throughout the document?

9. **Revise**: Meet with your group members – preferably in person or via conference call – to discuss the paper's strengths and weaknesses. Each person should come to the meeting having read the full document and with notes about their individual assessment of the document. Discuss issues that stand out in terms of content, organization, style, voice and tone (see Chapter 5 for a review of voice and tone) and come to conclusions about these items so that everyone in the group is working towards the common goal(s). When there is a difference in ideas, discuss the pros and cons to try to achieve group agreement. Repeat this process until all group members are satisfied with the paper (Duke University, 2013).

Providing Feedback

Steps 8 and 9 of the writing process – read and revise – will involve providing feedback. As a group member, you're responsible not only for taking the lead on researching and writing various sections, but also for providing and receiving feedback. As a peer reviewer, you need to read the work of others with a critical lens so that you can provide feedback about the strengths of someone else's writing as well as the areas for improvement. Your feedback should be justified. Be specific in your comments by pointing to specific examples within the original text. You may be feeling anxious about providing feedback to your peers because you don't want to ruin friendships over negative or harsh commentary. You may feel bad about hurting your peer's feelings. While you need to be respectful of your peer, you need to move beyond a concern that your critique will hurt their feelings; you will then become a useful peer reviewer and make reader-informed comments that will improve the paper for everyone.

You and your peers may opt to provide feedback on the whole document or assign each other sections; your approach may depend on the time allotted as well as the length of the assignment.

When providing feedback, you can look at the paper in terms of the macro- and micro-levels, and you can take a direct or indirect approach. Macro-level items include things like argumentation and organization. Micro-level items include sentence-level concerns related to grammar, citations and spelling. In general, macro items are addressed before moving on to micro items. There's no sense fixing minor spelling errors when the content does not address the assignment's goal(s). Revisions and proofreading of micro-level issues can be done on a later version of a draft.

In terms of approaches, direct feedback includes suggestions to make an explicit change. For example, 'delete this redundancy' or 'clarification is needed for this point'. Indirect feedback is often stated in the form of a question; for example, 'What do you mean here?'

See Table 8.1 for criteria to assess a peer's writing and questions to guide your feedback.

Table 8.1   Writing assessment criteria and feedback questions

Item level	What to look at	Questions to prompt feedback	Examples of Indirect (I) and Direct (D) feedback
Macro	Quality of content	Does this content fit directly with the assignment's goal?	How does this relate to your main topic? (I) You have digressed from your main point. Is this necessary? (D)

Item level	What to look at	Questions to prompt feedback	Examples of Indirect (I) and Direct (D) feedback
	Clarity and quality of argument	Is the argument well developed throughout the document? Is the argument clearly stated? How does a particular section support or explore the argument?	Have you clearly articulated the reasons for your main argument? (I) You have identified few reasons and provided insufficient evidence for your argument. (D)
	Adherence to assignment instructions/ goal	Is each part of the document justified/ warranted? Does each section of the document address the assignments' instructions/rubric/ goals?	How does this fulfil assignment expectation X? (I) This section insufficiently addresses expectation X. (D)
	Overall organization of the section	Are the ideas presented in a section clear? Is the section warranted?	Why have you included topic X here? (I) Topic X is irrelevant. Consider deleting it. (D)
	Organization of the paragraph(s)	Does the organization of the paragraph make sense? (Recall paragraph structure in Chapter 3)	What is the main point of this paragraph? (I) Consider paragraphs 2 and 3 as they deal with the same point. (D)
	Flow of ideas	Do I, as a reader, get a sense of the overall flow of ideas? Is one idea well connected to the next?	I am unclear about the logical progression of these ideas. (I) The two points you have identified don't seem connected to the third. Explanation needed. (D)
Micro	Word choice	Is slang used? Is jargon explained? Are acronyms defined? Do any words make no sense?	Does this word have a specific meaning in your discipline? (I) This is a colloquialism. Change to a formal word. (D)
	Sentence structure and grammar	Are there any sentences that don't make sense? Are there grammar errors?	This sentence seems overly long? Would splitting it up improve clarity? (I) This is a sentence fragment. You need to add a verb (D)

(Continued)

143

Table 8.1 (Continued)

Item level	What to look at	Questions to prompt feedback	Examples of Indirect (I) and Direct (D) feedback
	Transitions between sentences	Do sentences connect with one another?	This is an abrupt move from point A to B. How did you get here? (I)
		Are transitions used carefully and effectively?	You've changed the terminology. Maintain consistent terms. (D)
	Spelling errors	Are there any spelling errors?	Is this correct spelling for this word? (I) This is incorrect. Consult a dictionary. (D)

Receiving Feedback

It is natural to feel concerned about receiving feedback. You don't want to experience hurt feelings. You don't want to feel bad if someone didn't understand what you wrote. You *do* want to demonstrate that you are a strong contributor. Remember that your peers are trying to be constructive in their feedback, to provide a reader's perspective on your writing, and to, ultimately, improve the macro- and micro-levels of the paper prior to submission. The following are some things you can do to better prepare yourself to receive your peers' feedback on your writing:

- Be a thoughtful listener.
- Ask clarification questions.
- Keep the assignment's goals in mind as you receive feedback.
- Remember that the feedback you receive is not negatively reflecting on you as a person. Instead, the goal of the feedback is to make the paper as good as it can be.
- Be thankful that someone has taken the time to read your work. Reading a paper deeply and carefully and providing thoughtful feedback takes time and mental effort. Be appreciative of your peer's contribution to your improvement.

Be aware that most people find giving feedback difficult and have little practice at providing feedback. They are often learning to give good feedback, just as you are learning to receive it.

Common Frustrations and Pitfalls

Along with other types of writing tasks, there are some problems that need to be resolved in collaborative writing. If you are aware of the potential pitfalls at the outset, then you can avoid or resolve them. Make note of the following potential challenges:

- **Dividing the writing into pieces too soon**: We have already acknowledged that the divide-and-conquer approach can be effective for complicated and large writing tasks. But if you do this too soon (i.e., before a proper brainstorming or outlining), then you and your group members may run into trouble at a later point in the process. You will not benefit from everyone's ideas and diversity of opinion. Also, if you wait to divide up the writing tasks, then you will have more time to decide about style and format as a group. You may even opt to write a few sections while you're together to draft a 'template' about content development and writing style.

- **Procrastination**: It is worth reminding you that writing takes time. Collaborative writing takes even more time. You need to get to work early so that you'll have time to engage in a thorough and collaborative revision process. When working with others, you'll also have to balance everyone's schedules for online or face-to-face meet-ups and discussions. Group members need to keep in touch with each other if they are unable to meet as planned. You'll need to start early and adhere to a set working timeline so that each member can contribute feedback along the way. If you try to write your assignment at the last minute, you may risk submitting a final product that is inconsistent and sloppy in style.

- **Misinterpreting this writing as a solo endeavour**: While group work can be challenging, you must not fall into the trap of thinking that this is a solo effort. This is not your project alone, and you must not take it over. Since this is a group task, you must learn when to lead and when to follow. You must learn how to contribute and how to receive feedback. Remember that you're all working towards the same goal, and the work you produce should represent every group member's input.

- **Non-contributors**: Nobody likes the 'free-rider' – the group member who sits back through the process and rarely contributes. You will not gain anything if you expect your group members to do the majority of the work. If you yourself do not contribute, then you are taking credit for work that you didn't do, which is a form of academic dishonesty. Other reasons for non-contributors may relate to the way the people in the group interact with one another. For example, many non-English speakers may feel intimidated voicing their ideas to the group. They may require more time and encouragement to contribute.

- **Conflict resolution**: Conflicts are common when doing group work. You and your peers must learn how to get along with people you may not like or that you even disagree with. To promote collaboration, groups may opt to draft a group contract (or charter) at the beginning of the group writing task. Such contracts may prevent later problems from arising. Everyone should contribute to the contract, sign the contract, and adhere to its noted rules of behaviour during the collaborative work. You can articulate expectations for work progress, status updates and behaviour protocols, including for when conflicts occur, as well as for consequences for not abiding by the group contract. The charter could also be used to identify and assign specific roles to group members based on their strengths and interests, which could reduce conflict and encourage contributions. (See sample team charter for Devon's group in the Appendix E.)

- **Avoiding revising**: We know that the revision and proofreading tasks can be onerous. But if everyone contributes, the job will get done. At some points, for instance in proofreading, it might be helpful if one person checks for spelling errors, another checks for accuracy of citation style, and another checks for heading level formatting. However, identifying one group member to merge and edit the final document is too much. This is a large task and it's not fair for one person to take on this responsibility. If group members contribute ideas and revisions during the writing process through commenting on a shared document, then there will not only be a record of people's input, but also an easier pre-submission final review.

- **Focusing on the negative**: In providing feedback, it can be easy to fall into the 'fix this, fix that' trap. Providing only negative comments to your peers will not help them or your paper become stronger. Be concrete in your feedback by providing specific examples and suggestions for improvement. Justify your responses so that your peer can understand your point of view. Instead of writing 'I think your paragraph isn't good', you could write 'I didn't fully understand this paragraph. Could you be more explicit about how the ideas here support the argument?' Also, try to include positive comments whenever possible to encourage your group members (Duke University, 2013; University of North Carolina, 2017).

You can refer to the following form to evaluate your own performance within your group as well as your peers'. If you are writing for a course assignment, your professor may also provide you with a peer evaluation form. What kind of contributor are you?

Assessment of Individual Group Member Group Member's Name: _____				
	Low		**High**	
Categories	**1**	**2**	**3**	**4**
Planning				
Encourages others to participate				
Offers useful criticism				
Presents viable ideas				
Research				
Conducts primary and secondary research				
Helps others conduct research				
Shares research data with group in a timely manner				
Analyses data				
Writing				
Writes his/her share of the document, including various drafts				
Does his/her share of the word processing				
Provides useful peer critiques of others' writing				

Assessment of Individual Group Member
Group Member's Name: _____

Categories	Low		High	
	1	2	3	4
Helps prepare the final copy by effective editing and proofreading				
Group Meetings				
Attends group meetings regularly and on time				
Informs group members when unable to attend a group meeting				
Provides leadership in resolving conflicts				
Treats all group members respectfully				
Additional comments:				

From Speck, 2002, p. 80.

4. Reader's Practice

In the previous section, you learned about the group writing process, providing and receiving feedback, and frustrations and pitfalls. Focusing on providing feedback, read the following text and provide macro- and micro-level feedback to the writer. The text you see is one small paragraph taken from Devon's group project about planning a community garden. (Devon's group report is in Appendix F.)

Student's Text (8f)

The project network is the tool that will be use in the planning, scheduling and monitoring of project progress. See the initial network for the original network, which has an estimated duration of 34 days and a critical path (identified in red). The network was completed by hand. Once this was satisfactory, it was then integrated into the Microsoft project system. Any variance in the timeline, scope or budget could have a significant impact on the project.

Your Feedback

Compare your feedback with our feedback below.

Student Text 8f (annotated)

Student's Text (8f)

The project network is the tool that will be **use** in the planning, scheduling, and monitoring of project progress. See the **initial network** for the original network, which has an estimated duration of 34 days and a critical path (identified in red). The network was completed **by hand**. Once **this** was satisfactory, it was then integrated into the Microsoft project system. Any variance in the timeline, scope or budget could have a **significant impact on the project**.

Our Feedback

use→ used

, → the comma is required in the list here (after the word 'scheduling') because this text follows APA style

What is the initial network? Where can I find this as a reader?

What does 'by hand' mean? Who did this? For what reasons?

What is 'this'? The hand-written network?

And so? What is the impact? What are you going to do about it as a team?

Here is the revised version of the same text.

Student's Revised Text

The project network is the tool that will be used in the planning, scheduling, and monitoring of project progress. See the initial network below for the original network, which has an estimated duration of 34 days and a critical path (identified in red). The network was completed by hand, utilizing expertise of all team members to ensure completeness and accuracy. Once the project network was satisfactory, it was then integrated into the Microsoft Project system. Any variance in the timeline, scope or budget could have a significant impact on the project; therefore we request to be made aware of any deviations as soon as possible.

Comments

If you had to identify your strengths as a group member for a team charter, what would you write? Note them in the following box:

> **My Strengths**
>
> **What can I contribute to a group writing project?**

Now identify your weaknesses as a group member. Where will you rely on others for guidance and support? How will you overcome these weaknesses? Make note of your ideas in the box below:

> **My Weaknesses**
>
> **What do I need to overcome to better contribute to a group writing project?**

5. Revision of Devon and his Peers' Writing

Taking the advice of Francesca at the writing centre as well as their professors, Devon and his peers have made a conscious effort to make their combined text cohesive and consistent in format and style.

Francesca: Welcome back, Devon. I see you brought your group members with you today.

Devon: I did! I told them how valuable our last appointment was and asked them to come with me today. We somehow were able to make it work!

Francesca: Welcome, everyone! And what did you bring today?

Devon: As you may remember, our group is working on a project plan for a community garden. We came together as a group to identify the scope of the project. I mean, we were only going to prepare the plan for the garden, not the maintenance of it, for example. Even though we had individual pieces of writing done already – you know, the ones I showed you last time – we had more work to do before we were ready to write the full report. So, we brainstormed ideas together using lists and mind maps and outlines. We did all of that on white boards in the little group meeting rooms in the library.

Francesca: Great. Sounds good so far.

Devon: Then, we divided up some of the work, and set meeting times to discuss our findings.

Francesca: Did that strategy work?

Devon: It did! Honestly, I thought it was going to be so time-consuming, but it was good to come together after we had each done some work because we saw how our pieces were connected.

Francesca: Cool. Okay. So what did you bring in today?

Devon: We brought in our almost final draft. But this one section that we worked on together is what we want to show you because it really was a collaborative effort. The purpose of this section of our report is to show a progress update of our project. We could only write this section once we discussed the findings of each of our group members.

Francesca: Okay. Let's have a look.

Student Text 8g

STATUS REPORT JUNE 1, 2018: PROJECT IN PROGRESS

Progress Since Last Report

- Created blueprint
- Purchased equipment, accessories, plants/seeds, shed
- Built shed
- Laid soil and mulch
- Constructed fence
- Installed irrigation system

Problems and Issues Since Last Report

Since the last progress report, we have had a couple of new issues arising. Firstly, there have been some slight changes to the scopes regarding the quality of the fence and vegetables in the garden. Secondly, there have been some delays in the schedule due to bad weather and volunteers not showing up on time. Thirdly, our inventory of tools and seeds were stolen and damaged by critters, respectively. These new problems have caused us to modify the scope, budget, and schedule.

Cost and Scope Changes

The cost of the fence increased to **$303.85** because one of the volunteers, who is a contractor, recommended a couple of changes. First, it was recommended to use a gate instead of leaving an opening in the fence, and second, to use better quality posts as the planned posts would deteriorate after 2 seasons. Stronger posts will prevent further costs in the future as a result of fixing and/or replacing the fence or from damage to plants from fence failure. Finally, it was recommended that the perimeter of the fence be expanded to allow for some walking space. These changes in the quality of the fence did not increase the duration to build the fence as the process did not change significantly.

Additional costs were also incurred as a result of some of the tools being stolen and some of the seeds being eaten by critters. These issues were easily rectified by repurchasing the stolen items, which cost a total of **$213.89**. Replacing of the tools and seeds was not significant enough to cause any delays in the schedule. It was also decided upon to place the tools in the built shed and ensure that the doors were locked at all times when a volunteer was not present to prevent further theft. The cost of the lock was **$20.00**.

Scheduling Issues

Some volunteers were not showing up on time due to their personal schedules, so the amount of time they committed per day was decreased by roughly **1–2 hours**. This has been a cumulative trend and it is an understandable risk as these individuals are giving their free time for these activities. The result of this has led to the project being **1 day behind overall**.

Another factor that has increased the duration of the project is bad weather. Rainy days meant the volunteers were unable to work outside. The bad weather resulted in a waste of **2 days**.

We informed you of these delays as soon as they became known to us. These delaying factors were beyond project control.

Francesca:	Well, first of all, the structure is clear and logically ordered. It seems as though this report would be very useful. Also, I can see that there are no spelling mistakes and there are clear headings used! Nice! I also see that you've used 'we' more consistently in this document.
Devon:	Yeah, we decided to use 'we' throughout to take ownership of the report. We used 'you' to refer to the executive board members who will read this report.
Francesca:	Okay. I also notice that you have some good organization text cues such as 'firstly', 'secondly' and 'thirdly' in your first paragraph. But in the 'Cost and Scope Changes' paragraph, you've used 'first'. Choose one of these formats and keep them consistent throughout your document.
Devon:	Good point. Thanks. I guess we still have some proofreading to do!

6. Summary of Key Points

In this chapter you learned:

- about the purposes and benefits of collaborative writing,
- about the steps to follow in a collaborative writing project,
- how to provide constructive feedback about macro- and micro-level issues,
- how to receive and process feedback to advance your writing,
- common frustrations and pitfalls that come with collaborative writing, and
- about how to conduct self-evaluation and peer evaluation to assess contributions to group work.

7. References

Duke University. (2013). *Group essays*. Retrieved from https://twp.duke.edu/sites/twp.duke.edu/files/file-attachments/ws-group-essays-handout.original.pdf

Paré, A. (2014). Writing together for many reasons: Theoretical and historical perspectives. In C. Aitchison & C. Guerin (Eds.), *Writing groups for doctoral education and beyond: Innovations in practice and theory* (pp. 18–29). New York, NY: Routledge.

Speck, B. W. (2002). *Facilitating students' collaborative writing*. San Francisco, CA: Jossey-Bass. Retrieved from https://www.gpo.gov/fdsys/pkg/ERIC-ED466716/pdf/ERIC-ED466716.pdf

University of North Carolina. (2017). *Group writing*. Retrieved from http://writing-center.unc.edu/tips-and-tools/group-writing/

Note

1. In writing this book, in fact, we used Google Docs in a shared Google Drive to organize our individual and collaborative writing tasks. While each of us took the lead on writing a chapter, we made revisions, provided feedback through comments, and offered suggestions so that we were better reaching the goals we set for this book.

8. Your Notes

Table of Contents

Appendix A
Bellissima's Final Paper

Images of Identity: The Danish Muslim Cartoon Controversy in a Cultural Studies Framework

While they are often not considered to be a "serious" means of expressing personal or political viewpoints, the power of cartoon images as a form of social commentary should not be underestimated. A deceptively simple drawing can pass along an enormous range of ideas and values from the cartoonist to his or her intended audience, and in the right circumstances the impact of these meanings can be wide- ranging. Such is the case with the recent events surrounding the publishing of a series of cartoons, first in Denmark and later across the Western world, depicting the Prophet Mohammed in an unflattering light. According to the media, two opposing camps that are divided on the meaning of the caricatures have formed, with Muslims seeing the drawings as an attack on both their religion and their way of life, and Western countries viewing the Muslim response as an attack on free speech and democracy. Sociological analysis of this incident and its fallout is best done through an interpretation of Cultural Studies theory, because it is concerned with people's creation of identity and meaning as well as how audiences and cultural texts interact with one another. Application of this theory to the cartoon controversy will demonstrate how the creation of meaning from texts follows patterns laid out by such cultural theorists as Stuart Hall. By examining the impact of these cartoons through a Cultural Studies framework, the Muslim response can be seen as both a challenge to Western hegemony and an attempt to develop and define a Muslim identity.

This paragraph demonstrates rhetorical moves that set up the argument, which is enhanced by Bellissima's neutral but confident stance towards the material. She uses the language of her discipline well.

Good use of subordination to set up the topic and opposing viewpoint ('While …, cartoon images …')

Topic identification

It is 'images', not 'the power of images' that are a serious means …

This phrase refers to and builds on the previous sentence.

Context/Problem identified

Response to problem

Thesis

By examining … , the Muslim response' means that it is the Muslim response that is doing the examining.

Suggested revision to avoid dangling modifier error:

An examination of the impact of these cartoons through a Cultural Studies framework will show that the Muslim response can be seen …

A brief synopsis of the events that occurred is required to fully understand the theoretical ramifications that Cultural Studies presents on this issue. According to Peter Goodspeed's article titled "Clash of civilization's orchestrated: Global protests were anything but spontaneous", the cartoons in question first surfaced in the newspaper Jyllands-Posten in September 2005 (A16). The editor of the paper claimed he commissioned the cartoons in response to a perceived fear of the Muslim community by Danish illustrators, who supposedly refused to work on a children's picture book about Islam (ibid). Twelve drawings were published originally, and drew protest from the Danish Muslim community, who [which] were ignored by the Danish government; in response they took the original cartoons plus three additions to the Middle East to create support for their protest (ibid). The reason for this anger has to do not only with the unflattering light in which the Prophet was portrayed, but also with what some Muslims see as a religious taboo surrounding the depiction of Mohammed in any way (ibid). This resulted in a widely publicized Muslim condemnation of Denmark, including economic sanctions against it by Muslim countries, as well as public protests and attacks on Western embassies (ibid). Some elements of the Western media responded to this outrage by publishing the cartoons again, as well as criticizing a perceived Muslim hatred for free speech (ibid). Arab leaders were quoted as saying that the cartoons were an attempt by the West to "weaken and subjugate the Muslim world" and Western leaders who attempted to resolve the issue called the wide-ranging implications indicative of a "clash of civilizations" (ibid).

Upon reading this article, I immediately noticed several value- and history-laden terms being both quoted and used by the author that referred to the meanings of the cartoons in very different ways. However, if the cartoons were created by the same group of people, supposedly with the same intent behind the illustrations, why is there so much confusion over what these drawings represent? The answer lies at the centre of a key theory within the Cultural Studies framework created by Stuart Hall, whom many consider to be one for the "founding fathers" of the discipline. Hall developed the idea of encoding/decoding, which stated that audiences are not passive receptors of messages created and relayed through media, but rather interpret cultural texts differently based on their socioeconomic status, frameworks of knowledge, and other heterogenizing factors (Encoding, 93). Essentially, media texts are created by individuals or institutions and "encoded" with an intended meaning; then the texts' meaning are "decoded" by the audience of said text according to their aforementioned differences. Hall describes three different ways in which an individual can interact with a particular idea or value being passed through a text; he calls these dominant, negotiated, and oppositional readings (101–3). A dominant reading occurs when an audience member fully accepts the original meaning intended by the creator of the message (101); a negotiated meaning comes from a partial acceptance of the dominant values on a general level, while rejecting them in the specific instance in question (102); and a

---

Notice the introduction of the source and its integration into the text. Notice also Bellissima's critical stance towards the source.

Good topic sentence. It organizes the paragraph which is a concise summary of the problem event.

Bellissima uses MLA citation in this paper. The use of 'ibid' belongs in the Chicago citation style. The error occurs throughout and is only corrected once.

Pronoun errors: 'who' refers to people and therefore to 'community', while 'which' refers to things and refers back to protest.

Ambiguous pronoun reference. They can refer to both the Danish government and the Muslim community, provided we treat the two noun phrases as plural

This next paragraph gives a good example of how to use the language of the discipline in an extended paraphrase of a single source.

Vague reference, probably to Goodspeed's article, but several publications have been discussed. Identify by name.

Use of personal pronoun 'I' – potentially contentious. Conventional form of using third person or passive constructions are an option; e.g., 'Readers of the article might immediately notice several …'

Argument: First we get the research question and then the answer. This is a good rhetorical strategy.

Note the effective use of disciplinary vocabulary: encoding/decoding, passive receptors, heterogenizing factors, dominant, negotiated, oppositional.

oppositional reading completely rejects the meaning given by a text while also understanding it (103).

Encoding/decoding theory fits into the debate surrounding the meaning of the cartoons by categorizing the two "camps" typified into either a dominant or oppositional reading, with seemingly no negotiated positions possible. On the Western side, members of this group are shown as approving of these depictions of the Prophet because they represent the right to free speech without fear of reprisal; this was the stated intent of the editor of the Jyllands-Posten in commissioning these cartoons (Goodspeed, A 16). Muslims, first in Denmark and later in the Arab world, read the cartoons in a oppositional manner. They saw these representations as an attack on their religion and culture, as well as a symptom of Western racism and hatred for Muslims that was but one example of a variety of barriers facing their people in integrating into Western countries. This interpretation led to a reinterpretation by the West, reinforcing the notion that the cartoons represented free speech, and seeing Muslim reactions to them as indicative of the Arab world's backward and oppressive nature. Once the controversy became widespread, both sides of the debate seemed to agree on only one point; [:] that the cartoons were part of a "clash of civilizations" between the West and Islam that stretched back to the Crusades (ibid). These widely differing viewpoints show how differently a text can be interpreted, as well as underlying values and ideologies that influence how individuals create meaning.

One of the core issues at stake in this whole controversy is the nature of Muslim identity, and how both Muslims and those in Western societies view them Cultural Studies looks at the creation of identity within groups and among groups as one of its central interests. As Hall explains, the media plays a central role in creating and sustaining identities through the transmission of values and ideologies associated with the group being defined in three ways (qtd in Seidman, 137) First the media presents a series of "cultural codes" that are based on hierarchal sets of binaries such as normal/strange, dominant/submissive, and strong/weak (ibid). Then the media places individuals within sociodemographic categories such as race, gender, or ethnicity, and applies the binary sets to these groups by ranking them; as a result of this categorization, individuals will read the meanings in texts differently depending on what group they have been placed in, as well as the meanings and values associated with that group (ibid). Hall also argues that our modern society is marked by this distinguishing of difference, and results in numerous intra-categorical conflicts and divisions that help form the identity of individuals belonging to that group (*Introduction*, 598). Bhabha also brings in an important idea that will be developed later, that the creation of identity in cultures is accomplished by repeating the same meanings over and over until they become naturalized; furthermore, these meanings must be directed at "the Other", a term which is recurrent in Cultural Studies (qtd in Davies, 103).

Margin annotations:

In this paragraph, Hall's encoding/decoding theory is shown to be relevant to the topic.

Bellissima analyses the situation and proposes two opposing camps, using neutral language, again assuming a confident stance.

Punctuation error: Using the semi-colon implies that there is an independent clause on either side of the semi-colon. Instead we have a subordinate clause after the semi-colon. A colon would work very well because it introduces what 'the point' refers to.

This next paragraph is well structured in the first half.

Subject verb agreement error: media is plural

Spelling error: hierarchical

This complex idea from Hall would be better understood if it were followed by an example, in particular one that relates to the cartoons incident.

Here Bellissima loses control of the paragraph structure. The use of the word 'also' is a clear indicator that she is gathering together other sources for support of her point. Presumably she is finding it hard to incorporate the sources here. The complexity of this theoretical material might better have been addressed in a second paragraph instead of this brief gloss.

All of this theorizing has <u>practical application</u> despite its sometimes <u>abstract nature</u>. Hall's theory of <u>culture codes</u> within the media relating to <u>binaries</u> is seen in Western representations of Muslims as backwards, oppressive, and fanatically religious as opposed to the West's advanced free, secular society. Even the presentation of "the West" versus "Muslims" is indicative of the media's <u>categorization</u> of individuals based on types like race or gender, or in this case, religious and national affiliations. Within these broad <u>categories</u>, individuals are expected to accept what has been defined as their group's <u>values and ideologies</u>; Muslims who speak out in favour of the cartoons or Westerners who disapprove of them are seen as deviant from their groups. Therefore those in the West who accept the <u>dominant ideologies</u> passed through the cartoons use the stereotypical ideal of the Muslim to create their <u>identity</u> in opposition to that stereotype; Westerners thus become the <u>binary opposite</u> of the imposed Muslim identity. "<u>The Other</u>" is a central figure on both sides of this debate; this term refers to an <u>idealized oppositional presence against which your own identity is constructed</u>. Hall's idea of <u>division and conflict</u> as central to <u>the creation of identity</u> also proves useful here, as both Muslims and Westerners have constructed themselves as part of the previously mentioned <u>"clash of civilizations" ideology</u>. The explicitly confrontational nature of this discourse helps divide those involved in the cartoon controversy into <u>two entrenched camps</u>, with the West and Christianity on one side and Muslims and Islam on the another.

The creation of a Muslim identity in relation to the West is steeped in a long history dating back to Christianity's first major encounters with Islam during the Crusades of the medieval period. The discourses used by the Europeans to discuss their Islamic foes then have become resurrected now to serve different purposes. Edward Said in his work *On Orientalism* discusses how and why this particular power arrangement has come to be. Western nations, through cultural texts such as the mass media and literature, create "knowledge" about groups considered to live in the "Orient" (primarily the Middle East and Southeast Asia) as a way of gaining dominance over people categorized as Oriental (qtd in Storey, 79). The discourses created by the West allow them to assign meanings to the category "Oriental", meanings that place people of Arab heritage in a position of submission and inferiority (ibid). By looking at the cartoons from this theoretical perspective, they come to represent one example of a long series of discourses designed to denigrate Muslims and assign them Western values, thus allowing the West to assume a dominant position in the interaction between cultures. As the cartoons were disseminated through newspapers, they show the power of the globalized Western media to shape cultures on a global scale due to their wide range and pervasiveness (Giroux, 252); in this case the discourse of Orientalism was distributed not only to Western cultures, but across the planet. Through transnational media outlets, the West gains access to almost all cultures, including Arab culture; Arabs who view these hegemonic ideas about their own traditions are almost certain to respond in a

---

This next paragraph is a good piece of model academic writing. The argument is focused strongly through careful word choice that builds a topic thread (marked by underline).

The topic sentence explicitly declares the purpose of the paragraph: the application of theories to the incident under study.

Sentences build on each other throughout, picking up on the idea introduced in the previous sentence. The paragraph has good cohesion.

Note the use of helpful metadiscourse: in this case, therefore, thus.

Strong conclusion reinforcing and expanding upon Bellissima's initial thesis.

The topic sentence signals the purpose of the next explanatory paragraph.

Sets up source well.

Good paraphrase of source.

Dangling modifier: The pronoun 'they' stands for cartoons, but it is not the cartoons that are doing the looking.

Suggested revision: 'If the cartoons are viewed from this theoretical perspective, they …'

Should it be among?

Explains the significance of the source.

oppositional manner. As will be shown, the cartoons do more than attack the religious sensibilities of Muslims; they attack the Muslim identity as a whole.

Some newspaper articles have questioned the seemingly extraordinary response to the cartoons of the Prophet, calling them extreme and pointing to the riots and attacks on embassies as the product of religious extremists (Goodspeed, A 16). However, the nature of Islam is complicated, and has to do with more than simple religious affiliation for many Muslims. Stuart Hall helps to explain the complicated process by which people associated themselves within their categorical identities based on their differences, and politicize those differences to represent themselves and their culture (*Introduction*, 601). If we view the world as a hegemonic structure with the West as dominant, then the ways in which the West tries to make its values prevalent throughout all other cultures in order to maintain hegemony becomes apparent (Seidman, 137). This Western incursion into Muslim culture brings with it dominant ideas that belittle Islam and treat it as inferior; in response to this portrayal of their community, a solidarity movement takes places among Muslims centered on their religious traditions. This one facet of their identity becomes predominant because it is the main idea that the West centres on when constructing Orientalism; religion thus comes to represent Muslim culture as a whole, and becomes a political and cultural marker. Those of Arab heritage then use Islam as a way to show defiance to Western hegemony, and challenge attempts by Europeans to place them in submissive positions both within Arab countries and in the Muslim diaspora.

The fixing of Muslim identity to the religion of Islam is both prevalent and useful for individuals in this category to resist oppression. However, Cultural Studies recognizes that identities are never static, and with today's rapidly changing world, cultures face a variety of challenges to their traditions and values. The issue of globalization is closely studied by this theoretical position [anthropomorphism], as the movement of people and ideas around the globe has an enormous impact on both the creation of cultural identities and the influence of cultural texts on new audiences. Hall characterizes modern societies as being in a state of "constant, rapid, and permanent change" (*Introduction*, 599). The Muslim influx of immigrants into Europe in recent years demonstrates this, with previously insular societies of racially homogeneous bloodlines suddenly inundated with people from very different cultures and value systems. European nations have scrambled to adjust to this new presence in different ways, with some attempting to integrate Muslims into their own culture, while others allow for a more multicultural approach. This challenge to a clearly defined Western identity that is white and Christian has resulted in a variety of conflicts, both intellectual and physical, between newly settled Muslims and their European neighbours. Muslims in the diaspora also face a challenge to their identity and values, with some responding by isolating themselves in miniature enclaves of Arab culture, and others attempting to blend with Western society (Goodspeed, A 16). It is this integration of cultures that proves most interesting from a Cultural Studies standpoint.

Vague pronoun: the cartoons? The response?

Punctuation error: unnecessary comma.

Avoid use of the collective pronoun 'we' in academic writing.

subject – verb agreement error

Good introduction of example demonstrating the point being made.

Statement identifying the significance of this point, with reference back to the central thesis.

As cultures intermingle as a result of our globalized modern world, traditional identities break down and are replaced by new ones in a kind of cultural dialectic. Hall produces the idea of the "post-modern subject", and individual who has no "fixed, essential, or permanent identity" (*Introduction*, 598). While it is doubtful that many Muslim immigrants have acclimated to their adopted culture to such a degree, the possibility of that kind of integration is there. While the politicization of Islam is helpful in resisting Western attempts at dominating Muslim culture, it can also act as a dominating force in and of itself by forcing individuals who subscribe to it to accept other cultural values that they may not agree with (Seidman, 137). And just as some Muslims begin to accept some Western values despite criticism from their peers, some Westerners have moved to accept the Muslims as part of their national communities. However, the normal attitude towards Muslims among much of the European media seem to be a kind of "siege mentality". Iona Davies reports that television shows in America that depict "the Other" tend to show them as predatory invaders who seek to overrun "natural" British citizens (106).

Confusing example: America? British citizens? | Pronoun agreement error.

Publishing the Danish cartoons can bee seen as a defiant act by someone who was frightened of loosing their cultural identity to outsiders; in a way, challenging an Islamic identity is a response to the challenge that new Muslim arrivals present to a fixed European identity. It is unlikely that the cartoons would ever have arisen in a world where globalization did not test Western culture. As Mercer states, "identity only becomes an issue when it is in crisis, when something assumed to be fixed, coherent, and stable is displaced by the experience of doubt and uncertainty" (qtd in Hall, *Introduction*, 597). Cultural Studies allows us to read the cartoons in the historical context they were created in, and thus understand the motivations behind those who created them and those who decoded their meaning.

Again, concluding the idea explored in the paragraph by referring back to the thesis.

An interpretation of the cartoons through the theorization of Cultural Studies scholars proves to be most useful in coming to an understanding of how different groups within society are able to create meaning and an identity from the cultural texts they are exposed to. Rather than showing a more structural model of society, with a submissive majority being blindly influenced by dominant elites, Cultural Studies presents a more optimistic view of the world. Minoritized groups are able to resist oppression through interpreting the dominant culture in their own way. Even though the actual process of interpretation may be more complex than Hall's original three-part model allows (Hermes, 267), this simplified form of analysis can still yield a wealth of understanding about how individuals interact with texts. And, while the term "Cultural Studies" becomes increasingly broad and applicable to a wide range of theoretical types (ibid), The basic principle of understanding how people make meaning through various media forms remains central. However, as this field expands to become and interdisciplinary type of sociological analysis, it must be careful to remember its roots in neo-Marxist economic determinism and incorporate this historically venerable theory into itself (Storey, 191). Whatever theoretical problems this

Concession

Acknowledgement of a counter-claim, followed by a rebuttal that reasserts the original claim.

Digression into ideas that have not been explored in this paper. Inappropriate in a conclusion paragraph.

discipline might face, it proves to be both a formidable academic tool for under- .... Vague pronoun.
standing the impact of cultural texts on audiences, as well as a practical and
applicable way of addressing current and relevant social issues like the Danish
cartoon controversy.

Works Cited

Davies, Ioan. *Cultural Studies and Beyond: Fragments of Empire.* London:
Routledge, 1995. Print.

Giroux, Henry. "Doing Cultural Studies: Youth and the Challenge of Pedagogy."
*Cultural Studies and Education: Perspectives on Theory, Methodology, and
Practice.* Eds. Ruben A. Gaztambide-Fernandez, Heather A. Harding, and Tere
Sorde-Marti. *Harvard Educational Review 64.3* (1994): 2004. 278–308. Print.

Goodspeed, Peter. "'Clash of Civilizations' Orchestrated: Global Protests Were
Anything but Spontaneous." *National Post* 9 Feb. 2006. Web.
4 March 2006. <http://web.lexis-nexis.comremote.libproxy.wlu.ca>

Hall, Stuart. "Encoding/Decoding." *The Cultural Studies Reader.* Ed. Simon During.
New York: Routledge, 1993. 90–103. Print.

---, "Introduction: Identity in Question." *Modernity: An Introduction to Modern
Societies.* Eds. Stuart Hall, David Held, Don Hubert, and Kenneth Thompson.
Oxford: Blackwell Publishers, 1996. 596–601. Print.

Hermes, Joke. " A Concise History of Media and Cultural Studies in Three Scripts:
Advocacy, Autobiography, and the Chronicle." *The Sage Handbook of Media
Studies.* Eds. Hohn D. H. Downing, Dennis McQuail, Philip Schlesinger, and Ellen
Wartella. London: Sage Publications, 2004. 251–270. Print.

Seidman, Steven. "Stuart hall and British Cultural Studies." *Contested Knowledge:
Social Theory Today* 3rd ed. Oxford: Blackwell Publishing, 2004. 143–141. Print.

Storey, John. *Cultural Theory and Popular Culture: An Introduction.* 3rd ed. Harlow:
Prentice-Hall, 2001. Print.

Appendix B
Justin's Paragraph and Text Annotated

Justin's Revised Paragraph

The second reason why sign languages should be considered real languages is because the learning process is similar to spoken languages. **[TOPIC SENTENCE]** In fact, it has been shown that children can even learn to sign faster than they can learn to speak. **[ELABORATION]** Deaf infants may begin to sign as early as 8 months old, while hearing infants usually begin saying their first words at around 12 months old (Anderson & Reilly, 2002, p. 99). **[DEVELOPMENT]** Interestingly, hearing infants can also be taught to sign, and do so before they are able to speak. **[DEVELOPMENT]** Their knowledge of sign language has even been shown to assist them with verbal language acquisition later on (Goodwyn et al., 2000, p. 98). **[DEVELOPMENT]** This is evidence that sign languages are real languages because all children, both deaf and hearing, can acquire them quickly as long as there is proper exposure. **[INTERPRETATION]** In other words, communication via signing, and not by speaking, appears to be the more instinctive form of human communication. **[INTERPRETATION]** In the case of hearing children, it is only after they are sufficiently exposed to spoken languages that these languages replace their sign language use. **[CONCLUSION]**

Justin's Revised Text

Media and Missing and Murdered Aboriginal Women of Vancouver

Bourdieu, a prominent sociologist and social critic, analyzed the relationship between culture and media. He had a particular interest in television and journalism, and wrote a major text entitled *On Television* (1996).

In *On Television*, Bourdieu addresses the concept of censorship in media, and how this can be used as a political and cultural tool (Bourdieu, 1996). Specifically, he discusses the concept of symbolic violence. By this, he is referring to the complicit relationship between media outlets and their viewers. Media, especially television, tends to focus on strong headlines and extraordinary news instead of providing the information that will help the general public and will support their democratic rights (Bourdieu, 1996). In this sense, Bourdieu acknowledges how what is shown in the media is purposeful as it is designed to influence the public in a particular way.

Another major theorist on media is David Guantlett. Guantlett focuses on the relationship between media, gender, and identity. In his major work, he discusses how media portrayals shape ideas of masculinity and femininity, as well as appropriate gender roles (Guantlett, 2002). He also compares how the expected gender roles were portrayed through media in the past, as well as how these portrayals change over time. His work is key to this project because it not only addresses the ways in which media influences society, but also incorporates gender identity, which can be connected to the theme of violence against women. According to one source, media shapes Canadian identity by its focus on both the maintenance of a national identity and on influencing Canadian market and cultural choices (Filion, 1996). This means that media in Canada works to establish what constitutes our culture as well as what is apart from it, which has implications on who we view as Canadian and who we do not.

Since media is so intimately connected to identity, it follows that media also plays a role in the development and maintenance of stereotypes. Media impacts how certain groups of people are judged, and it can become hard for viewers to distinguish between real and fictional media portrayals. One study examined the impact of true and false media representations on viewers and found that what viewers accept as true depends on viewer motivation as well as gender (Murphy 1998). Female viewers tended to reject false stereotypes more frequently than men, but there was still acceptance by many women (Murphy, 1998). Identity and stereotyping are important parts of this research project as I want to determine how the media defines Aboriginals as well as how Aboriginals view themselves in relation to the rest of Canada.

A few authors have discussed the relationship between Aboriginal Canadians and the media. One author examines the powwow and how this

Justin shows awareness of the reader by identifying the role of one scholar ('a prominent sociologist') and the impact of his work ('a major text'). These references also establish Justin's credibility as someone who understands the recognized scholars in his field.

Summary of source material.

Significance of this source material.

Transition to new idea with reference to an addition ('Another major theorist …')

Ensure correct spelling of cited authors' names

Metadiscourse identifying for the reader the role this information will play in this project.

Use of a supplementary source and a parenthetical citation, relegating this information to a less prominent status.

Topic sentence, followed by development.

Identifying the significance of this source information for Justin's project. Note use of personal pronoun 'I'.

Topic sentence, followed by development using two summarized sources.

serves as a form of media that allows Aboriginals to participate in a cultural ⋯⋯ and political discussion (Buddle, 2004). Buddle also addresses how anthropologists are becoming increasingly interested in cultural forms such as the powwow as a way to analyze the relationship between cultural exchange, media, and cultural production. Another study looked at the history of Aboriginal news portrayal in Canada as well as how the dominant media discourse contributes to the maintenance of white power and perpetuation of stereotypes and social inequality between Aboriginals and non-Aboriginals (Harding 2006). Aboriginal stereotypes are often negative and tend to assimilate various Aboriginal groups into one homogenous identity (Harding, 2007). Various stereotypes are involved in this portrayal, including that all Aboriginals are victims and that they are dependent on others to lead them and care for them (Harding, 2007). Perpetuation and acceptance of stereotypes results in misinformation, and promotes the idea that mainstream Canadian culture is very different from Aboriginal culture.

Appendix C
Literature Review Sample Text

Introduction

Drug tourism, particularly *ayahuasca* tourism, is becoming increasingly popular in the Peruvian Amazon. Westerners come flocking in to the area, spending significant amounts of money on expensive *ayahuasca* resorts and 'authentic' curandero (native healer) experiences, hoping to find spiritual fulfilment and profound healing that they believe are inaccessible through ordinary western means. This research project focuses on the phenomenon of *ayahuasca* tourism through the lens of the popular *ayahuasca* resorts, particularly that of Blue Morpho Tours outside of Iquitos. The literature review that follows outlines the key framework for understanding entheogen tourism, and provides a multidimensional perspective for its interpretation. First, the review looks at entheogens themselves, defining the effects and uses of *ayahuasca* and its primary psychedelic component, DMT. Within this section, traditional shamanic uses of *ayahuasca* are considered, as well as the changing role of the Amazonian shaman and the rising popularity of new shamanic practices or "neo-shamanism" in both South America and the west. The second overarching area of study is that of tourism, specifically the category of "spiritual tourism" that *ayahuasca* tourism falls under. Though there are certainly many potential benefits to spiritual and indigenous tourism, this review also highlights the overly negative consequences of cultural appropriation and the romanticization and objectification of the native "Other" that is involved. Finally, the topic of identity will be explored, specifically spiritual identity, and the ways in which *ayahuasca* tourism serves to reconstitute western spiritualties. This final section of the literature review

Justin introduces the topic directly without preamble or overly wide contextualization.

Backing up this statement with evidence from a source and a reference/citation would be more effective.

This is a clear identification of research project focus, but the reader may want to know why this area/particular resort was chosen as a focus site.

Outline of the paper is presented here.

Good use of organizational key words (first, second…).

The use of first, second … presents the blueprint (or road map) for the paper.

What does this represent? Acronyms must always be written out in full first.

looks at the ways in which the use of entheogens shape western spiritual encounters. However, though some previous research has been done on this topic, much work on the subject remains to be done. My own research intends to examine the ways in which westerners experience their own culturally-mediated hallucinogenic visions and spiritual formations, and how they "bridge the gap" between this and the indigenous context in which the drugs are administered.

Entheogens

Ayahuasca, along with hallucinogens such as mescaline, psilocybin, and LSD among others, are sometimes placed in a special category of psychoactive substances known as entheogens. Derived from the Greek *entheos*, meaning "the divine within" (Blainey 2016), entheogens are used for spiritual or religious purposes as a means of connecting with the sacred through non-ordinary states of consciousness. Entheogens are defined by Ron Cole-Turner (2014) as "psychedelic drugs known to facilitate the occurrence of mystical states" (642). Though entheogens are integral to religious traditions such as Santo Daime (MacRae 1998, Blainey 2016), and are recognized by many as the catalyst for powerful transcendent experiences (Tupper 2006, Richards 2014), scholars of religion have only recently begun to take the study of entheogen-inspired spiritualties seriously, as until a few decades ago "there was little understanding of the uniqueness of entheogens and most so-called recreational drugs were viewed as inebriants that at best offered hedonistic pleasures" (Richards 2014: 654).

While scholars like William Richards (2014), Dennis McKenna (2004), Kenneth Tupper (2008) and Strassman (2001) are enthusiastic about the potential that entheogenic substances such as *ayahuasca* have for healing and spiritual enlightenment, others are not so sure. Indeed, Brush et al. (2003) and Sklerov et al. (2005) among others warn against the unsupervised, naïve use of *ayahuasca* and other similar substances, stressing the importance of context and proper preparation for their use. Though the psychiatric benefits of *ayahuasca* and other entheogens have been praised extensively (Palmer 2004, McKenna 2012, Schenberg et al. 2015), Marlene Dobkin de Rios and Roger Rumrill (2008) note that they can also negatively affect mental health in serious ways if not taken in a proper context. It is clear that the benefits and drawbacks of entheogens, as well as their potential for mobilizing 'authentic' spiritual experiences is still much debated today, and more research on the matter remains to be done.

Ayahuasca and DMT

Ayahuasca is a hallucinogenic brew or tea made from the *Banisteriopsis caapi* vine, native to the Amazon basin, and translated as "vine of the soul," or more ominously, "vine of the dead" by its indigenous users (Harner 1973,

---

Margin annotations:

Again, Justin clearly outlines the sections of the literature review. The reader may be asking why? Or so what? The reader will want to see justification for Justin's approach.

This is vague. What are they?

Is the paper equally highlighting the benefits and consequences? If not, why not?

This is vague. What did the previous research find?

Why? For what purposes? The significance of this research has not been made explicit. Justin has identified his purpose here. Again, the reader is left unclear why this research is important or what its wider significance is.

The use of headings helps the reader keep track of the action. The reader can refer back to the introduction, too, to be reminded of the text's blueprint.

It would be easier to read if the subject of the sentence (Ayahuasca) were closer to the verb (are). There are too many words between the subject and verb. A revision could be: Along with hallucinogens such as mescaline, psilocybin, and LSD, Ayahuasca is …

Subject and verb do not agree here. It should be: Ayahuasca is…

This is a lengthy, cumbersome sentence. Dividing it into two sentences would be easier to read.

Too many quotations used in this paragraph.

Justin uses 'other' often in his text. This leaves the reader wondering what these 'other' things are. It would be better if Justin provided an example (or several) rather than leave the reader guessing.

What does 'they' refer to here? This can be misinterpreted.

This idea is introduced but not developed sufficiently. The reader probably wants to know what these 'serious' negative effects could be.

Schenberg et al 2015). Known as yage in Columbia, quechua in Ecuador and Peru, and cadpi in Brazil, the plant has been used by many South American peoples for hundreds of years (Harner 1973, McKenna 1999). *Psychotria viridis* is typically added to the mixture and seen as integral for its success, as it is the psychedelic component, consisting of the powerful hallucinogen N,N-dimethyltryptamine, more commonly known in the west as DMT (Pinkeley 1969, Strassman 2001). Though structurally DMT is closely related to the more well-known hallucinogens mescaline (found in peyote), psilocybin, and LSD (lysergic acid diethylamide tartrate) those who have experienced the effects of DMT typically describe it as being far more powerful than other mind-altering substances, and significantly more effective spiritually (Harner 1973, Strassman 2001). DMT can be injected, inhaled, or taken orally, however for the hallucinogenic effects to occur when ingested it must be administered with an MAO (monoamine-oxidase) inhibitor, such as the *Banisteriopsis caapi* vine (McKenna and Towers 1984, Tupper 2006). When injected or inhaled, effects last from five to fifteen minutes. When taken orally the effects are significantly longer, typically lasting over three hours (Pickover 2005).

Due to its classification as a schedule I drug in the United States, and schedule III drug in Canada, little research has been done concerning the effects of DMT on humans (Tupper 2006). One of the few studies the subject, and potentially the most famous psychedelic study of the twenty-first century was conducted by Dr. Rick Strassman (2001) at the University of New Mexico's School of Medicine, who was granted permission to monitor the physiological effects of DMT in healthy adults. Over the five-year course of the project, Dr. Strassman and his team administered approximately four hundred doses of DMT to sixty volunteers. The results of the study were published in his book *DMT: The Spirit Molecule*, the source of inspiration for the later documentary of the same name (2010). Both the book and the film include personal accounts from volunteers who participated in the study. The notion that DMT is "the spirit molecule" comes from the fact that those who have experienced its effects often report having highly spiritual (though not necessarily religious) encounters, often describing having felt a "sense of pure being" and "oneness" with the universe (Strassman 2001: 244). In addition, DMT is a chemical compound found throughout nature, including the human body, thought to be produced naturally by the pineal gland (though not necessarily confirmed), a pinecone-shaped section of the brain often referred to as "the seat of the soul" (Strassman 2001, Johnston 2009, McKenna 2012).

Shamans and Ayahuasca Use

The use of *ayahuasca* in the Peruvian Amazon, as well as other parts of South America, is typically linked with shamanism. Indeed, traditional shamanic practices in the Amazon utilize *ayahuasca* as one of the main ritual

---

Why has Justin defined LSD here? He should have defined this acronym at first mention.

Incorrect punctuation for however. Instead, Justin should have written:

… or taken orally; however, for the hallucinogenic effects …

The name should be mentioned first, then the acronym.

Topic sentence introduces idea of DMT research.

Punctuation (a comma) is missing here.

Sentence too long.

This should be a period. A new sentence could begin with: Dr. Strassman was granted …

Incorrect transition: how is the idea in this sentence an addition to the previous idea? They seem unrelated.

This paragraph is poorly developed. It ends on a statement identifying information from a source, but fails to indicate why this information is important or significant. A re-ordering of the sentences in this paragraph may help, plus a conclusion tying this information to the research purpose.

This paragraph effectively examines the concept introduced, shamanism. Sources are well integrated and summarized, and an appropriate quotation is drawn out and cited.

components, sometimes accompanied by tobacco, either *Nicotiana rustica* or *N. tibacum*, as a means of enhancing the hallucinogenic experience (Kensinger 1973, Wilbert 1987). Though shamanism has been conceived of as one of the world's oldest religious (Vitebsky 2000), there is significant debate among scholars regarding varying definitions of shamanism. Originating from the Tungus (also known as the Evenk) of Eastern Siberia, the word "shaman" (*hamán*) is now applied to hundreds, perhaps even thousands of religions worldwide (Heinze 1991, Bowie 2000, Vitebsky 2000). While notable western scholars of shamanism such as Piers Vitebsky (1995, 2000), Ioan Lewis (1989), Jane Atkinson (1989, 1992) and Joan Halifax (1991) believe that a broad definition of shamanism that incorporates multiple traditions across the globe is necessary for a comprehensive understanding of the practice, Russian and Scandinavian-based scholars such as Åke Hultkrantz (1993) and S.M. Shirokogoroff (1982 [1935]) argue that the use of the term "shamanism" should be restricted to its original context. Generally, the western perspective posits that there can be said to be many different "shamanisms," just as there are many monotheisms (Atkinson 1992, Vitebsky 2000). However, as the anthropologist of religion Fiona Bowie notes, an overly broad definition of shamanism is problematic, as "believing [it] to mean almost anything is ultimately to mean nothing" (2000: 191).

Most western scholars would agree that shamanism is not a religion as such, but rather a system of beliefs, rituals, practices and myths – multiple characteristics that vary across space and time (Atkinson 1989, Bowie 2002). There can be several kinds of shamans, fulfilling a variety of roles including those of doctor, priest, mystic, social worker, psychoanalyst, hunting consultant, astronaut, poet, magician, and many more (Eliade 1964, Vitebsky 2000).

New Shamanism

Eliade's recognition of a generalized shamanism, manifest in various forms throughout the "primitive" world (1964) laid the foundation for a variation of shamanism that could be realized in any culture, even among westerners. In recent decades, the western world has expressed a growing sense of fascination with shamanism, to the point of attempting to become "shamans" themselves (Bowie 2000, Wallis 2003, DuBois 2009).

[information has been omitted from the original for the purpose of this book]

Ritual Use of Ayahuasca in the Amazon

Numerous studies have been conducted on the traditional uses of *ayahuasca* in the Amazon, namely by Alfred Métraux (1943), Richard Evans Schultes, and more recently by Donald Joraleman and Douglas Sharon (1993), and Marlene Dobkin de Rios, who spent over forty years living with

Note in the remaining text how subheadings of various levels are used to effectively identify the topics and guide the reader through each level, as identified in the introduction.

Note also the way sources are summarized, how material is used to provide definitions, and how quotations are sparingly used to good effect. Note how some sources are cited in parenthetical citations while in other instances the scholars' names are included within the sentences.

shamans and *ayahuasqueros*. Though studies of *ayahuasca* rituals among indigenous groups in the Amazon reveal many similarities, there are also significant differences. For instance, Kenneth Kensinger (1973) emphasises the group solidarity among the Peruvian Cashinahua, wherein the drinking of *ayahuasca* or as they call it, *Nixi pae* ("the vine of drunkenness") is always a communal event.

[information has been omitted from the original for the purpose of this book]

> Note the use of transitions and metadiscursive language such as 'for instance', 'however', 'though some scholars would deny …', 'In order to … we must first examine …'. This language helps guide the reader through a lengthy text.

Tourism

Until fairly recently, the study of tourism in anthropology and other social sciences was not seen as a legitimate academic pursuit, and was rather considered to be frivolous and even trivial (Mathews and Richter 1991, Larfant 1993). However, by the mid-1970ss to early 1980s multiple anthropological studies on the subject had begun to surface, and tourist studies today is an ever-increasing field of study (Dann et al. 1988). Perhaps one of the most pressing questions in the study of tourism today is how it should best be defined in relation to other forms of travel.

[information has been omitted from the original for the purpose of this book]

Tourism as Pilgrimage

Hoggart (1992) defines pilgrimage as the "travel to sacred placed undertaken in order to gain spiritual merit or healing or as an act of penance or thanksgiving" (236). Though some scholars would deny that modern tourism has anything to do with pilgrimage, condemning tourism as an inherently superficial, capitalist venture devoid of any true meaning or authenticity, (Boorstin 1964, Barthes 1984), most scholars believe that the line between the two is not so clear. Indeed, MacCannell (1973) and Singh and Singh (2009) argue that the line has been blurred to the extent that tourism and pilgrimage are virtually indistinguishable. Many anthropologists of tourism draw from Victor and Edith Turner's (1987) study of Christian pilgrimages, as well as from Victor Turner's (1969) deconstruction of ritual and rites of passage to show that tourism, like the pilgrimage, is a process of "sacrilization" (Senn 2002, Chambers 2010).

> Effective identification of the grouping of sources together.

[information has been omitted from the original for the purpose of this book]

Spiritual Tourism

Spiritual tourism is a distinct form of tourism that is characterized by an intentional search for spiritual benefit that corresponds with religious practices (Norman 2011). What distinguishes spiritual tourists however is their lack of "traditional religiosity," travelers who participate in religious practices and yet usually "have little or no everyday connection with the practices or traditions in which they are taking part" (ibid: 1). Spirituality, though certainly an umbrella term for a diverse set of beliefs, traditions and practices, is defined by Halstead and Mickley (1997) as a process of dynamic integrative growth that ultimately leads to the discovery of values, meaning and purpose in life.

Use of a paraphrase from source material to provide a definition of term.

[information has been omitted from the original for the purpose of this book]

The Problem with Authenticity

One of the primary reasons why westerners are so enamoured with *ayahuasca* tourism and shamanism is because they represent the notion of an "authentic" spiritual experience that is unavailable to them at home or through ordinary religion. Bruno Latour (1993) notes that modernity brought with it the notion of a "Great Divide" between nature and culture, a conceptual division between the natural, "primitive" world of the past, and the advanced, technologized world of "civilization."

[information has been omitted from the original for the purpose of this book]

Cultural Appropriation

Use of informal emphatic language to draw attention to a specific point.

A very real issue with indigenous tourism and the western consumption of *ayahuasca* is the notion of cultural or spiritual appropriation. Kulchyski describes cultural appropriation as "the practice on the part of dominant social groups of deploying cultural texts produced by dominated social groups for their own (elite) interests," (614)

Use of a quotation to provide a definition of a term.

and therefore highlighting power differentials between the source culture from which the authoritative (western) culture "borrows" from. Shand (2002) and Gorbman (2000) note the various kinds of harm associated with cultural appropriation, including the undermining of the community's integrity and values, as well as the ways in which the cultural object itself is distorted and altered through unequal exchange.

[information has been omitted from the original for the purpose of this book]

Spiritual Identities

Despite all of the negative consequences associated with ayahuasca tourism, the question remains as to whether there is also the potential for genuine spiritual growth at a resort like Blue Morpho. Essentially, can the appropriation of cultural-specific spiritual practices truly be used to the benefit of other? Or does this form of intellectual theft or "biopiracy" simply do more harm than good?

Effective use of rhetorical questions.

Though this is certainly a difficult question to answer, we should perhaps first look at the western context of psychedelic use. The birth of "neo-primitivism" in the west can be traced back to the 1950s and 1960s "cult of naturalness" and hippie frenzy (McGregor 1988), a time when a fascination with magic, ritual, tribal lore and psychedelics were beginning to surface as an attempt to return to an aesthetic of the ancient past, and reconnect with the powers of nature (Roszak 1969).

[information has been omitted from the original for the purpose of this book]

Changes in Spirituality Among Ayahuasca Users

In order to understand what kinds of changes in spirituality or other mental states users might be experiencing as a result of ingesting *ayahuasca*, we must first examine *who* these people are. Indeed, like western practitioners of neo-shamanism, *ayahuasca* tourists are typically people who seek to gain control over their lives, expand their views of reality, and get in touch with their inner selves (Bowie 2000).

[information has been omitted from the original for the purpose of this book]

While Dobkin de Rios and Rumrrill believe that *ayahuasca* use is more likely to add to these psychological issues rather than help alleviate them, others have a very different point of view. For instance, anthropologist Winkelman (2005) conducted an extensive study on *ayahuasca* tourists in Manaus, Brazil, interviewing 15 men and women who had come to South America in search of emotional and spiritual development, and a connection with the sacred through nature. The study concluded that the participants experienced overwhelmingly positive benefits as a result of their experiences with *ayahuasca*, including help with drug addictions, alleviation of depression, the discovery of inner peace and increased open-mindedness, and even assistance in the recovery from cancer. Indeed, while similar benefits from entheogens have been noted elsewhere (Holm 1982, Fisher 2005, Smith 2005, Richards 2014), much research on the subject remains to be done. Indeed, the question of how westerners mediate between the ritual practices associated with the traditional use of *ayahuasca*, and their own culturally constructed psychedelic experiences remains to be seen.

Effective balancing of contradictory points of view to indicate attempt at neutrality by Justin.

Classic (clichéd?) wording to indicate the current study is necessary.

Direct introduction to the goal of this current study.

Works Cited

Atkinson, J.M. 1989. *The Art and Politics of Wana Shamanship.* Berkley, CA: University of California Press.

Atkinson, J.M. 1992. "Shamanism Today." *Annual Review of Anthropology.* 21, 307-30.

Bowie, Fiona. 2000. *The Anthropology of Religion: An Introduction.* Oxford: Blackwell Publishers.

Blainey, Mark. 2016. "Mind-Altering Re-Enchantment in the West: Ethnographic Perspectives on the Santo Daime Religion and Its Ayahuasca Sacrament." *Religion and Culture Seminar*, Wilfrid Laurier University. Nov. 25, 2016.

Brush, D. E. et al. 2004. "Monoamine Oxidase Inhibitor Poisoning Resulting from Internet Misinformation on Illicit Substances." Journal of Toxicology: Clinical Toxicology, 42(2) 191-195.

Butler, Richard and Tom Hinch. 2007. "Introduction: Revisiting Common Ground," in *Tourism and Indigenous Peoples: Issues and Implications*, 1-14. Amsterdam: Elsevier.

Castaneda, Carlos. 1968. *The Teachings of Don Juan: A Yaqui Way of Knowledge*. Berkley: University of California Press.

Cole-Turner, Ron. 2014. "Entheogens, Mysticism, and Neuroscience." *The Potential Religious Relevance of Entheogens: Zygon*, 49(3), 642-651.

Cohen, E. 1988. "Authenticity and Commoditization in Tourism." *Annals of Tourism Research*, 12(1).

D'Amore, Lou. 1988. "Tourism: The World's Peace Industry," in *Proceedings of the First Global Conference: Tourism, A Vital Force for Peace*. Montreal: Lou D'Amore Associates.

De Rios, Marlene Dobkin and Roger Rumrrill. 2008. *A Hallucinogenic Tea, Laced with Controversy: Ayahuasca in the Amazon and the United States*. Westport: Praeger Publishers.

Drury, Neville. 1999. *Exploring the Labyrinth: Making Sense of the New Spirituality*. St. Leonards: Allen and Unwin.

DuBois, Thomas. 2009. *An Introduction to Shamanism*. Cambridge: Cambridge University Press.

Eliade, Mircea. 1964. *Shamanism: Archaic Techniques of Ecstasy*. Princeton New Jersey: Princeton University Press.

Eliade, Mircea. 1962. "The Yearning for Paradise in Primitive Tradition." *The Making of Myth*, edited by Richard M. Ohmann. New York: Putnam.

Fisher, Gary. 2005. "Treating the Untreatable." *Eminent Elders Explore the Continuing Impact of Psychedelics*, edited by Roger Walsh and Charls S. Grob, 103-118. New York: State University of New York Press.

Geertz, W. Armin. 2004. "Can we move beyond primitivism?" *Beyond Primitivism: Indigenous Religious Traditions and Modernity*, edited by Jacob K. Olupona, 37-70. New York: Routledge.

Gorbman, C. 2000. "Scoring the Indian: Music in the Liberal Western." *Western Music and Its Others: Difference, Representation and Appropriation in Music*, edited by G. Born and D. Hesmonndhalgh, 234-253. Berkley: University of California Press.

Halifax, Joan. 1991. *Shamanic Voices: a Survey of Visionary Narratives*. New York: Arkana, Penguin.

Hall, Michael. 2007. "Politics, Power and Indigenous Tourism." *Tourism and Indigenous Peoples: Issues and Implications*, edited by Richard Butler and Tom Hinch, 305-318. Amsterdam: Elsevier.

Halsted, M.T. and J.R. Mickley. 1997. "Attempting to Fathom the Unfathomable: Descriptive Views of Spirituality. Seminars in Oncology Nurisng, 113(4), 225-230.

Harner, Michael. 1973. "The Sound of Rushing Water," in *Hallucinogens and Shamanism*, 15-27. New York: Oxford University Press.

Harner, Michael. 1980. *The Way of the Shaman: A Guide to Power and Healing*. San Francisco: Harper & Row Publishers.

Holm, Nils G. 1982. "Ecstasy Research in the 20th Century: An Introduction," in *Religious Ecstasy*, 7-26. Sweden: Almqvist & Wiksell.

Hultkrantz, Ake. 1993. "Introductory Remarks on the Study of Shamanism." *Shamanism: an International Journal for Shamanic Research*, 1(1), 3-14.

Huxley, Aldous. 1954. *The Doors of Perception*. New York: Harper & Brothers.

Ingles, Pamela. 2002. "Welcome to my Village: Hosting Tourists in the Peruvian Amazon." *Tourism Recreation Research*, 27(1), 53-60.

Jakobsen, Merete Demant. 1999. *Shamanism: Traditional and Contemporary Approaches to the Mastery of Spirits and Healing*. Oxford: Berghahn.

Kensinger, Kenneth M. 1973. "Banisteriopsis Usage Among the Peruvian Cashinahua." *Hallucinogens and Shamanism*, edited by Michael Harner, 9-14. New York: Oxford University Press.

Kulchyski, P. 1997. "From Appropriation to Subversion: Aboriginal Cultural Production in the Age of Postmodernism." *American Indian Quarterly*, 21, 605-620.

Langdon, E. Jean. 1979. "Yagé Among the Siona: Cultural Patterns in Visions." *Spirits, Shamans, and Stars: Perspectives from South America,* edited by David L. Brownman and Ronald A. Schwarz, 63-80. Paris: Mouton Publishers.

Latour, Bruno. 1993. We *Have Never Been Modern.* Trans. Catherine Porter. Cambridge: Harvard University Press.

Leary, Timothy. 1968. *The Politics of Ecstasy.* Berkley: Ronin Publishing

Levi-Strauss, Claude. 1963. Effectiveness of Symbols. Structural Anthropology. Pp. 186-205. Basic Books.

Lewis, Ioan. 1986. Religion in Context: Cults and Charisma. Cambridge: Cambridge University Press.

Lewis, Ioan. 1989 [1971]. *Ecstatic Religion: A Study of Shamanism and Spirit Possession.* London: Routledge.

Lindquist, Galina. 1997. *Shamanic Performances on the Urban Scene: Neo-Shamans in Contemporary Sweden.* Stockholm: Stockholm University Press.

Little, Kenneth. 1991. "On Safari: The Visual Politics of A Tourist Representation." *The Varieties of Sensory Experience: A Sourcebook in Anthropology,* edited by David Howes, 148-163. Toronto: University of Toronto Press.

Luna, L.E. 1984. "The Concept of Plants as Teachers Among Four Mestizo Shamans of Iquitos, Northesastern Peru." Journal of Ethnopharmacology, 11(2), 135-156.

MacCannell, D. 1973. "Staged Authenticity: Arrangements of Social Space in Tourist Settings." *American Journal of Sociology,* 79, 589-603.

Macy, Terry and Daniel Hart. 1996. *White Shamans and Plastic Medicine Men.* United States: Native Voices.

McGregor, Gaile. 1988. *The Noble Savage in the New World Garden: Notes Towards a Syntactic* of Place. Toronto: University of Toronto Press and Bowing Green: Bowing Green State University Popular Press.

McKenna, Dennis. 2004. "Clinical Investigations of the Therapeutic Potential of Ayahuasca: Rationale and Regulatory Changes." *Pharmacology and Therapeutics,* 102, 111-129.

McKenna, Dennis. 2012. *The Brotherhood of the Screaming Abyss.* New York: North Star Press.

Métraux, Alfred. 1943. "The Social Organization and Religion of the Mojo and Manasi." Primitive Man, 16(2), 1-30.

Meyer, C.J. and D. Royer. 2001. *Selling the Indian: Commercializing and Appropriating American Indian Cultures.* Tucson, AZ: University of Arizona Press.

Nash, Dennison. 1996. *Anthropology of Tourism.* Connecticut: Pergamon.

Notzke, Claudia. 2006. *"The Stranger, the Native and the Land": Perspectives on Indigenous Tourism.* Ontario: Captus Press.

Richards, William A. 2014. "Here and Now: Discovering the Sacred With Entheogens. *The Potential Religious Relevance of Entheogens: Zygon,* 49(3), 652-665.

Roszak, Theodore (1969) *The Making of a Counter Culture: Reflections on the Technocratic Society and Its Youthful Opposition.* Garden City: Doubleday, 47.

Seiler-Baldinger, Annemarie. 1988. "Tourism in the Upper Amazon and its Effects on the Indigenous Population." *Tourism: Manufacturing the Exotic,* edited by Pierre Rossel, 177-193. Copenhagen: International Work Group for Indigenous Affairs.

Senn, C.F. 2002. "Journeying as Religious Education: The Shaman, the Hero, the Pilgrim and the Labyrinth Walker. *Religious Education,* 97(2), 124-140.

Singh, Shalini and Tej Ver Singh. 2009. "Aesthetic Pleasures: Contemplating Spiritual Tourism." *Philosophical Issues in Tourism,* edited by John Tribe, 135-153. Bristol: Chanel View Publications.

Shirokogoroff, S. M. 1982 [1935] *Psychomental Complex of the Tungus.* London: Kegan Paul, Trench, Trubner & Co. Ltd.

Smith, Huston. 2005. "Do Drugs Have Religious Import? A Forty Year Follow-Up." *Eminent Elders Explore the Continuing Impact of Psychedelics,* edited by Roger Walsh and Charls S. Grob, 223-240. New York: State University of New York Press.

Strassman, Rick. 2001. DMT: *The Spirit Molecule.* Rochester: Park Street Press.

Townsend, Joan B. 2005. "Individualist Religious Movements: Core and Neo-Shamanism." *Anthropology of Consciousness.* 15(1). 1-9.

Tramacchi, Des. 2006. "Entheogens, Elves and Other Entities: Encountering the Spirits of the Shamanic Plants and Substances." *Popular Spiritualties,* edited by Lynne Hume and Kathleen McPhillips. England: Ashgate Publishing.

Tupper, Kenneth. 2009. "Ayahuasca Healing Beyond the Amazon: the Globalization of a Traditional Indigenous Entheogenic Practice." Global Networks, 9(1), 117-136.

Turner, Victor. 1969. *The Ritual Process: Structure and Anti-Structure.* Chicago: Aldine Publishing Company.

Vitebsky, Piers. 1995. *The Shaman: Voyages of the Soul, Trance, Ecstasy and Healing from Siberia to the Amazon.* London and Basingstoke: Macmillan in association with Duncan Baird Publishers.

Vitebsky, Piers. 2000. "Shamanism." *Indigenous Religions: A Companion,* edited by Graham Harvey. London: Cassell.

Wallis, Robert J. 2003. *Shamans/Neo-Shamans: Ecstasy, Alternative Ideologies, and Contemporary Pagans.* London: Routledge.

Wilson, Bryan. 1988. "Secularisation: Religion in the Modern World." *The World's Religions*, edited by Sutherland et al., 953-966. London: Routledge.

Wilbert, Johannes. 1987. *Tobacco and Shamanism in South America.* New Haven: Yale University Press.

Winkelman, M. 2005. "Drug Tourism or Spiritual Healing? Ayahuasca Seekers in Amazonia." *Journal of Psychoactive Drugs,* 37(2), 209-218.

York, Michael. 2001. "New Age Commodification and Appropriation of Spirituality." Journal of Contemporary Religion, 16(3), 361-372.

Zinger, H. 1969. *The Future of Tourism in the East Caribbean.* Washington: Zinder & Associates.

Znamenski, Andrei A. 2007. *The Beauty of the Primitive: Shamanism and the Western Imagination.* Oxford: Oxford University Press.

Appendix D
Scholarship Proposal Sample

Eva Hibbert's Initial Brainstorm

<u>Title</u>: *Canada* ....

<u>Introduction</u>:

<u>Possible Hook</u>:

1. When preparing for exercise, most participants in sports simply enter the change room without a second thought, but for number of folks? Entering a change room can be a scary/alienating experience.

2. Dr. Freeman's recommendation: Traveling around the world as a member of the <u>*Canadian*</u> national boxing team, ~~I have entered many change~~ rooms. Often experienced a sense of alienation from being told that I'm in the wrong room. When I returned to train at the University during the exhibition of The Change Room Project (CRP), [Describe]. Immediately those ~~corrections~~ stopped entirely. ~~Repeatedly observed...~~ I decided to return to the university to learn more about this phenomenon for my master's.

Identifying my topic:

My research examines how people relate to their bodies and each other in the change room. Specifically, my research intends to look at how bodies which challenge a dimorphic gender binary experience the space of the change room and expands to inquire how these experiences are shaped by racism, ableism and ~~fat phobia~~ a culture that...[?].

Eva is exploring one way to engage the reader through emotional connections (pathos) – sharing similar experiences.

Eva is exploring a different way to engage here: by establishing her credibility (ethos) as someone who has experienced something *different* which bears studying.

Identifying a possible 'gap'?

Why is this research relevant?

Gender trouble in men's vs. women's rooms is becoming a growing issue (stat?) (source)

Provides a barrier to using athletic and recreational facilities and programs (source)

For trans and gender non-conforming [Define jargon] the change room is a space that high incidence of violence and harassment

While gender neutral bathrooms are being used as a solution, gender neutral solutions aren't likely to offer big solution

> Because infrastructure for men and women's rooms are already in place. Expensive and unlikely to be converted to gender neutral. (source)

> Also, gender neutral raises safety issues and barriers for *Canadians* eg muslim women

Identify the niche: Unaddressed: what to do? *Canada* hasn't figured out a solution to this societal puzzle.

Fill the niche: My research question asks what is the most effective/economically feasible approach to improve perceptions of inclusion and safety of participants using men's and women's change rooms. I hypothesize that

LITERATURE REVIEW: My work builds on...

Gender differentiated spaces: Cavanaugh [Queering washrooms] (expand) more.

TransGender in physical activity: (more) Sykes, Hargie et al.

+ Also

Body size in physical activity: Sykes. (more)

Ability in physical activity spaces: (more)

Racism in physical activity spaces: (more)

What comes close to my work?

Identify the gap: My work is original because... + gap Canada?

THEORETICAL FRAMEWORK & METHODS: This is how I will go about doing my research... Theoretical Framework: Ahmed 2006, Butler ( ) , Critical Race Theory ( )

Here's how I will do the research:

Margin notes:

A certainty claim? Exploring ideas for logical development of topic (logos). Will need literature review for support.

Exploring wider implications of the possible gap?

Drafting a potential review focus

Potention themes for lit review

Addressing credibility as a researcher (ethos)

Identify research subjects – who? How?

Interviews them how: Kvale 1995 +

Focus Groups:

Transcribing interviews according to protocol from Mishler 1991, 1995

This is why I've chosen these methods… + +

From this data I hope to establish an understanding of how different bodies experience change rooms, and what are the biggest barriers.

Timeline and Feasibility: How will I deliver what I promise? Justify location.

> Eva is considering credibility (ethos): why am I a good bet to successfully do this research?

Who will do the work? I will. What is my expertise? Identify skills necessary to deliver this.

RELEVANCE: [another alternative subheading name?]

Why is this worth doing? It will make a contribution to scholars, this research will improve foundation addressing…? Gender in both locker rooms and physical activity spaces, gender differentiated, improve literature intersectional analysis, offer literature addressing strategies for improving inclusion in these spaces. This research will benefit…?

> Expanding outwards – significance of work.

Eva Hibbert's First Draft (with student's original comments and professor's feedback)

Assessing and Improving Inclusion in Canadian University Change Rooms.

While serving on the Canadian women's boxing team, and as a three-time Canadian champion, I have visited change rooms around the world. As an androgynous female athlete, entering the women's change room can be an alienating experience. I am regularly met with nervous or hostile stares and often directed to the men's change room. In 2015, returning to the city between competitions, I observed a phenomenon that compelled me to return to the university to pursue a Master's degree.

> Professor (P): REMINDER: The draft includes all necessary elements (rhetorical and structural), but as you carry it through possible further revisions keep them in mind. What you want is a proposal which says: my subject is important; my anticipated results will be important, both for scholarship and practice; my method will allow me to achieve that result; I have the capabilities needed.

Entering the change room at the the university's Athletic Center, I observed that the reactions I'd grown accustomed to were replaced with welcoming nods from other women in the change room. At this time, an installation for the Pan-Am Games, The Change Room Project (CRP) was on display (Fusco et al. 2015). Large posters with quotations from lesbian, gay, bi, transgender, intersex, and queer (LGBTIQ)

participants were mounted in visible areas. These quotations gave change room users an opportunity to look inside the vulnerability that LGBTIQ often experience in this space. For example, "In the change room I dress as

> Student (S): I need to make a decision about my focus. Gender deviant – describe. Expressions of sex and gender that are

quick as possible. I'm afraid if I make eye contact, I'll get beat up (John, transgender athlete)." My Master's research pursues the hypothesis that the CRP offers a model which can alter perceptions of diverse bodies, previously rendered unintelligible in the change room (Sykes 2011).

not immediately recognizable as male or female, such as transgendered and intersex genders. (gender ambiguous (GA).

Literature Review: Discomfort in change rooms has been identified as the primary barrier to LGBTIQ participation in sport (Hargie 2017; Keogh 2006; Whittle 2007). However, little scholarship been devoted to understanding how the change room is experienced by a diversity of LGBTIQ individuals. My research expands scholarship's comprehension of these experiences.

P: You might explain a bit more how looking at one model (university's CPR) will provide that knowledge

While several scholars have examined how LGBTIQ bodies navigate gendered space in women's washrooms (Cavanaugh 2010) and sport (Travers 2011; Caudwell 2007), little literature examines the experiences of these bodies in the space of the change room. My research aims to directly address this gap with an examination of how diverse LGBTIQ navigate a space fraught with such vulnerability. A dearth of literature addresses how existing change rooms can be made more inclusive for LGBTIQ members. My research examines the CRP as a potential model for mediating relationships between change room users.

P: Expand or rephrase

S: I NEED TO ADD TO SIGNIFICANCE – CAN I REDUCE HERE?

Methods:

My analysis is informed by a queer feminist framework which presupposes that discrete, binary constructions of sex and gender cannot explain the biological and social spectrum of sex and gender expressed by humanity (Halberstam 1998; Butler, 1990, 1993; Monro, 2005). During the fall I will be enrolled in a research methods course CTL1018H (Introduction to Qualitative Inquiry) to help me consolidate my methodology. I anticipate conducting 12–15 semi-structured, qualitative interviews to elicit personal experience (Thorpe 2015). In order to examine interviewee reactions to the CRP, I anticipate drawing upon the photo elicitation method; including photos of the CRP installation in the interview (Harper 2002; Atkinson 2009). My research will be supervised by C. Fusco, who has written extensively on change room spaces and is the creator of the CRP (Fusco et al. 2015; Fusco, 2005; 2006). As an apprentice coach in a boxing gym, I have access to a number of contacts who represent diversity in the LGBTIQ community. My own experience in change rooms offers me sensitivity to help identify and reduce interviewee discomfort.

P: the methods section has to show that the methods use will result in a project which can generate the findings which you say will result, given time and resources available

P: categories

P: listed as 2011 in bibliography

S: Do I need a comma between intext citations?

S: I think I can draw a few words out here

S: Check date

S: SEE I don't think I can get rid of defining this all together.

Significance: We, as scholars, are aware that LGBTIQ participants experience discomfort in change rooms, but do not yet understand how to diminish this discomfort. This case study will improve the literature by helping to characterize the nature of these challenges. The change room is a space where a lack of progress for LGBTIQ individuals is most evident, due to the vulnerability of nudity. My research presupposes that the CRP offers a model to mediate this space, and seeks to further examine the CRP's potential for making the change room a more inclusive space for all bodies, regardless of difference. from that, it needs to show you will fill a gap in the literature; you say you will, but might expand on that a bit plus, ideally, the research outcome should not only contribute to academic understanding, but also to applied practice; how could the relevant non-scholars use your findings? Again, you touch on that, but it might be more explicit

Allowable Inclusion

This section offers an explanation for the length of time which I took to complete my undergraduate degree at the University. This degree was completed in 12 years (between fall 2005 and spring 2017). My professional career, as a representative of the Canadian national boxing team, led to this delay in completion. As early as elementary school, I was identified as both a gifted student and a promising athlete. From an early age, both educators and coaches encouraged me to simultaneously pursue academic aspirations and athletic goals of competing for Canada at the Olympic Games.

Aware that my career as an athlete was biologically constrained to span of to to three Summer Olympics cycles (which occurs once every four years), I decided to temporarily prioritize my athletic goals over my academic course work. In accordance with this decision, I pursued course work whenever it was possible to do so without compromising the quality of my athletic and academic results. In early 2007 I was identified by Boxing Ontario and Boxing Canada as an athlete with considerable potential. Shortly thereafter I moved to Windsor, Ontario to train on a full time basis with a noteworthy and internationally recognized coach, Charlie Stewart. As a result, I was not enrolled in any courses in 2008 and 2009.

P: No.

P: What literature? Specify. Feminist? Queer?

S: • Significance:

S: • The outcome of my research will be a better understanding of how to improve GA individuals' experiences in the change room.

• Looking at one model the university's CPR model, will provide that knowledge.

P:• From that, it needs to show you will fill a gap in the literature; you say you will, but might expand on that a bit

• Plus, ideally, the research outcome should not only contribute to academic understanding, but also to applied practice; how could the relevant non-scholars use your findings? Again, you touch on that, but it might be more explicit

P: Or a diversity

S: Reduce to 1/3 of page

Returning to the city, I continued my degree part time in 2010. In early 2011, my standing had accelerated quickly and more frequent competitions required my course load to be reduced. My transcripts reflect this reduction in the late withdrawal of two courses in spring of 2011. In 2012, after failing to qualify for the London Olympics, I returned to school on a full time basis. From the fall of 2013 to early 2016, I was training and competing full time in preparation to qualify for the 2016 Olympics. In 2016 from winter to summer I trained and competed full time as the Olympic alternate for the Canadian women's national boxing team in the middleweight division.

After retiring from competitive boxing in the spring of 2016 I returned to complete my undergraduate degree on a full time basis. My cumulative GPA, earned two consecutive full course load semesters, demonstrates my capacity for achieving as a full time student. I will be pursuing my Master's degree as a full time student.

Bibliography:

Atkinson, Michael. 2010. "Fell running in post-sport territories." *Qualitative Research in Sport and Exercise* 2(2): 109–132.

Butler, Judith. 2011. ·· S: Or 1993? How to cite published another edition?

Bodies that matter : on the discursive limits of "sex" /

Butler, Judith. 1990. *Gender Trouble: feminism and the subversion of identity.* New York: Routledge.

Caudwell, Jayne. 2007. "Queering the Field? The complexities of sexuality within a lesbian-identified football team in England." *Gender Place and Culture* 14(2): 183–196.

Cavanagh, Sheila L. 2010. *Queering Bathrooms.* Toronto: University of Toronto Press.

Fusco, Caroline. 2012. "Critical Feminist/Queer Methodologies: Deconstructing (Hetero)Normative Inscriptions." In *Qualitative Research on Sport and Physical Culture*, edited by Michael Atkinson and Kevin Young, 151–166. Bingley: Emerald Group Publishing.

Fusco, Caroline et al. 2015. "The Change Room Project." *Hart House.* Accessed May 2017. http://harthouse.ca/the-changeroom-project/.
·········· S: should I list these from most recent? Check Chicago style.

Fusco,···

Caroline. 2006. "Inscribing healthification: governance, risk, surveillance and the subjects and spaces of fitness and health."

Fusco, Caroline. 2005. "Cultural Landscapes of Purification: Sports Spaces and Discourses of Whiteness." *Sociology of Sport Journal* 22: 282–309.

Halberstam, Judith. 1998. *Female Masculinity.* Durham: Duke University Press.

Hargie, Owen et al. 2017. "'People have a knack of making you feel excluded if they catch on to your difference': Transgender experiences of exclusion in sport." *International Review for the Sociology of Sport* 52(2): 223–239.

Harper, Douglas. 2002. "Talking about pictures: a case for photo elicitation." *Visual Studies* 17(1): 13–26.
··········· S: Include first name with et al?

Keogh, Peter et al. 2006. "Lambeth LGBT Matters: The needs and experiences of Lesbians, Gay men, Bisexual and Trans men and women in Lambeth."
··· Need help formatting

Monro, Surya. 2005. "Beyond Male and Female: Poststructuralism and the Spectrum of Gender." *International Journal of Transgenderism* 8(1): 3–22. ....

Sykes, Heather. 2011. *Queer Bodies: Sexualities, Gender & Fatness.* New York: Peter Lang.

Thorpe, Holly. 2012. "The Ethnographic (I)nterview in the Sports Field: Towards a Postmodern Sensibility." In *Qualitative Research on Sport and Physical Culture,* edited by Michael Atkinson and Kevin Young, 79–99. Bingley: Emerald Group Publishing.

Travers, Ann and Jillian Deri. "Transgender inclusion and the changing face of lesbian softball leagues." *International Review for the Sociology of Sport* 46(4): 488–507.

Whittle, Stephen et al. 2007. "Engendered Penalties: Transgender and Transsexual People's Experiences of Inequality and Discrimination." *The Equalities Review.* Accessed May 2017. www.pfc.org.uk/pdf/EngenderedPenalties.pdf.

S: Is this the correct format?

+
+
+

- *Nominalization* abstract noun that would like to be an adjective = **WRITE TO BE MORE DIRECT.**
- Nominalizations depersonalize it. – keep my voice. Too stiff – how can we say everyone is welcome.

This paragraph begins by establishing an emotional connection to the reader (sharing a personal anecdote, identifying a common emotional reaction). It also establishes Eva's credibility as someone who has experienced the phenomenon which she will explore in her research.

Eva Hibbert's Final Draft

Exploring Inclusion in Canadian University Change Rooms

Despite boxing for Team Canada and visiting change rooms around the world, as an androgynous lesbian athlete, entering the women's change room provokes anxiety for me. I am regularly met with nervous or hostile stares and often directed to the men's change room. In 2015, returning home between competitions, however, I observed that the reactions I had grown accustomed to were replaced with welcoming nods from other women in the change room. At that time, an installation for the Pan-Am Games, The Change Room Project (CRP)[1], was on display. Large posters with quotations from lesbian, gay, bisexual, transgender, and intersex (LGBTI) participants were mounted in visible areas. These quotations alerted change-room users to the vulnerability that LGBTI often experience in the change room. My Master's research, commencing in the Fall of 2017,

Now, Eva describes the specific phenomenon of interest (the Change Room Project).

Clear identification of the research project's goal.

181

explores the possibility that the CRP offers a model which can make the change room more inclusive of diversity.

Literature Review: Discomfort in change rooms has been identified as a barrier to inclusion of LGBTI in sport[2, 3, 4]; however, little literature has been devoted to understanding how this discomfort is experienced[5].Scholarship examines how LGBTI individuals navigate gender-exclusive space in washrooms[6], in physical education classes[7], and in sport[8, 9]. With the exception of Fusco[2, 3, 10, 11], little literature attends to LGBTI experiences in the change room. Although a number of North American universities are currently adding all-gender change rooms[12, 13], a dearth of literature examines how *existing* change rooms can engage discourses to widen the boundaries of gender identifications. My research intends to explore the CRP as a promising model for assisting diverse LGBTI participants to navigate a space that is fraught with vulnerability.

Establishing the topic with statement of the problem. This is followed by the identification of a gap ('little literature has been devoted to …').

Methods: My analysis is informed by a queer, feminist theoretical framework, which presupposes that a discrete binary category of male/female cannot explain the diversity of gender expressed by humanity[14, 15, 16]. Following the completion of my proposal (Spring 2018) and ethics review (Fall 2018), I anticipate collecting 200–300 anonymous, optional surveys from an LGBTI-positive Facebook forum which I moderate named "All-In." These surveys will ask participants for demographic information and about their use the change room. From these surveys, I intend to recruit 12–15 volunteers representing a diverse LGBTI community. These volunteers will be classified into those who use the change room frequently, occasionally and avoid altogether. In the first phase of the semi-structured interview, I will explore their experiences in and expectations of the change room. In the second phase of the same interview, I will explore how they experience methods currently used by universities to address LGBTI discomfort in change rooms, such as all-gender change rooms and the CRP. To do this, I anticipate using the photo elicitation method[17] and drawing upon images of CRP quotations; for example, "Me, by myself in a locker room changing on my own is not predatory in any way… but I still feel anxious about it: Elise, lesbian"[1]. My research will be supervised by Dr. C. Fusco, who established the CRP and is a leader on scholarship in this field. My own experiences in change rooms provide me with sensitivity to help identify and reduce interviewee discomfort. I am currently enrolled in a research methodology course (EXS5510) that will consolidate my methodology for this research. I anticipate completing my data collection by December 2018.

Establishing credibility of the researcher by describing a plausible study methodology.

Further establishing ethos by citing connections of this project to established scholar and to personal and academic experiences.

Outcomes: The change room is a space where a lack of progress for LGBTI individuals is most evident due to the vulnerability of nudity and bodies in gender-exclusive spaces. By characterizing the nature of LGBTI experiences in the change room, my proposed research may provide practical recommendations for scholars, policy makers, and communities seeking to make physical activity more accessible to all Canadians. In November, 2017 I presented a paper comparing the CRP to various strategies for making change rooms more inclusive at the peer-reviewed North American Society for the Sociology of Sport conference. I plan to continue this of research with a PhD degree beginning Fall, 2019. I submitted abstracts to present preliminary research at the Sexuality Studies Assoc. conference in 2018. I hope to publish my research in a diversity of fields; sexuality studies, women studies, and sport sociology.

Identifying significance of the project and reasserting her credibility as an emerging scholar.

References

1. Fusco, C., Milman, D., De Lisio, A. (2015). "The change room project." *Hart House*. Retrieved from http://harthouse.ca/the-changeroom-project/.
2. Fusco, C. (1998b). "Lesbians in locker rooms: The subjective experiences of lesbians in sport." In G. Rail (Ed.), *Sport and Postmodern Times* (pp. 87–116). New York, NY: SUNY.
3. Fusco, C. (2002). "Bent on changing? Imagining postmodern possibilities for locker rooms." *Canadian Women Studies Journal, 21*(3), 12–29.
4. Hargie, O., Mitchell, D., Somerville, I. (2017). "'People have a knack of making you feel excluded if they catch on to your difference': Transgender experiences of exclusion in sport." *International Review for the Sociology of Sport, 52*(2), 223–239.
5. Whittle, S., Turner, L., Al-Alami, M. (2007). "Engendered penalties: Transgender and transsexual people's experiences of inequality and discrimination." *The Equalities Review*. Retrieved from www.pfc.org.uk/pdf/EngenderedPenalties.pdf.
6. Cavanagh, S. L. (2010). *Queering bathrooms*. Toronto, ON: University of Toronto Press.
7. Sykes, H. (2011). *Queer bodies: Sexualities, gender & fatness*. New York, NY: Peter Lang.
8. Caudwell, J. (2007). "Queering the field? The complexities of sexuality within a lesbian-identified football team in England." *Gender Place and Culture, 14*(2), 183–196.
9. Love, A. (2014). "Transgender exclusion and inclusion in sport." In J. Hargreaves & E. Anderson (Eds.), *Routledge Handbook of Sport, Gender and Sexuality* (pp. 376–383). Abingdon, VA: Routledge.
10. Fusco, C. (1998a). "Setting the record straight: The experiences of lesbian athletes." *Atlantis: A Women's Studies Journal, 23*(1), 69–79.

11. Fusco, C. (2006). "Inscribing healthification: Governance, risk, surveillance and the subjects and spaces of fitness and health." *Health & Place, 12*, 65–78.
12. Cauterucci, C. (2017). "UC Berkeley gym plans to open an all-gender locker room next fall." *Slate*. Retrieved from http://www.slate.com/blogs/xx_factor/2017/06/01/uc_berkeley_s_gym _plans_to_open_an_all_gender_locker_room_next_fall.html.
13. Ritchie, K. (2017). "Toronto schools open gender-free washrooms." *Now Toronto*. Retrieved from https://nowtoronto.com/lifestyle/class-action/toronto-schools-open-gender-free-washrooms/.
14. Butler, J. (1990). *Gender trouble: Feminism and the subversion of identity*. New York, NY: Routledge.
15. Butler, J. (1993). *Bodies that matter: On the discursive limits of "sex."* New York, NY: Routledge.
16. Halberstam, J. (1998). *Female masculinity*. Durham, NC: Duke University Press.
17. Harper, D. (2002). "Talking about pictures: A case for photo elicitation." *Visual Studies, 17*(1), 13–26.

Appendix E
Devon's Team Charter

TEAM CHARTER

Mission Statement

Through the alignment of our individual goals and embedded within the values of integrity, respect, and dedication, we strive to be a cohesive and focused team in which the whole is greater than the sum of the parts. Our mission is to ensure that each team member performs to the best of their ability and develops a thorough understanding of the fundamentals of project management in order to successfully manage complex projects across multiple functions in the future.

......Clear identification of group's mission.

Strengths and Weaknesses

Student 1 - Barbara

Identification of each member's personal characteristics which may be helpful in allocating assignment of work.

- Strengths: Versatile - able to adapt to any situation, good time management skills, dependable, punctual, team player - willing to take on additional responsibilities for the success of the team
- Weaknesses: Takes on too many responsibilities, attempts to please everyone, has high expectations for the group, likes having a plan/details in place

Student 2 - Andrew

- Strengths: Thorough, comfortable with Excel, quick learner, punctual, responsible for actions, reliable
- Weaknesses: Tends to spend too much time on unnecessary details, which can waste time; limited availability because of coop program commitments

Student 3 - Devon

- Strengths: Attention to detail, good writing skills, confident presenter, effective time management, conducting research
- Weaknesses: Limited availability for meeting times due to school and work schedule, impatient

Student 4 - Chloe

- Strengths: Attention to detail, financially inclined, idea generator, able to drive thoughtful discussion in group meetings, strong research skills
- Weaknesses: Has high expectations of others, likes to speak directly and honestly, has a busy schedule until second half of semester

Student 5 - Lilly

- Strengths: Creativity, idea generation, time management, organizational skills, attention to detail, decision-making, conscientiousness, reliability
- Weaknesses: Perfectionism, conflict-avoidance, sometimes easily frustrated with others, takes on too much

Values

- Respect
- Authenticity
- Accountability
- Honesty; Integrity
- Leadership
- Dedication
- Creativity
- Cooperation
- Learning; education
- Transparency

Reminder to attend to these important elements of collaborative work.

Point form and direct makes it easy to read.

Goals

- Perform to the best of our abilities and achieve a minimum grade of 80% on projects (case study, final report, presentation)

- Complete individual tasks on time and in accordance with university policies
- Work together to accomplish our goals
- Learn and apply key project management concepts to our work
- Gain knowledge that will be relevant and meaningful to our future careers
- Work with academic integrity

Strategies

Leadership Model

- The leadership position will be shared by all team members throughout the course of this term. The leadership role will rotate based on which team member has the most significant skills and expertise on the topic for each meeting
  - Leader expectations:
    - Will moderate discussion
    - Set agenda in advance of each meeting and distribute to team at least 2 hours before the scheduled time
    - Maintain track of time throughout meeting
    - Keep other team members on track
    - Follow up on outstanding items
  - Follower expectations:
    - Respect leader at all times
    - Contribute willingly to tasks
    - Speak when appropriate to do so
    - Follow through on assigned deliverables
    - Ask for help when needed

Roles and Responsibilities

- Roles and responsibilities will be devised and agreed upon by all group members. Task roles will be assigned according to each individual team member's strengths and interests. General roles throughout the course of the project will be as follows:
  - Barbara: Timekeeper
  - Andrew: Tech Specialist
  - Devon: Editor
  - Chloe: Scheduler
  - Lilly: Master of Google folder
- Work will be equally distributed among all five (5) team members. Team members will have an opportunity to volunteer to work on specific

Identification of framework and specifications of each person's role and expectations are concisely presented.

sections of the project. Any unassigned project tasks will be assigned by the team to individual team members subject to a vote of majority on agreement

Expectations

- Be cognizant of everyone's schedules and remain flexible as much as possible
- Be present and on time for all meetings; inform the group via email or text as soon as possible if there are circumstances under which you will be late or unable to attend
- Come prepared to all meetings; ensure necessary research and resources are collected ahead of time and available to present to the rest of the group
- All group members will have an opportunity to share their ideas
- All group members will take an active role in numerous aspects of the project
- Any concerns will be brought forward to the rest of the group as and when they arise
- Group members will be supportive and offer advice or guidance to other group members where required

Conduct ....

Check – why different formatting here?

- Meeting conduct/norms:
    - Face-to-face meetings will take place as deemed required by the team based on assignment due dates and requirements
    - Meetings will take place in the Hall's central space (or elsewhere on campus as agreed upon by the team)
    - Work product will consist of action items from previous meetings
    - In between face-to-face meetings, we will maintain email communication
    - If meetings go off-track, Lilly will be responsible for reminding team members of meeting objectives and deadlines
- Timelines
    - Project timelines will be determined by all team members during the team meeting for that project/task. Timelines will be based on:
        - Requirements of the project/task
        - Team members' schedules
    - Project timelines will allow for a minimum of 2 days (48 hours) for finalization (editing/formatting)

- Work ethic
  - Team members will carry out assigned tasks on time and to the best of their ability
  - Work produced will be professional
  - All team members will encourage quieter members to speak up by asking questions to engage everyone
  - Team members will refrain from badmouthing the project/task or any other aspects related to the work of the group
- Code of conduct

  - Communicate professionally and respectfully with one another in face-to-face meetings and via email
  - Show respect for all team members at all times by:
    - Actively listening to all team members (i.e. not on computer or phone while others are speaking)
    - Ensuring all members get a chance to speak
    - Not being derogatory or overly critical of ideas and suggestions
    - Arriving to meetings on time and not leaving abruptly throughout
    - Not using cell phones or other communication devices or social media when the meeting is in progress (unless it is an emergency)
  - Provide constructive feedback where possible
    - Team members will provide constructive feedback to one another and offer input on work produced to achieve team goals
    - All team members will be asked for their feedback at the end of each meeting

Conflict Resolution

Identification of methods for resolving problems.

- Voicing concerns and addressing issues as soon as they appear
- Talking about the issues amongst all group members; vote of majority on issues of contention
- Involving an individual from outside the team (e.g., Dr. Professor) if necessary to provide a non-judgmental opinion on the situation, whatever it may be
- Allowing time after each meeting for a recap of the meeting events and any concerns that may have arisen

Charter Violation Procedures

Identification of repercussions of problems and violations of team charter.

Violations of the charter will result in penalties/courses of action as determined by the other group members and penalties/courses of action will vary depending on the severity of the violation. Penalties/courses of action will range from having to bring in treats for the other group members to involvement of the professor of the course.

Signatures

I have participated in the development of this charter and agree to all terms as outlined above. Any request for modifications must be made in writing and submitted to all team members for review and a vote of majority will apply to any changes.

Team Member Name	Team Member Student #	Team Member Signature
Barbara		
Andrew		
Devon		
Chloe		
Lilly		

Commitment of all members to the charter is demonstrated through signature.

Date: _____

Appendix F
Devon's Group Report
The Non-Profit Organization
Vegetable Garden

Table of Contents

Table of Contents is expected for a report like this.

Learn how to create an automatic table of contents in Word or other word processing programs.

Headings follow the assignment guidelines and expectations.

Project Scope

Consistent formatting in terms of heading levels and spacing throughout the document.

Title

The Organization Vegetable Garden

Objective

The Vegetable Garden project has been approved to plan, design and build a vegetable garden at the current The Organization location. The purpose of the project is to establish a vegetable garden that will produce organic produce to supplement the food requirements to prepare meals for the The Organization program, which supports approximately 350 clients. Historically, The Organization has sourced produce from local farmers and as a result the cost for produce is significant and in some cases, there is the inability to establish the organic nature of the produce. The Organization' goal is to provide the best quality, organic and locally-sourced foods for their meals and therefore the Vegetable Garden Project is a means to do this. By having a vegetable garden on site, The Organization will be able to better leverage their resources in terms of volunteers and donations to reduce the costs associated with sourcing produce for their meals.

Deliverables

- Land prepared and ready for planting
- Equipment procurement and setup
- Plant and seed procurement
- Plans as requested by The Organization

Bullet point style is appropriate for the report genre.

Milestones

- Contact list created and donations secured – 24/Apr/2018
- Creation of blueprint – 26/Apr/2018
- Purchase of equipment, accessories and plants/seeds – 27/Apr/2018
- Shed and shelving built – 1/May/2018
- Creation of documentation template – 3/May/2018
- Installation of soil and mulch – 8/May2018
- Fence construction – 18/May/2018
- Installation of irrigation system and water hookup – 18/May/2018
- Seeds and seedlings planted – 25/May/2018

Technical Requirements

- Soil testing must meet the Ministry of Environment standards for human-grade food crops

- Irrigation hose must be capable of handling water pressure up to 50 PSI
- Irrigation system must include an emergency shut off valve
- Minimum shed dimensions of 7x7x6 Ft. (length x width x height)
- Minimum plot size of 20x20 Ft.
- Plot must be located at least 15 Ft. from the road
- No pesticides or non-organic products are to be used in the planting process
- Gloves should meets one-size-fits-all criteria
- Fencing must be at least 3 Ft. in height and not restrict airflow
- Blueprint must be created in and be modifiable in Microsoft Excel
- Documentation template must be created in and be modifiable in Microsoft Word

Limits and Exclusions

This project is limited to the scope defined above under the section: objective. As this project is being completed on a pro-bono basis with the utilization of volunteers, we do not guarantee any of the workmanship, but we will ensure that work is performed to the best of our ability throughout the duration of the project. Limits and exclusions include but are not limited to the following:

- Ongoing maintenance and upkeep of the vegetable garden
- Replanting of any plants that perish
- Damage to plants or physical structures as a result of the weather, animals or vandalism
- Breakdown/failure of items purchased/rented
- Protection of plants from insects, birds and rodents

Review with Customer

This project has been reviewed and approved by Desiree Smith, Executive Director and Rachael Hardy, Manager of The Organization.

Effective use of table to present large amount of information concisely

Communication Plan

Author	Target Audience	Objectives	Channels	Frequency	Setting
Project Manager	The Organization Leader	Negotiate project scope, including deliverables, timeline, and budget	Face-to-face meeting	Once	The Organization Office

(Continued)

(Continued)

Author	Target Audience	Objectives	Channels	Frequency	Setting
Project Manager	The Organization Leader	Provide project status updates at one-third and two-thirds through the project timeline	Face-to-face meeting	Twice	The Organization Office
Project Manager	Suppliers	Negotiate best pricing for supplies required. Do not go over the maximum estimate. Try to negotiate discount.	Face-to-face meeting	Once at the beginning of the project	Supplier's Location
Project Manager	Labor	Ensure volunteers are aware of the project scope and deliverables. Educate volunteers on the work breakdown structure (WBS).	Face-to-face meeting	Once before the project begins; once near the start of the project; ongoing communication with labor crew	The Organization Garden
Financial Lead	Project Manager	Provide financial status update to project manager.	Email	Weekly	Every Monday
Volunteer Coordinator	Project Manager	Provide updates on volunteer training, progress, and tasks achieved regarding preparation and planting of garden	Email or Face-to-face meeting	Weekly	Every Monday
The Organization Leader	Community Members	Connect with the The Organization community to share information about the preparing and planting of the garden. Share news of project completion at the end of the project.	Email or newsletter	Once before the project begins and once at the end of the project	Via The Organization network

Document Change Control

The following is the document control for revisions to this document.

Version Number	Date of Issue	Author(s)	Brief Description of Change
V1.0	July 2017	Project Manager	Approved version

Project Priority Matrix

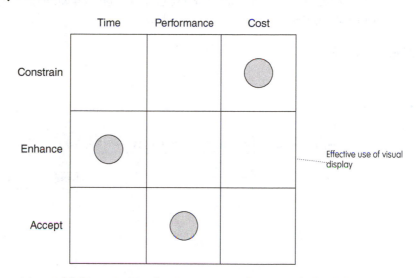

The priority matrix establishes priorities for time, cost and scope, which all have an impact on the overall quality. Given that the project is under a strict deadline to ensure that planting takes place no earlier or later than May 24th 2018, the only available option is to optimize time. Cost is constrained because the budget available to complete the project is fixed based on the donation received by The Organization. It is acceptable to not meet the original parameters for the performance criterion as 2018 is the first year that The Organization will have a vegetable garden and as such, will be using the 2018 year as a test platform from which to learn for future years. The priority matrix has been established in cooperation with the Meals on Wheel's goals, and therefore it is not anticipated that there will be any significant management implications as a result.

Work Breakdown Structure

The work breakdown structure (WBS) represents the selective outline for this project. The deliverables were determined as part of project scope section above. Please be aware that a WBS is not a project plan or a project schedule. It only provides detailed information on the given initial scope and on the final deliverables that need to be implemented to achieve the project goals and objectives. Should there be any scope changes in this project, the WBS will be updated as required.

Acronym has been defined.

Acronym has been used appropriately.

Network

The project network is the tool that will be used in the planning, scheduling and monitoring of project progress. See the initial network below for the original network, which has an estimated duration of 34 days and a critical path (identified in red). The network was completed by hand, utilizing expertise of all team members to ensure completeness and accuracy. Once the project network was satisfactory, it was then integrated into the Microsoft Project system. Any variance in the timeline, scope or budget could have a significant impact on the project; therefore we request to be made aware of any deviations as soon as possible.

Paragraphs are structured appropriately to provide the reader with description and explanation of complex content.

Initial network

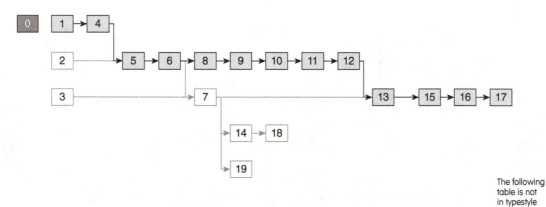

The following table is not in typestyle of others

Initial Network Key

ID	Task Name	Duration (days)	Early Start	Early Finish	Late Start	Late Finish	Slack (days)	Critical Activity
0	Project	34	9/Apr/18	24/May/18	9/Apr/18	24/May/18	0	N/A
1	Research plants, research contact list, create contact list, upload to SharePoint	5	9/Apr/18	13/Apr/18	9/Apr/18	13/Apr/18	0	Yes
2	Test soil, check land, estimate soil/mulch	5	9/Apr/18	13/Apr/18	16/Apr/18	20/Apr/18	5	No
3	Confirm water supply, select location for shed/bin	0.5	9/Apr/18	9/Apr/18	4/May/18	4/May/18	19.5	No
4	Contact network for donations	5	16/Apr/18	20/Apr/18	16/Apr/18	20/Apr/18	0	Yes
5	Determine seed requirements	0.5	23/Apr/18	23/Apr/18	23/Apr/18	23/Apr/18	0	Yes

196

ID	Task Name	Duration (days)	Early Start	Early Finish	Late Start	Late Finish	Slack (days)	Critical Activity
6	Select seeds to purchase	0.5	23/Apr/18	23/Apr/18	23/Apr/18	23/Apr/18	0	Yes
7	Create blueprint	0.5	24/Apr/18	24/Apr/18	7/May/18	7/May/18	9	No
8	Buy everything, rent rototiller	1	24/Apr/18	24/Apr/18	24/Apr/18	24/Apr/18	0	Yes
9	Clear debris	3	25/Apr/18	27/Apr/18	25/Apr/18	27/Apr/18	0	Yes
10	Till land	0.5	30/Apr/18	30/Apr/18	30/Apr/18	30/Apr/18	0	Yes
11	Level land, level ground for shed	2	30/Apr/18	2/May/18	30/Apr/18	2/May/18	0	Yes
12	Lay down soil/ mulch	3	2/May/18	7/May/18	2/May/18	7/May/18	0	Yes
13	Install posts for fence/irrigation	5	7/May/18	14/May/18	7/May/18	14/May/18	0	Yes
14	Set up bin, build shed, put shelving together	3	24/Apr/18	27/Apr/18	21/May/18	24/May/18	19	No
15	Install wire, install sprinkler heads, install hose, hook up water supply	3	14/May/18	27/May/18	14/May/18	17/May/18	0	Yes
16	Write names on stakes, insert stakes in ground	0.5	17/May/18	17/May/18	17/May/18	17/May/18	0	Yes
17	Plant seeds/ seedling, water plants	5	18/May/18	24/May/18	18/May/18	24/May/18	0	Yes
18	Put tools in shed	0.5	27/Apr/18	27/Apr/18	24/May/18	24/May/18	19	No
19	Discuss documentation with The Organization, create documentation template, upload to SharePoint	1	24/Apr/18	25/Apr/18	24/May/18	25/May/18	21.5	No

Schedule   [information has been omitted from the original for the purpose of this book]

Resources

Budget

INITIAL BUDGET

Item	# Needed	Cost Per Unit	Total Cost
General Items			
Gardening Gloves	20	$5.66	$113.20
Sunscreen	5	$8.99	$44.95
Foam Kneeling Pads	10	$15.99	$159.90

INITIAL BUDGET

Item	# Needed	Cost Per Unit	Total Cost	
Small Pots for Transporting Plants	40	$2.00	$80.00	
				$398.05
Small Hand Tools				
Wooden Stakes	50	$1.10	$55.00	
Pruning Sheers	5	$23.98	$119.90	
Cultivator (Loosening land)	2	$39.98	$79.96	
Hand Trowel (for digging holes for plants)	10	$9.48	$94.80	
Hand Spade	5	$31.98	$159.90	
Garden Rake	2	$40.98	$81.96	
Shovel	3	$19.97	$59.91	
				$651.43
Large Gardening Tools				
Wheelbarrow	3	$89.98	$269.94	
Shed (10x10)	1	$1,206.35	$1,206.35	
Shelving	2	$396.75	$793.50	
Garbage Bins	3	$20.97	$62.91	
Rain Catching Barrel	1	$99.00	$99.00	
Compost Bin	1	$54.97	$54.97	
				$2,486.67
Irrigation System				
Hose for Irrigation (100ft)	2	$16.28	$32.56	
Misting Tower (aka sprinkler)	6	$49.99	$299.94	
				$332.50
Fencing				
Chicken Wire	3	$37.95	$113.85	
Posts	3	$14.00	$42.00	
				$155.85
Plants and Seeds				

INITIAL BUDGET

Item	# Needed	Cost Per Unit	Total Cost	
Tomato Plants	80	$8.75	$700.00	
Butternut Squash	1	$4.49	$4.49	
Green Cabbage	2	$1.00	$2.00	
Carrots	4	$54.00	$216.00	
Celery	1	$3.49	$3.49	
Cucumber	144	$8.82	$1,270.08	
Beets	10	$3.49	$34.90	
Leeks	40	$1.25	$50.00	
Green Onions	2	$4.49	$8.98	
Red Onion	1	$3.49	$3.49	
Spinach	3	$1.89	$5.67	
				$2,299.10
Soil and Mulch				
Mulch	4	$189.00	$756.00	
Soil	4	$159.00	$636.00	
Rent Rototiller	1	$70.00	$70.00	
				$1,462.00
Subtotal				$7,785.60
Tax on all Items				$1,012.13
Budget Reserve				$800.00
Management Reserve				$1,000.00
Total Cost				$9,597.73

The initial budget detailed above gives a good indication of the amount of money required to implement the project using a top down estimation approach. Although the project is considered to be time constrained and not cost constrained, the budget was allocated keeping in mind your commitment to clients and community. Your overall corporate strategy was reviewed when drafting the original budget, and the following considerations were made:

Writer refers to table.

1. Costs are not constraining the project, but it is important to be cost conscious when shopping. Sale options were chosen whenever possible, as long as the quality of product was not compromised.

Numbered lists are used appropriately in the report.

2. You have expressed in our communication that this project is seen as a pilot year to determine whether the benefits of growing outweigh the costs of purchasing. For that reason, only the bare essentials were purchased.

In our initial project planning, The Organization identified a high likelihood of receiving donations in the form of seeds and plants from various nurseries and hardware stores. However, at the time of drafting the initial budget, fundraising had not come in from any community sources in sponsorship for the garden, and thus were not estimated or included. If donations are received during the duration of the project, this will be reflected on the final budget.

Consistent use of personal pronouns.

Because of your extensive roster of volunteers eager to assist in the garden project, billable labor hours were not incurred. As discussed in project design, The Organization volunteer coordinator will be responsible for scheduling all labor resources needed.

A Management Reserve of $1,000 was included in the initial budget to cover any unforeseen expenses that may arise during the duration of the project. At approximately 10% of the total budget, this represents a reasonable number to allocate as this is The Organization' first attempt with a community garden, and many unforeseen challenges might arise. For example, the soil sample could be sent out for testing only to find the topsoil is highly contaminated. In such an instance, the scope of the project will change, and the Management Reserve would be used for land reclamation and the purchase of additional soil.

A Budget Reserve of $800 was allocated to the initial budget as well. This amount will be used to cover the expenses of change management or risk management surrounding the "Irrigation" and 'fencing' work packages. The cost of an irrigation system and fencing are budgeted at $332.50 and $155.58 respectively, however, these estimates are considered to be conservative. The Budget Reserve will help to absorb any costs associated with necessary upgrades to the irrigation system and fencing.

Finally, it should be noted that the budget was not turned into a time-phased budget, as most activities happen over a short few days. It would be difficult to evaluate how the budget was being spent over short periods of time, and thus was not included.

Risk Management

Step 1: Risk Identification

The following is an exhaustive list of all potential risks that could arise during the duration of the garden project:

The writer is pointing the reader to specific information.

Risk Breakdown Structure

Risk Category	Risk #	Risk
Technical	1	Quality of soil is found to be compromised, unable to produce high quality vegetables without land reclamation
	2	The plant varieties chosen did not do well in the area (becomes obvious before project is turned over to The Organization)
	3	Unable to prevent critters (rabbits, mice, snails, etc.) from getting into the garden and eating plants
External	4	Unexpected frost after May 24 (Date of Planting)
	5	Inclement weather pushes back schedule as volunteers cannot work outside when raining
	6	Summer is unseasonably cold, and garden produces minimal yield, making the overall project unsuccessful
	7	The Organization organization unhappy with the yield/setup of garden
	8	Rototiller not available for days needed, holds up schedule
	9	Local community feels the garden is a 'free-for-all.' Helps themselves to vegetables as they wish
	10	Excessive flooding due to topography of where the garden plot is located
	11	Health and Food Safety regulations have not been considered when implementing a "farm to table" program for The Organization' customers
	12	Not Enough or too much sun
	13	Vandalism
Organizational	14	The Organization unable to secure the minimum funding required for garden project
	15	Local garden centers unable/unwilling to donate seeds and seedlings to project
	16	Project does not generate enough interest among the volunteers
	17	Volunteers are not physically fit enough to garden for extended periods of time
	18	Volunteers lack gardening know-how
	19	Volunteer(s) get(s) hurt while gardening
	20	No leadership established among the volunteers. Difficult to keep volunteers motivated
	21	Conflict among members of the volunteer community, makes scheduling volunteer hours more difficult
	22	Difficulty communicating what has been done (and what needs to be done) to volunteers from one day to the next
	23	Estimated plot size not large enough to make vegetable yield worthwhile
	24	Underestimated the increased cost in water and hydro bill

Step 2: Risk Assessment

Risk assessment is easily measured using a Risk Severity Matrix. The graph below captures all identified risks based on the likelihood of occurring and the impact its occurrence would have on the garden project. For simplicity purposes, the matrix uses risk numbers from the Risk Breakdown Structure (RBS) above.

Risk Severity Matrix

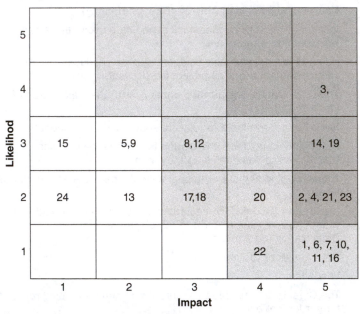

Step 3: Risk Response Development

It is clear that there are many potential risks associated with the garden project, but many are low impact and unlikely to occur. For the purposes of a Risk Response Development, only those risks identified as "High Risk" (dark blue in color) will be analyzed further in terms of appropriate response and contingency plan.

Appropriate use of text cue for emphasis and identification of a key point.

Risk Event #	Response	Contingency Plan	Trigger
2	Retain	Purchase additional plants of strains proven to do well	Plants die within first week of being in ground (before turnover to The Organization)
3	Mitigate	Install a more efficient fence, capable of keeping rodents out	See bite marks on the plant leaves or vegetables

Risk Event #	Response	Contingency Plan	Trigger
4	Retain	Replant as much as possible using money from Management Funds	Plants dead after overnight frost
14	Avoid	Have them pay upfront before work begins.	No trigger
19	Transfer	Ensure The Organization has the proper liability insurance to cover accidental harm to volunteers	Near-misses in the garden with volunteers
21	Mitigate	As part of volunteer orientation to garden, do team building exercises	Internal strife
23	Retain	Mark as a lesson learned for next season	Report from The Organization indicates harvest not big enough to be worthwhile

Status Report April 2, 2018: Planning process

Since the Garden Project was approved, our team has worked efficiently to prepare the plan for the garden.

Charter and project Scope ·· Capitalization error

The charter and project scope have been finalized and sign-off has been completed.

Work Breakdown Structure (WBS)

We have developed the WBS. The WBS highlights the deliverables (e.g., preparing and planting the garden) and sub-deliverables (e.g., fencing, soil, irrigation, plants) of the project. The WBS also identifies the work packages (e.g., fencing, soil, irrigation, plants). Finally, the WBS lists the activities required in each work package.

Risk Breakdown Structure (RBS)

In collaboration with your management team and the volunteers, the RBS has been created. This includes three risk categories associated with this project: technical, external, and organizational.

Budget

The initial budget has been finalized and approved by you. The budget includes per unit cost estimates as well as total cost estimates for each activity grouping as well as additional supplies that carry over multiple activities (e.g., gardening gloves).

Current Status

Schedule

The project is set to begin on time and according to the established timeline.

Cost

The initial budget has been created and is in-line with our estimated overall project cost and cost limitations.

Scope

The established scope is unchanged. No scope creep has been identified.

Problems and issues since last report

No problems have been identified to date. The RBS will help the team mitigate future problems.

Status Report June 1, 2018: project in progress

Progress Since Last Report

- Created blueprint
- Purchased equipment, accessories, plants/seeds, shed
- Built shed
- Laid soil and mulch
- Constructed fence
- Installed irrigation system

Problems and Issues Since Last Report

Since the last progress report, we have had a couple of new issues arising. Firstly, there have been some slight changes to the scopes regarding the quality of the fence and vegetables in the garden. Secondly, there have been some delays in the schedule due to bad weather and volunteers not showing up on time. Thirdly, our inventory of tools and seeds were stolen and damaged by critters, respectively. These new problems have caused us to modify the scope, budget, and schedule.

Cost and Scope Changes

The cost of the fence increased to **$303.85** because one of the volunteers, who is a contractor, recommended a couple of changes. First, it was recommended to use a gate instead of leaving an opening in the fence, and second, to use better quality posts as the planned posts would deteriorate after 2 seasons. Stronger posts will prevent further costs in the future as a result of fixing and/or replacing the fence or from damage to plants from fence failure. Finally, it was recommended that the perimeter of the fence be expanded to allow for some walking space. These changes in the quality of the fence did not increase the duration to build the fence as the process did not change significantly.

Additional costs were also incurred as a result of some of the tools being stolen and some of the seeds being eaten by critters. These issues were easily rectified by repurchasing the stolen items, which cost a total of **$213.89**. Replacing of the tools and seeds was not significant enough to cause any delays in the schedule. It was also decided upon to place the tools in the built shed and ensure that the doors were locked at all times when a volunteer was not present to prevent further theft. The cost of the lock was **$20.00**.

The last cost incurred was the result of a scope change regarding the planned plant types. Your management team made the decision to change some of the plant types and varieties, which ultimately cost additional time and money. It took an additional **0.25 days** and **$108.00** to replace these plants.

The additional incurred costs were offset by some savings. Specifically, a donation of 50 tomato plants from local gardening centers was received, which allowed savings on money that was allocated to the purchase of these plants. The funds saved were used to repurchase the stolen tools and damaged seeds, and the remainder was used for the costs incurred from the fence. In total, **$437.50** was saved in view to these donations from the gardening center.

Scheduling Issues

Some volunteers were not showing up on time due to their personal schedules, so the amount of time they committed per day was decreased by roughly **1–2 hours**. This has been a cumulative trend and it is an understandable risk as these individuals are giving their free time for these activities. The result of this has led to the project being **1 day behind overall**.

Another factor that has increased the duration of the project is bad weather. Rainy days meant the volunteers were unable to work outside. The bad weather resulted in a waste of **2 days**.

We informed you of these delays as soon as they became known to us. These delaying factors were beyond project control.

Index

CPSIA information can be obtained
at www.ICGtesting.com
Printed in the USA
LVHW050909080223
738570LV00002B/31